AF711128

SENTENCING FRAGMENTS

Recent Titles in

STUDIES IN CRIME AND PUBLIC POLICY
Michael Tonry and Norval Morris, General Editors

Banished
The New Social Control in Urban America
Katherine Beckett and Steve Herbert

Policing Problem Places
Crime Hot Spots and Effective Prevention
Anthony A. Braga and David Weisburd

The Policing Web
Jean-Paul Brodeur

Punishing Race
A Continuing American Dilemma
Michael Tonry

The Toughest Beat
Politics, Punishment, and the Prison Officers Union in California
Joshua Page

The City That Became Safe
New York's Lessons for Urban Crime and its Control
Franklin E. Zimring

Children of the Prison Boom
Mass Incarceration and the Future of American Inequality
Sara Wakefield and Christopher Wildeman

Living in Infamy
Felon Disfranchisement and the History of American Citizenship
Pippa Holloway

Unwanted
Muslim Immigrants, Dignity, and Drug Dealing
Sandra M. Bucerius

SENTENCING FRAGMENTS

PENAL REFORM IN AMERICA, 1975–2025

Michael Tonry

OXFORD
UNIVERSITY PRESS

OXFORD
UNIVERSITY PRESS

Oxford University Press is a department of the University of Oxford.
It furthers the University's objective of excellence in research, scholarship,
and education by publishing worldwide. Oxford is a registered trade mark
of Oxford University Press in the UK and in certain other countries

Published in the United States of America by
Oxford University Press

198 Madison Avenue, New York, NY 10016,
United States of America

© Oxford University Press 2016

All rights reserved. No part of this publication may be reproduced,
stored in a retrieval system, or transmitted, in any form or by any means,
without the prior permission in writing of Oxford University Press,
or as expressly permitted by law, by license, or under terms agreed with
the appropriate reproduction rights organization. Inquiries concerning reproduction
outside the scope of the above should be sent to the Rights Department,
Oxford University Press, at the address above.

You must not circulate this work in any other form
and you must impose this same condition on any acquirer

Library of Congress Cataloging-in-Publication Data
Tonry, Michael H.
Sentencing fragments : penal reform in America, 1975–2025 / Michael Tonry.
p. cm. — (Studies in crime and public policy)
Includes bibliographical references and index
ISBN 978–0–19–020468–6 (hardcover : alk. paper) 1. Corrections—United States.
2. Prison sentences—United States. 3. Imprisonment—United States.
4. Criminal justice, Administration of—United States. I. Title.
HV9471.T653 2016
365'.70973—dc23
2015019053

1 3 5 7 9 8 6 4 2

Printed in the United States of America on acid-free paper

CONTENTS

PREFACE

NO ONE ADMIRES AMERICAN SENTENCING systems. They are arbitrary and unjust, they are much too severe, they ruin countless lives, and they have produced a shameful system of mass incarceration. Ten or 20 years ago, many people and most politicians would have dismissed those two sentences as polemic. Today they express mainstream views. Nearly everyone agrees. The *New York Times* and the *Wall Street Journal* publish interchangeable editorials decrying the system, condemning its excesses, and regretting what it has done. The Soros Foundation and Koch Industries fund major criminal justice reform initiatives aiming to repeal severe laws and facilitate offenders' reintegration into mainstream society. Conservative organizations like the Manhattan Institute, Justice Fellowship, the American Enterprise Institute, and the Texas Public Policy Foundation more often than not find common cause with liberal organizations like the American Civil Liberties Union, the Open Society Institute, the Sentencing Project, and NYU's Brennan Center.

Until the mid-1980s, American sentencing laws and practices resembled those in other Western democracies. Laws set outer limits on punishments that could be imposed but seldom prescribed them. Judges deciding individual cases sought to acknowledge wrongs done to victims and to fashion punishments that were just, appropriate, and as humane as they could be. Prison terms and incarceration rates were not greatly different from those in other English-speaking and Western European countries. Sentencing was seen as a somber business, an extraordinary exercise of state power that required discretion and judgment. Sentences were expected to be tailored to take account of the seriousness of crimes and of the characteristics and circumstances of individual offenders.

And then things went haywire. The center of gravity of American sentencing moved from the solemn confines of the courtroom to the emotional whirlpools of the campaign trail. Politicians competed to show who was tougher on crime. Hamfisted laws—three-strikes, mandatory minimums, truth-in-sentencing, life-without-parole—were enacted throughout the country. Some states enacted all of them. All enacted some. Those laws mandated the sentences that would be imposed for particular crimes and expressly forbade judges to take account of offenders' situations. The lengths of sentences those laws required are the major cause of current levels of imprisonment.

Exactly why things went haywire is a mystery except in the mundane sense that we know that legislators enacting laws in the 1980s and early 1990s meant for more people to be sent to prison and for longer times. It is unlikely that anyone foresaw or wanted the mass incarceration that resulted.

The explanation that legislators wanted tougher sentencing, however, begs the question of why they wanted that and enacted the laws that they did. No other country did anything remotely similar. Crime is a regrettable but predictable occurrence in all human societies. Crime rates rise and fall. Occasional horrifying and sensational crimes happen and provoke powerful emotions and for a time raise heightened public concern. All of that is part of the human condition.

Crime rates, for example, rose in all developed countries between the 1960s and the early 1990s, with rates of violent crime including homicide tripling and property crime rates quadrupling. Only American legislators responded with three-strikes and kindred laws; no other Western country did. Only in the United States did legislators enact laws that forbade judges to treat offenders justly, proportionately, and fairly.

The challenge now is to undo mass incarceration, repeal the laws that caused it, and once again empower judges to behave justly in individual cases. It is not an easy challenge, and despite nearly universal condemnation of American sentencing laws, it is not one that legislators have tried to address. There have in the past decade been many hundreds of changes in sentencing statutes, but they have barely nibbled at the edges. They have created narrow exceptions in harsh sentencing laws for first and minor offenders, narrowed criteria for revocations of probation and parole, and established new correctional treatment and "reentry" programs. Those changes are important, of course, to the individuals they affect and their loved ones, but they will not reverse mass incarceration or prevent the imposition of unjustly severe mandatory penalties.

Meaningful change will occur only when legislators throughout the country repeal the laws that produced mass incarceration and required sentence lengths of historically unprecedented severity, and enact laws authorizing the release of people now in prison who should not and need not be there. So far, except in Michigan more than a decade ago, no American jurisdiction has repealed a major mandatory minimum, three-strikes, life-without-parole, or truth-in-sentencing law. And no state has enacted new laws to permit reconsideration of the continuing need for confinement of people now in prison.

If and when legislators and other policy makers decide to unwind mass incarceration and reconstitute just sentencing systems, proven tools are available. A few states have created systems of "presumptive" sentencing guidelines that, evaluations clearly show, make sentencing fairer, more consistent, and more predictable. Standards for sentences are established for particular crimes. If judges believe some other sentence is called for, they can impose it, but have to give detailed reasons. Defendants and prosecutors can appeal the adequacy of the reasons given. Other states created successful systems of parole guidelines that worked in much the same way. Historically, reduction in prison crowding was one of the functions of parole release systems. Given the authority to consider the need for continuing confinement of people now serving long sentences, parole boards could once again perform that function.

American citizens and voters are ready for change. Countless public opinion surveys show that Americans do not consider crime or drug abuse to be major problems and would rather that public money be spent on treatment programs than on prisons. California voters enacted referendums that greatly narrow the scope of that state's three-strikes law, with retrospective application, and require diversion of many drug-dependent offenders to treatment. Voters in four states and the District of Columbia approved marijuana decriminalization. In the end, though, voters and referendums will not unwind mass incarceration or remake sentencing into the individualized human process it should always have been. Only legislators can do that. So far they have failed.

Michael Tonry
Bologna, September 2015

ACKNOWLEDGMENTS

INDIVIDUALS WRITE BOOKS, OCCASIONALLY STANDING on the shoulders of giants, and always benefitting from what others have taught them. In trying to understand and improve American sentencing policies and practices for more than four decades, I learned many things from many people. Two, Norval Morris of the University of Chicago and Harvard's Lloyd E. Ohlin, were mentors and inspirations. Having even one loving and demanding mentor is great good fortune. Having two is a blessing.

Norval Morris thought long and deeply about sentencing processes and norms before others did, and beginning in the 1950s offered ideas that remain influential. More mundanely, in the 1970s he suggested to a young post-doc that sentencing law and policy would be a promising specialization for a beginning academic. The coast was clear; no one in the United States then paid much attention to the subject and only David A. Thomas did so in England.

Lloyd Ohlin taught me that sentencing and punishment are complicated human processes. In his 1950s work on the American Bar Foundation surveys of criminal justice administration, he learned and showed something that American policy makers forgot, or pretended to forget, after the early 1980s. Almost all practitioners want to act humanely, justly, and constructively. They resist and often evade rigid and unjust laws. The signature sentencing laws of the 1980s and

1990s—three-strikes, mandatory minimums, truth-in-sentencing, life-without-parole, and their kindred—are cruel on their faces and as a result are applied erratically and inconsistently.

My tutors included many of the pioneers of the short-lived sentencing reform movement of the 1970s and 80s that sought to make sentencing fair, consistent, predictable, and humane. They include Marvin Frankel, Kay A. Knapp, Dale Parent, and Douglas Amdahl in Minnesota; Roxanne Lieb, David Boerner, and Norm Maleng in Washington State; David Factor, Kathy Bogan, and Hardy Myers in Oregon; John Kramer, Robin Lubitz, and Richard Conaboy in Pennsylvania; Thomas Ross and Robin Lubitz in North Carolina; and Peter Hoffman of the U.S. Parole Commission.

Many thoughtful academics have worked on sentencing subjects in the last three decades. I cannot mention all from whom I received instruction. There are too many. Foremost among them are Hans-Jörg Albrecht, Andrew Ashworth, Alfred Blumstein, Eric Blair, Jean-Paul Brodeur, Alessandro Corda, Anthony Doob, Antony Duff, Daniel J. Freed, Richard S. Frase, Arie Freiberg, Andreas von Hirsch, Roger Hood, Josine Junger-Tas, Cecelia Klingele, Krzysztof Krajewski, Britta Kyvsgaard, Miklos Levay, René Levy, Wayne Logan, Marc Mauer, Marc Miller, Daniel S. Nagin, Joan Petersilia, Stan C. Proband, Kevin R. Reitz, Frank Remington, Julian V. Roberts, Sebastian Roché, Tapio Lappi-Seppälä, Michael E. Smith, Sonja Snacken, Kate Stith, Peter J. P. Tak, David A. Thomas, Thomas Weigend, Nigel Walker, Ronald Wright, and Dirk van Zyl Smit. All are or were good friends, all repeatedly attempted to save me from error in earlier books and articles, and most read drafts and provided ideas, criticisms, and leads.

At the University of Minnesota, I have been helped greatly by David Zopfi-Jordan, who with limitless patience tracked down fugitive and not-so fugitive sources. Reece Almond, Chad Pennington, and numerous law students tested my ideas and kept me on my toes. Finally, the gifted poet, choreographer, and editor Su Smallen played an indispensable part in the creation of this book, as she has in everything I have written or edited in the last decade.

None of these people, alas, bears any responsibility for my mistakes and infelicities. Those are mine alone. I am more grateful than words can adequately express to all of these people for their friendship and guidance.

SENTENCING FRAGMENTS

I

Sentencing Matters

AMERICAN SENTENCING IS A DISASTER—unjust, unprincipled, arbitrary, overly severe, and absurdly expensive. Each state and the federal system has a crazy quilt of incompatible and conflicting laws, policies, and practices. For some cases, laws mandate punishments nearly everyone involved believes to be too severe. For others, they forbid judges to impose sentences that everyone involved thinks would be appropriate. And for a third set of cases, they authorize judges to do what they believe to be sensible and right. Three-strikes, life-without-parole, and mandatory minimum sentence laws exemplify the first set. Federal policies severely limiting use of community punishments and forbidding judges in most cases to take account of offenders' drug or alcohol dependence, family responsibilities, disadvantaged childhoods, and employment records illustrate the second. Drug courts, restorative justice initiatives, and new rehabilitation programs illustrate the third.

Sentencing matters. Life, liberty, and property are at stake. Convicted offenders and victims care about it for obvious reasons. Judges and prosecutors want to act justly and do what is right. Policy makers hope or believe judges' decisions can enhance public safety and reinforce important social norms. Civil rights advocates worry that members of disadvantaged minority groups unfairly bear the brunt of harsh laws. People of all political persuasions believe that many current laws are unjust and that too many people are in prison.

Recent laws and practices have been largely ineffective and exorbitantly expensive. Those are good reasons to overhaul American sentencing, but by themselves they are not enough to motivate major changes. Financial shortfalls in state budgets have led many states in recent years to make modest changes in order to save money. When the good times again roll, budgetary pressures will weaken. Political inertia and resistance to change are powerful; concerns about inefficiency and waste seldom overcome them.

No meaningful progress will be made in reducing mass incarceration, rampant racial and ethnic disparities, or injustice in individual cases until sentencing laws and practices are overhauled. That will not happen until a critical mass of opinion recognizes that what America is doing to many convicted offenders is wrong and unjust, that punishments are often cruelly severe, and that lives are being ruined for no good purpose. New systems need to be built that are just, rational, and cost-effective. Doing that will require repeal or radical pruning of severe laws and creation of new policies and institutions.

As recently as 50 years ago, sentencing and punishment were important state responsibilities that, like education or public health, were neither particularly controversial nor a major focus of partisan politics. Notorious crimes and cases involving celebrities from time to time attracted attention, of course, but for the most part, like hospitals and schools, courts did their work out of the public eye. For much of the twentieth century, there was a distinctive American approach that was humane, hardheaded, and practical. Indeterminate sentencing, as it was called, existed in every jurisdiction. It was predicated on the desirability of tailoring decisions to fit offenders' circumstances and characteristics. Rehabilitation of offenders was the primary aim and incapacitation the fallback, subject to general agreement that punishments should be no more severe than was minimally necessary.

Like all human institutions, indeterminate sentencing was imperfect, but much of the time it produced reasonable results. Judges decided whom to send to prison and parole boards decided when prisoners were released. Judges and parole board members tried to make just and defensible decisions, and generally believed they did. The system contained safeguards. Redundancy was seen as a virtue. Judges' hands were seldom tied by prosecutors' decisions about charges or by mandatory minimum sentence laws. Judges could usually specify the maximum sentence a prisoner might serve, and sometimes the minimum, but parole boards set release dates. Sometimes parole boards set dates based on a judgment that the sentence was idiosyncratically or unreasonably severe, sometimes because they had more and better information, and sometimes because the offender's behavior in prison showed his or her criminality to have been fundamentally out of character. Then as now, two-thirds of people sentenced to prison *for the first time* never went back. Also then as now, two-thirds of those *released each year* recidivated; that's because most of those released each year are chronic drug and property offenders on a treadmill.

Support for indeterminate sentencing dissolved in the mid-1970s. Liberals charged that it gave too much discretion to judges and parole boards and produced results that were inconsistent, unpredictable, often unjust, and sometimes racist. Conservatives complained that the system was too lenient and insufficiently oriented toward retribution, deterrence, and incapacitation. Both groups believed that rehabilitative programs were seldom effective.

In retrospect, it is clear that there were problems that needed fixing, but also that the criticisms were overblown. There were disparities, but far fewer than under current mandatory minimum sentence and truth-in-sentencing laws. Blacks and Hispanics were overrepresented among prisoners, but far less than they were later in the 1980s and 1990s, and less than in the twenty-first century. Rules could have been clearer and procedures fairer, but developers of parole and sentencing guidelines had been working on that since the mid-1960s. Only a handful of states in 2015 had well-developed sentencing rules. In most states, latitude for judicial idiosyncrasy is no less than it was under indeterminate sentencing except when specific sentences are mandated by legislation.

In the two decades after 1975 every state and the federal government radically overhauled its laws and policies. Until the mid-1980s, most changes sought to remedy the perceived weaknesses of indeterminate sentencing. They focused on improving consistency, predictability, and fairness. In the ensuing decade, many changes sought to give more power to prosecutors, reduce judicial discretion, and make punishments harsher, without much concern for fairness or justice. By 1996, a third of states abolished parole release, and an overlapping third established sentencing guidelines. Every state enacted mandatory minimum sentence laws. States that did not already have life-without-possibility-of-parole laws enacted them. More than half the states enacted three-strikes laws requiring minimum terms of 25 years to life for many third-time felons. More than half enacted truth-in-sentencing laws that forbade release from prison until offenders served at least 85 percent of their nominal terms. Beginning in the early 1990s, many jurisdictions began to reestablish rehabilitative programs. Drug, mental health, and other problem-solving courts came first and in 2015 numbered in the thousands. Restorative justice, community justice, prisoner reentry, and new rehabilitative programs followed.

Some states and the federal government made all those changes. All states made at least several. Sentencing systems in every jurisdiction became too complicated, too mechanical, and too harsh. Sentencing almost everywhere became less consistent. Often it is arbitrary. It is unprecedentedly severe and disproportionately ensnares black and Hispanic Americans. It has produced prison populations seven times larger than before 1975, and an imprisonment rate that once exceeded 750 per 100,000 population and still topped 700 in 2014. That is seven times the average of other developed Western countries. No one celebrates or much admires what four decades of sentencing "reforms" have wrought.

Many well-known conservatives in recent years acknowledge those problems, even though in earlier times they promoted the laws that produced them. "There is an urgent need to address the astronomical growth in the prison population, with its huge costs in dollars and lost human potential," wrote Republicans Newt Gingrich and Pat Nolan (2011), announcing the formation of Right on Crime, a justice reform group. "We can no longer afford business as usual with prisons. The criminal justice system is broken, and conservatives must lead the way in fixing it."[1]

The web page of Right on Crime, under the heading "What Conservatives Are Saying," contains a long list of similar statements. Kentucky senator Rand Paul: "Our federal mandatory minimum sentences are simply heavy handed and arbitrary. They can affect anyone at any time, though they disproportionately affect those without the means to fight them. We should stand and loudly proclaim enough is enough. We

[1] This and the following quotes are taken from http://www.rightoncrime.com/the-conservative-case-for-reform/what-conservatives-are-saying/.

should not have laws that ruin the lives of young men and women who have committed no violence."

Grover Norquist, head of Americans for Tax Reform: "Mandatory minimums have become a sort of poor man's Prohibition: a grossly simplistic and ineffectual government response to a problem that has been around longer than our government itself."

Former Texas governor Rick Perry: "The idea that we lock people up, throw them away, never give them a chance at redemption, is not what America is about. . . . I believe we can take an approach to crime that is both tough and smart. . . . There are thousands of non-violent offenders in the system whose future we cannot ignore. Let's focus more resources on rehabilitating those offenders so we can ultimately spend less money locking them up again."

Dave Keene, former president of the National Rifle Association and chairman of the American Conservative Union: "Everybody forgot what the mission in our society of the criminal justice system is. It's not simply to punish people. It's not simply to extract retribution. It's to provide a safer society. And to treat people humanely."

Ohio Senator Rob Portman: "Incarcerating people who don't pose a threat is a really inefficient use of resources. . . . What do you end up with? You end up with broken families. You end up with communities that are being plagued with more violence and more crime. And you end up with people not reaching their God-given potential."

Utah congressman Chris Cannon: "In this whole thing, nobody is being soft on crime. . . . The system has a very strong tendency to change [offenders] for the worse. Everybody knows that, I think. Our current system is fundamentally immoral."

Similar heartfelt, emotive language about lost human potential, ruined lives, unintended consequences, heavy-handed laws, ineffectual policies, and immorality appears regularly in position papers of the American Civil Liberties Union, the Open Society Institute, and other liberal law reform groups. That high-profile conservative Republicans say the same things could signal the beginning of a fundamental shift away from the tough-on-crime attitudes of recent decades. The time may soon be ripe for major changes.

Liberal and civil liberties groups are paying increased attention to sentencing and punishment. George Soros's Open Society Foundations late in 2014 announced a $50 million grant to the American Civil Liberties Union for work to reduce prison populations. The Brennan Center of New York University has launched a series of high-profile national initiatives. Long-time nonpartisan reform organizations like The Sentencing Project and New York's Vera Institute of Justice have been revitalized.

Mainstream organizations not traditionally focused on criminal justice policy have become more engaged. The Council of State Governments has worked with governors and legislatures on "justice reinvestment" efforts in 20 states to reduce prison populations and use the savings to create more effective community programs. In the 1980s and 1990s, only two major American foundations, the Edna McConnell Clark Foundation, specializing in prisoners' rights litigation, and the Annie E. Casey Foundation, focusing on youth justice, emphasized criminal justice policy. Other major foundations—Ford, Rockefeller, MacArthur—refused to become significantly involved; the subject was too contentious. In this century, that has changed. The Pew Charitable Trusts and the MacArthur Foundation, for example, have initiated major, long-term efforts to reduce excessive use of imprisonment and create more humane and effective programs. Many smaller foundations followed, and some led.

Change is underway. It is far too soon, however, to declare victory or predict with any confidence that major changes will be made. Voters and courts have acted boldly, but legislators and executive branch officials have not. Many talk the talk; few walk it. Elected officials have mostly made minor changes to laws that provoke major criticisms, do unnecessary harm, lock up too many people, and waste too much money.[2] Most politicians appear still to be immobilized by fear that they will be called "soft on crime," even though crime has not been a major issue in a presidential election since 1988 and seldom arises in statewide elections.

[2] Most major criminal justice reform organizations issue annual summaries of important legislative developments. These include the American Civil Liberties Union (2012), the Brennan Center (Roeder, Eisen, and Bowling 2015), The Sentencing Project (Porter 2014, 2015), and the Vera Institute of Justice (Subramanian and Delaney 2014; Subramanian, Moreno, and Broomhead 2014). All express optimism, but subject to caveats like this one from the Vera Institute: "The restrictive scope and application of recent reforms—including narrow criteria for eligibility and the discretionary nature of some revised sentencing policies—suggest that the impact of reform may nevertheless be limited" (Subramanian and Delaney 2014, p. 201).

Voters have approved major changes. In 2014, Gallup Poll results showed that less than 2 percent of Americans considered crime and violence America's most serious problem; drug abuse ranked lower. Sixty-one percent of California voters in 2000 supported Proposition 36, requiring that most people convicted of a first or second nonviolent drug offense be offered probation with drug treatment instead of a prison sentence. Sixty-nine percent of California voters in 2012 passed another Proposition 36, this time sharply narrowing the state's three-strikes law, and making the changes retroactive. Fifty-nine percent of California voters in 2014 approved Proposition 47, another retroactive narrowing of the three-strikes law. More than ten thousand inmates became eligible for resentencing.

Citizens have for a decade been changing marijuana laws in ways that legislators would not. Colorado and Washington voters approved legalized sale of marijuana in 2012. So did Alaska, Oregon, and District of Columbia voters in 2014. As 2015 began, medical use of marijuana was legal or authorized in 24 states and the District of Columbia. Approval in the first five states—Alaska, California, Maine, Oregon, and Washington—was by ballot initiatives and referendums. Only later were legislatures in 10 states emboldened to make the move themselves. Medical marijuana use is legal in Alaska, Arizona, Montana, and Nevada, "red" states that typically elect conservative Republicans. Another 11 states have authorized medical use of cannabidiol, a nonhallucinogenic cannabis compound.

Judges also have acted boldly. In *People v. Superior Court (Romero)*, 13 Cal. 4th 497, 533 (1996), a California Supreme Court composed entirely of members appointed by conservative Republican governors, using tortured reasoning, empowered judges to disregard the three-strikes law. In a long series of decisions beginning in the 1990s, the US Supreme Court, dominated by conservatives since the 1970s, reduced the severity of federal and state sentencing laws and guidelines. In *Koon v. United States*, 518 U.S. 81 (1996), the court weakened the rigid federal guidelines by broadening judges' discretion to depart from them. In *United States v. Booker*, 543 U.S. 220 (2005), the court decided that "mandatory" federal guidelines were unconstitutional and made them advisory. In *Blakely v. Washington*, 542 U.S. 296 (2004), the court forbade state judges to impose sentences more severe than guidelines authorized unless the defendant pled guilty to a more serious offense or a judge or jury found that he had committed one. A series of cases, including *Kimbrough v. United States*, 552 U.S. 85 (2007), fundamentally weakened the federal "100-to-1" law punishing crack cocaine offenses much more severely than powder cocaine offenses, and made the decisions retroactive. In *Graham v. Florida*, 560 U.S. 48 (2010), and *Miller v. Alabama*, 132 S. Ct. 2455 (2012), the court declared mandatory sentences of life without the possibility of parole for juveniles unconstitutional. It is hard not to conclude, even in this era of "strict construction" of judicial authority, that the courts recognized that the laws were fundamentally unjust and that executive branch officials and legislatures were politically incapable of changing them.

That skepticism is warranted. Little, for example, has happened at the federal level to roll back mass imprisonment even though the Congress in 1984–96 enacted every major form of tough-on-crime legislation. There have been a few ballyhooed executive branch changes, but they have been more symbolic than substantive.

Attorney General Eric Holder, for example, obtained reams of publicity in 2014 for announcing an initiative that may lead to clemency for more federal prisoners. Its scope is exceedingly modest. Eligibility is limited to *nonviolent first offenders who have already served 10 years in a federal prison*. The criteria are italicized, despite copy editors' efforts to persuade writers not to use italics for emphasis, because they are so niggardly. In no other developed country could nonviolent first offenders receive a 10-year, real-time sentence. In many, the longest possible prison sentence for any crime except murder or treason is 12 or 14 years, and that almost always includes a one-third or greater reduction for good behavior. With the possible exception of perpetrators of immense financial frauds, no one should serve 10 years in prison for a nonviolent first conviction. Holder's initiative, if it is carried out, will diminish unjustifiable human suffering in a small number of cases. That is a good thing, of course, but it will have no significant effects on mass imprisonment or federal sentencing.

The US Sentencing Commission received favorable media attention and enjoyed much self-congratulation in 2007 and 2014 for modestly shortening prison sentences for some drug offenders, potentially retrospectively.[3] Press releases pronounced that wrongs would be righted. Here too, however, the changes are modest and partial. Under the 2014 change, for example, no releases are authorized before November 2015; people who the commission in April 2014 decided had already served unjustly long sentences would remain in prison for at least another 18 months. The commission, moreover, did not acknowledge that it was merely and only partly correcting its own policy mistakes. The commission had earlier made guideline-required sentences for many drug offenses longer than the already-severe lengths mandated by federal laws.

Holder's and the commission's initiatives are steps in the right direction, but small and cautious. Should someone someday write a successor to President John F. Kennedy's Pulitzer Prize–winning *Profiles in Courage* (1956), which celebrated political figures who risked their careers to do what they believed to be right, neither Attorney General Holder nor the US Sentencing Commission will be among the honorees. Bold decisions are needed. Federal officials have been loath to make them.

Legislatures have done little better, merely nibbling at the edges of the problem. Reports issued by the National Conference of State Legislatures list many hundreds of changes to sentencing laws since 2000, but almost all are minor.[4] A recent report issued by a coalition of sentencing reform advocacy organizations observes that the limited scope of the changes so far "runs the danger of institutionalizing mass incarceration at current levels" (Austin et al. 2013, p. 1). The changes typically slightly narrow the scope of mandatory minimum sentence laws or carve out exceptions for some first offenders, narrow the grounds for parole and probation revocation for breach of technical conditions, or broaden grounds for parole release of people convicted of minor crimes. Those changes are important to people whose lives they affect and to their families, but they do not fundamentally alter American sentencing systems. No state legislature has repealed a three-strikes, truth-in-sentencing, or life-without-possibility-of-parole law. Except in Michigan

[3] The stories of the federal sentencing guidelines, the US Sentencing Commission, and these changes are told in chapter 3.

[4] The National Conference of State Legislatures for many years compiled annual summaries (of uncertain comprehensiveness) and maintains a searchable database beginning with developments in 2010.

in 2002, no state has repealed broad-based mandatory minimum sentence laws for drug and violent crimes.

The two best-known amendments to severe sentencing laws are, despite major publicity, modest. The US Congress in 2010 amended the 100-to-1 crack cocaine sentencing law to reduce the differential with powder cocaine to a still indefensible 18-to-1; it continues to produce unjustifiable racial disparities in sentencing of black and white drug offenders. The New York Legislature in 2004 and 2009 amended the Rockefeller Drug Laws but left many of their severest provisions in place. Imprisonment of drug offenders is declining in New York and in the federal system, but that is primarily because prosecutors are becoming less aggressive. The declines could easily have occurred without the statutory changes once prosecutors decided to change their ways of doing business.

The size of the American prison population is the clear, unambiguous evidence that nothing fundamental has changed. The number of people locked up in state and federal prisons increased continuously through 2010, fell slightly in 2011 and 2012, and resumed its upward climb in 2013. The Pew Charitable Trusts in November 2014, on the basis of state corrections department projections, predicted a 3 percent increase in the number of state prisoners by 2018.

When crime rates began their steep quarter-century decline in 1991, prisons and jails held 1,219,014 inmates. By 2008, after the imprisonment rate peaked, the number of inmates had nearly doubled to 2,308,390. Prisons and jails held 2,306,000 inmates in 2013 (Carson 2014; Minton and Golinelli 2014).

The imprisonment rate for state and federal prisons and county jails rose continuously from 1973 until it peaked at 756 per 100,000 population in 2007. Since then it has fallen, but primarily because the overall US population has grown. The rate was 709 at the beginning of 2014. Those numbers are unprecedented in American history and unparalleled in any other developed country. In 1973, when the rise in imprisonment began, the rate was 160 per 100,000, a level around which it had fluctuated since 1930.

Imprisonment rates in the United States have been seven times higher than the average of all developed Western countries since 2000, and four to ten times higher than those in individual countries, as table 1.1

shows. Many developed countries—for example, Canada, Germany, France, and Italy—have long had rates around 100 per 100,000. The lowest, under 70, are in the Netherlands and the Scandinavian countries. The highest, New Zealand, is around 190, followed by England and Wales, Spain, and Portugal, all below 150.

TABLE 1.1. Imprisonment rates, selected countries, January 1, 2014*

Country	Imprisonment rate per 100,000 population	Country	Imprisonment rate per 100,000 population
United States	709 (12/31/13)	Australia	130.0 (6/30/12)
Russia	450 (9/1/13)	France	118.3
Ukraine	324.4 (2013)	Belgium	115.5
Lithuania	314.6	Canada	113.4 (9/30/11)#
South Africa	294.0 (8/20/13)	Austria	104.2
Latvia	256.8	Italy	102.9
Estonia	230.0	Switzerland	86.9
Poland	205.2	Ireland	86.6
New Zealand	192.0 (6/30/13)	Germany	77.5
Hungary	180.6	Norway	69.9
Czech Republic	158.4	Denmark	67.1
England & Wales	147.1 [1/1/13]	Netherlands	60.8
Spain	143.6	Sweden	57.3
Portugal	137.0	Finland	55.2

Sources: For continental Europe: Council of Europe 2014; for Australia, Canada, New Zealand, South Africa, and Ukraine: Walmsley 2014; for the United States: Carson 2014; Minton and Golinelli 2014; for Russia, Aebi and Delgrande 2014, table 1.

*Except where noted otherwise. #The Canadian source count of 118.0 includes youth confinement, which has been netted out.

No country since 1990 has had higher imprisonment rates than America's. The closest competitors, Russia, Ukraine, Lithuania, and South Africa, lock up many fewer of their residents. Those are not places, however, with which most Americans would ordinarily want their country equated in terms of justice, human rights, or commitment to the rule of law. Except for Russia and the United States, the countries which in 1990 had rates above 300 have substantially reduced them. South Africa's, for example, has fallen by 50 percent. Those in most of the former Warsaw Pact countries of Eastern Europe and former Soviet Socialist Republics have fallen by at least a third, and often by half or more. After the collapse of the Iron Curtain and dissolution of the Soviet Union in the early 1990s, governments in those countries viewed reduction in imprisonment rates as a symbol of their commitment to Western human rights ideals. Most resolved to reduce the number of people in prison substantially. Nearly all succeeded. So far, overall, American governments have not much reduced their prison populations, even though numbers in some individual states have fallen.

I. Why Are So Many Americans in Prison?

The use of imprisonment in the United States rose as it did primarily because legislators enacted laws that were meant to send more people to prison and for longer. There is no doubt about that. It is what policy makers at the time said they wanted.[5] Sometimes politicians' statements of what they hope to accomplish need to be taken with a grain of salt. Not this time. No other plausible explanation can be offered for the enactment of broadly drafted mandatory minimum sentence, three-strikes, truth-in-sentencing, and life-without-parole laws, and others requiring imprisonment and longer terms for repeat and "dangerous" offenders. The aim was to put more people in prison, though most likely no one foresaw or really wanted things to get as far out of control as they have.

Researchers have investigated the factors that caused American prison numbers to balloon since 1973.[6] The primary cause is a set of

[5] Why American crime control and sentencing policies evolved as they did is a subject for a different book. A large, sophisticated, and contested literature is developing (e.g., Lerman and Weaver 2014; Murakawa 2014; Gottschalk 2015; N. M. Moore 2015). The short answer is that American politicians willed that it be so. The reasons why they made that choice are, in my view, entangled in the history of American race relations, evangelical Protestantism, and distinctive constitutional features of American government (Tonry 2004, 2009*b*).

[6] Chapter 2 traces the development of American sentencing policy since 1975.

laws mandating more and longer prison sentences that were mostly enacted in the 1980s and early 1990s. Other factors contributed, especially during earlier periods (Blumstein and Beck 1999; Raphael and Stoll 2013; Travis, Western, and Redburn 2014, chap. 3):

- In the 1970s, imprisonment rates increased partly because crime rates increased and there were therefore more cases to be dealt with.
- In the 1970s and 1980s, the attitudes of judges, prosecutors, and parole board members about crime and criminals, like those of Americans generally, became harsher. This was reflected in more aggressive prosecutions, more prison sentences, longer terms, and more revocations of probation and parole.
- In the 1980s and 1990s, the War on Drugs sent many hundreds of thousands of people to prison.
- Parole release was eliminated in many states. Where it survived, parole boards became much more risk averse at a time when sentencing became a major political issue, delaying release for most prisoners and in many states revoking parole of more than half of those released, primarily because of violations of technical conditions.
- Two-thirds of people admitted into prison in recent years in some states were parole and probation violators. The numbers are huge, but because their time in prison is typically short, they are not a major cause of population increases.
- Since the mid-1980s, longer prison terms required by harsh sentencing laws have been the primary reason why prison populations increased.

California's original three-strikes law provides vivid evidence. People convicted of a third strike, which could include any felony, no matter how minor, and many misdemeanors, received a minimum 25-year sentence. They were required to serve 85 percent of the sentence—at least 21 years and 3 months. The ballot initiative was approved in 1994. As I write these words in mid-2015, not one person has been released because their three-strikes sentence has been completed. The first possible expiration will occur late in 2015 or early in 2016.

It is reasonable to wonder whether rising, or high, American crime rates are the explanation for high rates of imprisonment. Changes in rates and patterns may be one reason citizens and politicians at various times became preoccupied with crime, but they are at most only a small part of the explanation. Crime rates increased significantly from the 1960s through 1991, but that happened in every developed country (Eisner 2008; Tonry 2014). Nowhere else, however, did sentencing laws and the use of imprisonment change radically (Tonry 2007). There is no causal relationship between rising crime rates and either enactment of harsher laws or increases in imprisonment rates (Lappi-Seppälä 2008). American politicians chose to increase use of imprisonment.

American crime rates are not the explanation for contemporary levels and patterns of imprisonment. Rates have been falling since 1991 and in any case have long been lower than in many developed countries except for homicide and offenses involving guns. Rates for violent offenses generally, however, including robberies, rapes, and assaults, are not higher than those in other countries with which the United States would ordinarily be compared (van Dijk, van Kesteren, and Smit 2007).

Even if all sentences imposed on people convicted of violent offenses were ignored, the United States would still have by a wide margin the highest imprisonment rate among developed countries. In 2011, as table 1.2 shows, 47.8 percent of sentenced offenders in state and federal prisons had been convicted of violent offenses. The rest were convicted of property, drug, and other nonviolent offenses. Extrapolated to the total imprisonment rate, including jails, the American imprisonment rate for nonviolent crimes alone was in recent years nearly 400 per 100,000. That is 2.5–6 times higher than the total rates of other developed countries, including their violent offenders.

Locking up so many people, hundreds of thousands for decades and lifetimes, does damage to them in prison and afterward and also hurts their children, families, and communities.[7] Imprisonment in America diminishes ex-prisoners' prospects of achieving economic success and law-abiding lives, and being good partners and parents. It costs vast amounts of money that would be better left in taxpayers' pockets or spent on other, more constructive things. It disproportionately burdens

[7] The research findings summarized in this and the following four paragraphs are discussed at length with extensive documentation in the 2014 National Academy of Sciences report on causes and consequences of high rates of incarceration (Travis, Western, and Redburn 2014, chaps. 3 and 5).

TABLE 1.2. Federal and state prisoners sentenced to 12 months or more, 2013, by offense

Offense	State	Federal	Total	Percent
Total	1,314,900	193,775	1,508,675	100
Violent	707,500	13,600	721,100	47.8
Property	247,100	11,500	258,600	17.1
Drug	210,200	98,200	308,400	20.4
Public order	140,200	69,200	209,400	13.9
Other	10,000	1,200	11,200	0.7

Source: Carson 2014, tables 14, 15.

minority communities and impedes progress toward a time when race no longer matters.

Some might believe these are regrettable but necessary prices to pay in order to have a safe society. However, overwhelming and largely uncontested evidence shows that much of the punishment American courts impose and corrections institutions deliver is ineffective. There is no credible evidence that lengthy prison sentences are more effective deterrents than short ones, and there is little evidence that imprisonment is a better deterrent than many community punishments.

Even the seemingly self-evident claim that imprisonment reduces crime because it incapacitates known offenders is subject to major qualifications. Large numbers of offenders would stop even if they were not sent to prison. Many young people commit crimes but naturally desist, most while teenagers. The peak offending ages are the middle teenage years for property offenses and the late teenage years for violence. Even among the relatively few people who continue offending into their twenties, most stop by their early thirties. Some enter into long-term relationships or get married. Some start work and realize they have something important to lose. Some find God. All of these things are associated with stopping offending. Other offenders just burn out. Specialists refer to offenders' "residual criminal careers," the time during which they will continue offending. Most are short. These patterns mean that many younger people sent to prison need not have been if the aim was to prevent crime, and that comparatively little is gained from holding older offenders for long periods.

Other problems bedevil hopes for much crime prevention through incapacitation. Locking up many drug users and dealers has almost no preventive effects. That is because they are minor participants in complex markets and are quickly replaced by others who naively believe the risks to be low and the profits high. The successors are usually wrong on both counts, but learn that only when they too are arrested. The story is much the same for higher-level drug traffickers. Similar processes affect many gang members. Small fry in ongoing criminal networks are usually quickly replaced by willing new recruits, and higher-ups step into leadership roles as they become available. It is sad that there are many disadvantaged young people who feel they have little to lose by joining gangs or selling drugs and are influenced by deviant role models and peer pressures, but it's true.

These are all reasons to question the preventive effects, let alone cost-effectiveness, of imprisonment in America. They are strengthened by a crucial, recently emerging research finding. All else being equal, people sent to prison are more likely to commit offenses in the future than if they had been punished in some other way. Critics of imprisonment for two centuries have believed this to be true. The first famous prison reformer, the eighteenth-century Englishman John Howard, called prisons "schools for crime" because they exposed incomers to a criminal milieu and deviant values, provided hardened criminals as role models, and led to stigma that made a later law-abiding life harder to achieve. Empirical evidence now shows that these speculations are true (Nagin, Cullen, and Jonson 2009; Bales and Piquero 2011; Cullen, Jonson, and Nagin 2011; Villettaz, Gilliéron, and Killias 2014).

American sentencing systems are broken. Huge numbers of people are locked up, to a significant extent because of harsh laws enacted in the 1980s and 1990s. There is no persuasive evidence that having so many people in prison significantly reduces crime through its deterrent and incapacitative effects. Confinement of older prisoners has few preventive effects, but holding them becomes increasingly costly, especially for medical care. Prisoners are the only people in America with a constitutional right to state provision of adequate medical care. Prisoners age and deteriorate faster than people in the free community; their medical needs are greater.

American sentencing laws and practices must be changed. Failed policies must be abandoned, successful ones improved, and promising new ones developed. The things that need doing are straightforward. Many build on solid evidence of what does and does not work.

II. How Can Things Be Improved?

Reducing the scale of imprisonment and building just sentencing systems will not be easy. Three kinds of changes are required. First, many fewer people should be sent to prison and jail and for much shorter stays. Second, devices need to be established to shorten the sentences of many now in prison. Third, sentencing systems should be redesigned to permit judges to impose just and appropriate punishments in every case that comes before them. Chapter 6 sets out, explains, and justifies a series of concrete proposals for reinventing American sentencing systems. This section paints them in broad strokes. The overall objective should be to reduce the national imprisonment rate to the mid-1980s level of 350 per 100,000 by 2020 and to the 1973 rate of 160 per 100,000 by 2030.

California's recent Proposition 36 provides a dramatic example of the kinds of changes that are needed. Passed in November 2012 by a two-thirds majority, it significantly narrowed the range of offenses subject to a 25-year minimum sentence and authorized many previously convicted prisoners to petition for resentencing. It will result in shorter sentences for many sent to prison in the future, and shorten the terms of many already there. Before that, California's law potentially applied to thousands of offenders per year—anyone previously convicted of two drug or violent felonies, and newly charged with a felony of any type or with many misdemeanors. That breadth of the third "strike" explains why people received 25-year and longer sentences for such things as taking pieces of pizza in a school playground in one notorious case, stealing two golf clubs in a second, and shoplifting $153 worth of video tapes in a third.

After the referendum, only serious violent felonies are covered. More than 3,000 California prisoners serving three-strikes sentences for misdemeanor or nonviolent felony convictions became eligible to apply for resentencing. Superior Court judge David Danielsen on November 24, 2012, ordered the release of the referendum's first beneficiary, 62-year-old Kenneth Corley, who had served more than 16 years for nonviolent drug possession offenses.[8] San Diego County District Attorney Bonnie Dumanis was among those who attended a welcome-home party. Proposition 47, approved in 2014, has again narrowed the scope of California's three-strikes law.

Fundamental changes must attend not only to sentencing laws but also to the activities of police and prosecutors. The police initiate most criminal cases. Prosecutors decide whether and how to proceed with them. These processes are not merely mechanical. People decide what to do. For some kinds of crimes, those decisions are usually self-evident. Serious acts of violence, very serious property crimes, high-level involvement in drug distribution networks, major white collar crimes—all these almost always do and should result in arrests and prosecutions. For many other kinds of crimes, those decisions are not self-evident. Examples include drug possession, low-level drug sales, many property and public order crimes, most property crimes by young or drug-dependent people, and much violence among friends or acquaintances. For these and for many more serious crimes, prosecutors can often find more constructive ways to deal with cases than sending them to court.

A. Reducing the Flow into Prison

There are four basic ways to reduce the number of people sent to prison: pull back from overcriminalization; change police policies and practices; change prosecution policies and practices; change sentencing laws and guidelines. All should be done. The proposals discussed below build on current experience in the United States or other Western countries.

1. *Overcriminalization*. There is widespread concern that too much of American life has been criminalized. The concern is not politically partisan. Liberal organizations like the American Civil Liberties Union, conservative ones like the Heritage Foundation and the Texas Public Policy Foundation, and libertarian ones like the Manhattan Institute have been equally active and assertive. Technical critiques focus on the weakening and elimination in American law of mens rea (guilty mind) requirements in the legal definitions of crimes. These changes, some by

[8] The story is told in "First Inmate Set for Release under California 3-Strikes Law Revision," http://www.thecrimereport.org/news/crime-and-justice-news/2012-11-3-strikes-release.

legislatures, some by appellate courts, were meant to make it easier to convict suspected offenders, with the inevitable effects that more innocent people are convicted and that prosecutors are given greater leverage to coerce confessions.

Broader critiques challenge a trend in recent decades to define deviance up, to redefine social problems as criminal law problems. Conservative organizations highlight criminalization of "morally innocuous" business conduct. Liberals tend to focus on public order offenses, drug possession, low-level drug dealing, property crimes, offenses in schools, and immigration violations (which in most developed countries are civil law violations, not crimes). Most Western countries do not rely heavily on the criminal law to deal with drug abuse, relying instead on treatment and education. They reserve criminal prosecution for high-level traffickers, wholesalers, manufacturers, and importers. Few treat immigration law violators as criminals.

Overcriminalization is a large and complex subject and not a main subject of this book. Prison admissions will fall quickly and substantially if American policy makers fundamentally rethink the tactics used in the "war" on drugs, deemphasizing prosecution of possessors and low-level and user dealers, and reemphasizing treatment and prevention. Decriminalizing possession, use, and sale of small quantities of drugs, as four states and the District of Columbia did by referendums in 2012 and 2014 for marijuana, would make a big difference quickly. Forbidding or greatly constraining imprisonment of parolees and probationers for violation of technical conditions would quickly and substantially reduce prison admissions. Missing an appointment, failing a drug test, or drinking alcohol are almost never punishable acts when done by other citizens. Yet many probationers and parolees are sent to jails and prisons because of them (Kleiman 2009).

Schools' zero-tolerance and similar policies that effectively criminalize violations of school rules are a repudiation of their traditional function of socializing young people. Recent research shows that even a single arrest reduces the likelihood a young person will finish high school (Kirk and Sampson 2012).

Rescission of policies that lead to frequent referrals of young people to the police by schools would make a short-term difference in prison numbers, though probably not a large one. It would, however, produce long-term benefits in school completion and young peoples' successful navigation of the challenges of their teenage years. It would reduce the prevalence of adolescent criminal records and their stigmatizing and disqualifying effects on college and employment applications. Those would be good things in themselves. They are also associated with lower levels of subsequent criminality.

2. *Police.* Police officers in the nature of things must exercise discretion. They always have and always will. Police officers understand as well as anyone else that arresting and prosecuting teenage offenders does long-term damage. That's why many officers often decide to call young people's parents rather than arrest them for minor crimes. That's why young people with drug or mental health problems who have apparently committed more serious offenses are often taken home if there are reasonable prospects of privately supported treatment or care. Police often would rather solve a human problem than make an arrest. They understand that public treatment programs are underresourced and overloaded, and that private efforts to solve young people's problems are usually more promising.

Similar things happen with adults. If private mental health or drug treatment is available, police are often prepared to let it be given a try. Often, albeit more in earlier times than now, police break up minor fights between friends and in domestic incidents, cool things down, and forget it unless one of those involved wants something more to be done.

In the 1960s, police fundamentally changed their way of handling public drunkenness. The title of a famous book by Raymond Nimmer, *Two Million Unnecessary Arrests: Removing a Social Service Concern from the Criminal Justice System* (1971), tells the tale. Police long responded to public drunkenness by making an arrest for vagrancy, loitering, or being a public nuisance and locking drunks up for the night. It was burdensome, frustrating, and expensive, an ineffective revolving door. Over time police practice changed, and most public drunks picked up are now taken home, to a homeless shelter, to a detox center, or to a hospital as circumstances suggest.

Something similar needs to be done with most drug arrests. Many arrests are made only because the police make tactical choices to do so or because police departments use the number of arrests made as an indicator of officers' productivity. The potential supply of arrestees is not limitless, but it is enormous. Making undercover purchases in disadvantaged urban neighborhoods is easy. In 2012 there were more than 750,000 arrests nationally for marijuana offenses and more than 40,000 in New York City alone. There were 1,550,000 felony drug arrests in the United States altogether. In 2013, more than 300,000 people were serving prison sentences for drug offenses, and at least 100,000 more were in county jails. In the 1980s and 1990s, those numbers were substantially larger.

Many of those convictions and imprisonments have no positive effects at all. Most drug sellers arrested on street corners are quickly replaced. At the corner of Ninth and Concordia in Milwaukee in the mid-1990s, for example, 94 drug arrests were made within a three-month period. "These arrests," a police officer said, "were easy to prosecute and to convict. But . . . the drug market continued to thrive at the intersection" (Smith and Dickey 1999, p. 8). Many drug, minor property crime, and prostitution arrests are of drug-dependent people trying to feed their addictions. As with the mass public drunkenness arrests of earlier times, the doors revolve and revolve.

There are better solutions for the problems these people pose. For the drug-dependent, referral to treatment costs less than arrest and prosecution, and promises better results. For street-corner drug sellers, if arrests are made at all, referral to treatment, community penalties, and short jail sentences cost less than prison sentences and do less damage. Many of those arrests, however, simply should not be made.

More generally, for all but serious crimes police should make arrests only as a last resort. Private solutions are almost always better. Sometimes that may entail referrals to private treatment programs. Sometimes they may involve informal restitution, mediation, or referral to a restorative justice program, or other times to drug or mental health treatment. Police in the United Kingdom and Australia have long operated restorative justice programs that aim to help victims and offenders find a solution without formal prosecution (Wilcox, Young, and Hoyle 2004; Association of Chief Police Officers 2012). There are many ways police could reduce the number of arrests they make without compromising public safety. For that to happen, police need to abandon use of arrests as a measure of officers' performance, and police organizations need to develop new systems of referral and dispute resolution.

3. *Prosecution*. Prosecutors exercise discretion and always will.[9] They are not automatons and often look for ways to handle sympathetic defendants without prosecuting them. They could do much more. In places where police make unnecessary arrests, prosecutors can and often do dismiss them. They can refer drug-dependent arrestees to treatment and many other suspects to dispute resolution, mediation, and restorative justice programs. They can also adopt new strategic approaches for dealing with large numbers of cases.

Prosecutors in most Western countries operate formal programs for dealing efficiently with large numbers of cases that are too serious to ignore. Sometimes convictions result. Sometimes, from recognition of the stigmatizing effects of convictions, they do not. In Germany, for example, section 153a of the German Criminal Procedure Code authorizes "conditional dismissals" under which suspects make restitution, pay a sum of money, or perform community service in order to avoid a formal accusation and a trial. This option is available only with the consent of the suspect, but he or she need not admit guilt. Prosecution is suspended, and if the suspect complies with his or her obligations, the charge in due course is dismissed. Of criminal sanctions imposed by judges and prosecutors in 2012, 19.2 percent resulted from conditional dismissals.

Prosecutors in the Netherlands and Belgium operate "transactions" systems that are similar. The defendant is offered the opportunity to resolve the case by accepting the financial or community punishment they would have received if convicted. For most offenses, and all minor ones, the offer is made on a take-it-or-leave-it basis. Almost all suspects take it. There are no negotiations or haggling. No guilty plea is required. More than 90 percent of criminal cases are potentially eligible for transactions. In 2008, more than 26 percent of criminal cases resulting in sanctions were resolved in this way (68,290 of 260,228).

Prosecutors in Scandinavian countries and elsewhere in Europe operate "penal order" systems. These are similar to conditional dismissals

[9] The prosecutorial diversion systems mentioned in this section, and others, are discussed in detail in papers on individual countries in Luna and Wade (2012) and Tonry (2012a). Most have been in use for many years. On Germany, see Weigend (2001, 2016). On the Netherlands, see Tak (2001) and van de Bunt and van Gelder (2012). On Scandinavia, see Lappi-Seppälä (2007, 2016) and Asp (2012).

and transactions except that the defendant must plead guilty. Because criminal records are seldom publicly available, the implications of a conviction are less portentous than in the United States. The defendant is told what sentence will be imposed if he or she agrees to accept the penal order. Twenty percent of criminal cases prosecuted in Sweden in 2010 were dealt with in this way (50,920 of 259,612).[10]

All of these organized programs for informal prosecutorial resolution of cases could be established and implemented in the United States. As a practical matter, since *Bordenkircher v. Hayes*, 434 U.S. 357 (1978) and *Castle Rock v. Gonzales*, 545 U.S. 748 (2005), were decided by the US Supreme Court, discretionary prosecutorial decisions in the United States are not reviewable by courts. Individual offices could establish diversion programs on their own. Enactment of authorizing legislation as in Europe would be better. It would make the process more transparent. Either way, organized systems for prosecutorial handling and final disposition of cases too serious for outright dismissal would save money, reduce the volume of cases dealt with by courts, and reduce the number of people sentenced to imprisonment. Systems not requiring guilty pleas and convictions as in Germany, the Netherlands, and Belgium would reduce stigmatization and avoid the collateral effects of conviction which in the United States blight many offenders' lives. Such programs would also reduce prison populations.

A large fraction of cases coming to the attention of prosecutors should be handled through dismissals, informal diversions, and disposition through formal programs involving sanctions like those in Europe. Another large fraction, however, involving violence, large-scale property crimes, major drug trafficking activity, and white collar crimes will be prosecuted. For these cases, prosecutors need to rethink what they do and create better policies. The priorities are to moderate plea negotiation strategies and sentencing recommendations and demands. In most American jurisdictions, many drug and violent offenses are potentially subject to lengthy mandatory minimum sentences. Prosecutors, however, have unreviewable discretion to file charges or insist on guilty pleas to other offenses not subject to mandatory penalty laws. US Attorney General

---

[10] The Netherlands also recently adopted penal orders. Of 191,131 cases resolved by courts or prosecutors in 2012, more than a third resulted from transactions (20,719) or penal orders (44,448).

Eric Holder, for example, directed federal prosecutors early in 2014 to become much more discriminating in filing charges subject to mandatory minimums, and to use them only for serious and aggravated cases. That should become standard practice in all prosecutors' offices.

Something more is needed, though—a fundamental change in ways of thinking about the prosecutors' role. Just as police need to stop thinking about arrests as a primary measure of police productivity, prosecutors need to stop thinking about convictions and severe sentences as primary goals. They should instead be thinking about sensible and humane dispositions of cases that come before them and of sentences that are just and appropriate under the circumstances.

American criminal courts operate on the adversary legal system assumption that prosecutors and defense lawyers should aggressively promote their clients' interests. That is the appropriate function of the defense lawyer, but the prosecutor as representative of the state has broader responsibilities. The current approach leads both to unnecessarily aggressive prosecutions and to primary emphases on winning convictions and obtaining severe punishments. In continental Europe, by contrast, prosecutors in most countries are career civil servants and are part of the judicial branch of government. Individuals often work in both roles, sometimes alternating between them. Prosecutors have the legal status and ethical obligations of judges. In most of Europe, prosecutors do not plea-bargain and are ethically barred from proposing sentences. That is seen as uniquely the judge's function. For judges and prosecutors both, acquittal of the innocent is as important as conviction of the guilty.

Federal Court of Appeals judge Gerald Lynch (2003) has observed that American prosecutors, by contrast, because of plea bargaining and the intimidating effects of mandatory minimum sentence laws, have effectively supplanted judges both in determining guilt and in deciding sentences in more than 95 percent of cases. All of this is exacerbated by the partisan election of state chief prosecutors and appointment of federal ones, many of whom are politically motivated to be "tough on crime."

Election and partisan appointment of prosecutors result from provisions of American state and federal constitutions. The pertinent provisions are unlikely to change any time soon. The constitutional autonomy of the prosecutor, however, means that policies and priorities are uniquely his or hers to set. Current approaches and attitudes have produced the policies and practices that now exist, but they can be changed.

4. *Sentencing Laws.* Changes to policing and prosecution will not by themselves greatly reduce the prison population in the short term, although they can significantly reduce prison admissions. Changes in sentencing legislation are required. Mandatory minimum, three-strikes, and truth-in-sentencing laws result in many people being sent to prison who should not be locked up. Retail drug dealers are a prime example. These and life-without-parole laws result in many people being sent to prison for too long.

"Too long" is to some extent, but not completely, in the eye of the beholder. Most people probably agree with California voters that a minimum 25-year sentence for a minor violent, property, or drug offense is much too long. In recent decades, American prison sentences became much longer than they were before 1980, and there is no good reason why they should not be rolled back. The National Academy of Sciences Panel on Understanding and Controlling Violence in 1993 showed that the average American prison sentence per violent crime tripled between 1975 and 1989 (Reiss and Roth 1993). That increase occurred before any modern three-strikes and truth-in-sentencing laws had been enacted, mostly in 1993–96. The multiple would be substantially greater today.

American sentences are by far the longest in the Western world. In most countries, sentences longer than 1 year are rare, 1 or 2 percent of the total. For example, as table 1.3 shows, only 5–20 percent of convicted offenders are sentenced to imprisonment in seven Western European countries, including the four most populous: England and Wales, France, Germany, and Italy. Most sentences to imprisonment are for a year or less. In six of the countries, half to two-thirds of prison sentences are for terms of 6 months or less. Germany is the exception, but only because German law strongly discourages use of short prison sentences as serving little purpose yet severely damaging offenders' and their families' lives. In most of these countries, only 1–3 percent of offenders sent to prison receive sentences of 5 years or longer.

Even those numbers look misleadingly large. Few convicted offenders receive prison sentences at all. Germany imposes the highest percentage

Table 1.3. Length of prison sentences in months, selected countries, 2010

Country	Percent sentenced to prison	Of these, percent under 6 months	Of these, percent 6–12 months	Of these, percent 12–24 months	Of these, percent 24–60 months	Of these, percent 60–120 months	Of these, percent over 120 months
Austria	n.a.	56.1	16.7	11.9	2.0	1.2	n.a.
Finland	3.1	61.2	15.5	11.4	9.3	1.8	0.3
France	17.8	57.2	20.3	17.3	2.8	1.4	1.0
Germany	5.4	24.1	28.6	18.8	24.4	3.5	0.3
Netherlands	23	74.1	10.8	6.3	4.9	1.2	0.4
Sweden	9.6	60.6	14.2	14.3	5.4	3.1	n.a.
Switzerland (2007)	n.a.	87.1	3.4	2.6	4.5	0.4	0.1
England	7.5	52.7	17.4	12.6	11.4	3.8	0.7
United States	73.0 (2009)						

Sources: Europe 2007—Aebi et al. 2010; Europe 2010—Aebi et al. 2014, tables 3.2.3.1 and 3.2.7.1; United (offenses charged as felonies) (cases initially prosecuted as felonies).

of prison sentences of a 5 years or longer—3.5 percent. That is 3.5 percent of the 5.4 percent of convicted offenders overall who are sent to prison. In other words, less than one-fourth of 1 percent of all convicted offenders receive 5-year or longer sentences. In addition, prisoners in most European countries receive an automatic one-third reduction in their sentences, called "remission," basically the same as American "good time"—time off for good behavior.

In many countries, the maximum sentence that can be imposed for any single offense is 12, 15, or 20 years. LWOPs are unconstitutional in European countries. They conflict with European and national laws. In 2013, the European Court of Human Rights in *Case of Vintner and Others v. The United Kingdom* (nos. 66069/09, 130/10, and 3896/10) held full life sentences to violate the European Convention of Human Rights. The German Constitutional Court nearly 40 years ago declared full life sentences to violate the German constitution, and required that every prisoner be allowed to petition for release after at most 14 years, and regularly thereafter, under procedures that afforded a meaningful review of the need for continued confinement and a meaningful possibility of release (*lebenslange Freiheitsstrafe*, 21 June 1977, 45 *BVerfGE* 187).[11]

No reliable data are available that allow detailed comparisons between sentences imposed in the United States and other countries. Comprehensive national American data including both felonies and misdemeanors do not exist. The most recent national data, shown in table 1.4, cover only sentences imposed on people charged with felonies (though they may have been convicted of misdemeanors) in the 75 most populous counties in 2009. Overall, of people charged with felonies, 73 percent were sentenced to prison or jail, including 100 percent of murderers, 89 percent of robbers and rapists, 75 percent of property offenders, and 71 percent of drug offenders. Sentences are incomparably more severe than in Europe. Among people sentenced to state prisons, the mean sentences were 373 months for murder, 142 for rape, 90 for robbery, and 40 for property offenses. Most serious offenses are covered by truth-in-sentencing and mandatory

[11] Kommers (1997, pp. 306–13) provides an English translation of extracts from the opinion. Limits on maximum prison sentences and rationales by which courts in a number of European countries have forbidden full life sentences are discussed in detail in van Zyl Smit and Snacken (2009).

minimum sentence laws. Many offenders serve 80–90 percent of their nominal maximum terms.

Part of the explanation for long American sentences is that they are a residue of the movement away from indeterminate sentencing after 1975. In those systems, judges set maximum and sometimes minimum terms, but knowing that the time to be served would be decided by a parole board. Both maximums and minimums were usually shortened by at least a third by time off for good behavior, and parole boards released many prisoners as soon as they were eligible. In the most indeterminate systems, in California and Washington, judges decided only who went to prison; every sentence was "1 year to the maximum authorized by law." The maximum sentences judges announced in indeterminate systems often were long: 20, 30, or 40 years or life. For multiple offenses, sentences could be made consecutive, making it possible for judges to impose sentences measured in hundreds of years. Such sentences continue to be imposed even though parole lease is no longer possible in many states and for many offenders. An Alabama man convicted of rape in 2012, for example, received a sentence that included six consecutive 99-year sentences.[12] An Arizona man convicted of possession of child pornography was sentenced in 2003 to 200 years—20 consecutive 10-year sentences.[13]

Under indeterminate sentencing, every prisoner in some systems was eligible for parole release after serving 1 year, no matter how long the maximum sentence announced by the judge. Judges sometimes expressed their horror at particular crimes or their frustration that parole boards could second guess their decisions by imposing long but entirely symbolic sentences. Newspaper stories might report a 25-year sentence, or longer, but everyone involved knew the offender might be released after a year or some other much shorter period. A June 20, 1970, *New York Times* article reported a 1,500-year prison sentence for possession and sale of heroin, "the longest sentence in Texas history. Sentences of

---

[12] A *Los Angeles Times* article reported: "In Tuesday's sentencing, 25-year-old Mark Anthony Beecham was given 99 years each for six counts—first-degree kidnapping, two counts of first-degree rape and three counts of first-degree sodomy—plus 20 years for felony first-degree theft of property and 10 more for felony first-degree bail jumping" (Hubbard 2012).

[13] *State of Arizona v. Morton Robert Berger* (2006), Supreme Court of Arizona (no. CR-05-0101-PR).

TABLE 1.4. Felony sentences, US state courts, by type and length of confinement, 2009

Maximum mean sentence length in months, felons				
Conviction offense	**Percentage imprisonment**	**Incarceration**		**Percentage non-imprisonment**
		Prison	**Jail**	
All offenses	73%	52 mo.	5 mo.	27%
Violent offenses	83	91 mo.	6 mo.	17
Murder/nonnegligent manslaughter	100	373	n.a.	0
Rape	89	142	n.a.	11
Robbery	89	90	9	11
Assault	81	62	6	19
Property offenses	75	40 mo.	6 mo.	25
Burglary	79	52	7	21
Larceny	72	31	6	28
Motor vehicle theft	77	34	7	23
Fraud	71	47	5	29
Drug offenses	71	40 mo.	5 mo.	29
Trafficking	80	49	6	20
Other drug offenses	64	29	4	36

Source: Reaves 2013, tables 24–26.

1000 years and more have been given recently in cases of rape, robbery, and assault."

American judges and legislators under indeterminate sentencing were accustomed to thinking of sentences expressed in multiples of the numbers of their fingers and toes, even though in practice most sentences served were far shorter. In most other developed countries, by contrast, a one- or two-year sentence is long and 25- or 200-year sentences are impossible and unimaginable. That difference contributed substantially to lengthening sentences and increasing prison populations in the United States after support for indeterminate sentencing collapsed. Parole release was eliminated in many states and became much less common in the others.

Laws requiring long sentences have a sleeper effect. That is why no one by 2015 had been released under California's three-strikes law because his or her sentence has expired. For many years after such laws are enacted, newly admitted prisoners simply accumulate; their numbers are not offset by others being released. That is why American imprisonment rates rose for 16 years after crime rates peaked in 1991 and began a steep long-term decline. The ultimate effects are not yet known of the laws mandating decades-long sentences that were enacted between 1984 and 1996.

American imprisonment rates cannot fall substantially if so many people are sent to prison for such long times. Fixing that will require three major changes in sentencing laws. First, mandatory minimum sentence, three-strikes, and LWOP laws must be repealed or radically pruned so they affect only small numbers of people who present substantial threats of serious future violent behavior. Those laws that remain should be amended to specify sentences much shorter than the 5-, 10-, and 20-year and longer periods that are now common.

Second, sentence lengths need to be shortened substantially across the board. Other countries manage to punish offenders appropriately and proportionately with prison sentences measured in months and small numbers of years. Until the 1970s, American jurisdictions did too. They can again.

Sentencing lengths seem to be perceived by many American politicians as the equivalent of the third rail in a subway: touch it and you'll be electrocuted, or at least politically imperiled for defying harsh public attitudes. They are wrong, as large bodies of evidence have long made clear. Ordinary citizens vastly underestimate the severity of sentences, are less single-mindedly punitive than politicians believe, and are much more likely than politicians believe to support use of community penalties and referrals to treatment programs (Roberts et al. 2003).

Federal District Court judge James S. Gwin recently learned this, to his dismay. He imposed a much harsher sentence in a child pornography case than jurors thought appropriate:

> I asked each of the [12] Sheldon jurors—who were a cross-section of the community and who actually heard the case, saw the terrible images and videos, and met the defendant—to recommend

> anonymously what punishment Sheldon should receive. I put their responses away without examining them. Months later, I sentenced Sheldon within the guidelines range, but near the high end. Surprise came upon learning that my sentence was almost five times higher than the average of the jurors' sentence recommendations. (Gwin 2010, p. 173)

The mean average sentence recommended by the jurors was 20 months imprisonment; the median was 15 months. The federal guidelines required a prison term between 87 and 108 months. Gwin and six other federal trial judges replicated his effort in 22 cases. The median sentences recommended by jurors were 19 percent of the median guidelines sentences and 36 percent of the least severe sentences authorized.

Gwin's discovery surprises no one who is familiar with research on public opinion and knowledge. Asked whether judges' sentences are too lenient, too severe, or about right, large majorities of Americans in recent decades answer "too lenient." Yet when citizens are asked to indicate what sentences they would impose, almost always the sentences they specify are less severe than those judges impose (Roberts et al. 2003).

We know why: citizens believe sentences to be much less severe than they really are. Most Americans learn about criminal cases from media accounts, many involving sentences said by someone to be too lenient. Media accounts, however, deal primarily in sensational crimes. Courts handle few sensational cases and many mundane ones. When citizens learn more, and especially when they know the reasons behind judges' decisions in particular cases, they are much less critical. Judges think about crimes and criminals in all their human complexity. When citizens have sufficient knowledge to think in that way, they react in much the same way as judges do (Yankelovich 1991; Slobogin and Brinkley-Rubenstein 2014).

Research on deterrence makes it clear that differences in sentence lengths have no discernible effects on behavior. Research on incapacitation shows long sentences to be ineffective at preventing crime. Many people are confined who would have stopped offending in any case. Others are adversely affected by their prison experience and become more likely to commit crimes in the future. It is important that the criminal law and punishment reinforce fundamental social norms, but this can be done with a system of short sentences closely proportioned to the gravity of the offenses for which they are imposed.

Third, policy makers should strengthen and professionalize parole boards in jurisdictions that have them, and reestablish them where they do not exist. Experience with parole guidelines in the 1970s showed that they can effectively regulate parole release decisions and reduce unwarranted disparities in the lengths of prison sentences. Research on the ineffectiveness of correctional treatment programs in the 1970s undermined support for basing release decisions on rehabilitative considerations. Mountains of evidence have since accumulated, however, that show that many treatment programs can change people's lives for the good. Parole boards often have good reasons to conclude that there is no valid reason to keep someone in prison longer. Parole boards can also play an important and, in the large majority of states that do not have well-developed systems of appellate review of sentences, indispensable role in evening out disparities that result from judicial idiosyncrasy and caprice.

Revivified parole release systems might be of two different types. The two-thirds of states that retain parole release need to professionalize their parole boards, repeal most of the laws that make prisoners ineligible for release, and pass new laws making all prisoners currently in prison eligible to apply for release. Well-designed and managed guidelines systems can make decisions more consistent and decision makers more accountable.

Those states that do not have parole boards, and the federal government, should reestablish them. In indeterminate sentencing states they would play the same kinds of roles they traditionally played. In the handful of states with sentencing guidelines, their roles might be different. In states with presumptive guidelines, their authority might be restricted to consideration of applications for release of prisoners serving especially long sentences. The US Supreme Court's decision in *Blakely v. Washington*, 542 U.S. 296 (2004), already treats the upper bound of a presumptive guideline range as equivalent to a statutory maximum sentence. In advisory guidelines states, all of which lack meaningful systems of appellate sentence review, the parole guidelines should be designed to dovetail with the sentencing guidelines. If judges choose to impose sentences more severe than applicable sentencing guidelines specify, the parole board should have authority to review the adequacy of the judge's reasons and to set a release date from within the range specified in the guidelines. For especially long sentences, parole boards should have authority to evaluate the need for continued confinement of individual prisoners, and release those for whom need cannot be shown.

5. *Sentencing Standards.* It may seem odd to some readers that the subject of sentencing standards appears so late in this introduction.[14] That is because the overuse of the criminal law and imprisonment is now a widely recognized problem, and sentencing is the end of a long process that depends on laws legislatures enact and on actions of police officers and prosecutors. At the end of the day, however, judges decide sentences in cases in which the prosecutor has not negotiated a specific sentence (judges have power to reject negotiated sentences but seldom do). We know a lot about sentencing decisions and about how to help judges make them better and more fairly (Spohn 2008; Tonry 2013).

When support for indeterminate sentencing collapsed, "unwarranted sentencing disparities" were widely seen to be the fundamental problem. States tried to address it in many ways. One solution worked. First Minnesota, then other states including notably Washington, Oregon, North Carolina, and Kansas, adopted "presumptive" guidelines for sentencing. Depending on the offense and the offender's criminal record, guidelines specified ranges within which judges were expected to choose sentences for typical cases. If the judge believed a case was not typical, he or she could impose some other sentence but had to explain why. Defendants and the state could challenge that explanation by appealing to a higher court. The aim was to develop a body of appellate case law that over time would establish standards for difficult kinds of cases.

By every measure, presumptive guidelines succeeded. Evaluations showed that they made sentencing fairer and more consistent. They reduced sentencing disparities generally and in relation to defendants' race, ethnicity, and gender.

Most of the successful commissions adopted a "corrections capacity" constraint policy. This meant that the new guidelines were designed so

[14] The research findings on effects of sentencing policies summarized in this subsection are discussed at length with extensive documentation through their respective dates in Blumstein et al. (1983), Tonry (1996, 2013), and Travis, Western, and Redburn (2014, chap. 3).

that they would not result in more people being sent to prison than the prisons were designed to hold. The aim was not to limit the size of the prison population but to create a rational planning process. If legislators wanted to pass laws that would increase prison use, they certainly could, but they would have to allocate resources to increase the existing capacity. This too worked.

All of these states managed to balance their prison populations and capacities, and all experienced lower levels of population increase than national or regional averages. Minnesota and Washington, for example, had stable or gradually rising prison populations during the 1980s when the national rate doubled. North Carolina, for another example, elected to control the absolute level of its prison population and succeeded. In 1971, its imprisonment rate was the highest in the country. It was 32nd in 2013. Since the guidelines took effect in 1994, the North Carolina rate has been essentially flat, fluctuating between 340 and 370 per 100,000 population (Tonry 2013).

Other efforts to reduce sentencing disparities were markedly less successful. California, Arizona, Illinois, and a few other states in the late 1970s revised their criminal codes to spell out appropriate sentences for typical cases. This was soon shown to have little effect on disparities. No additional states enacted such laws.

Many states and an enormous number of local courts in the 1970s and 1980s established "voluntary" guidelines based on research on past sentencing patterns. The logic was that if judges were aware of the kinds of sentences offenders typically received for particular offenses, they would in the interest of consistency want to impose something similar. The reasoning was plausible, but proved to be wrong. Evaluations showed that such systems had few or no discernible effects on disparities or on sentencing patterns generally. Only a few states since then have created voluntary systems, and that has generally been because judges, prosecutors, or both waged successful battles against presumptive guidelines.

The US Sentencing Commission adopted a system of "mandatory" guidelines, which was disastrously unsuccessful. Highly detailed, mechanical, and severe, they provoked widespread resistance from prosecutors and judges. They largely eliminated the use of community sentences and forbade judges to take account of defendants' personal characteristics that most judges, and most people, believe to be ethically relevant. The guidelines were widely circumvented. Because the extent and forms of circumvention varied widely between judicial districts and courts, they produced massive disparities. They also led to an eight-fold increase in the federal prison population. The US Supreme Court, in the series of decisions already mentioned, gradually weakened the federal guidelines and finally, in *United States v. Booker*, 543 U.S. 220 (2005), converted them into a voluntary guidelines system.

There is a clear conclusion to be drawn. All states should create a sentencing commission and adopt presumptive sentencing guidelines. Well-designed and well-implemented presumptive guidelines systems reduce disparities, increase fairness and transparency, and enable jurisdictions to engage in rational policy and resource planning. The other approaches failed. Jurisdictions that want to make sentencing fairer and more consistent and to control or reduce the size of their prison population have a proven tool at their disposal to do so.

6. *Community Penalties.* If fewer offenders are imprisoned, credible, evidence-based community programs will be needed. Many already exist, but more are needed. Twenty years ago comparatively little was known about targeting and operation of successful programs, but that has changed. A vast evaluation literature shows what does and does not work in dealing with particular kinds of offenders. Many kinds of programs can reduce later offending. Drug and other problem-solving courts that try to target treatment effectively have proliferated. Drug abuse treatment and programs aimed at enhancing offenders' cognitive skills and empathy have been especially effective (MacKenzie 2006).

The need can be described in a few words: well-targeted, well-designed, and well-run programs. Correctional interventions, just like those in medical and mental health programs, need to address specific needs and deficits. One size seldom fits all. There are different kinds of drug dependence, sexual offending proclivities, mental handicaps, personality disorders, and deficits in educational and vocational skills.

Much in the preceding paragraph no doubt seems self-evident. I risk belaboring the discussion because the American experience with community programs has not in recent decades been a happy or successful one. Large-scale efforts in the 1970s to create new "alternatives to imprisonment" and in the 1980s to create "intermediate sanctions" are generally assessed as failures. Evaluations seldom demonstrated success either in addressing human problems associated with offending or in reducing it. Most new initiatives were swamped by "net-widening," the tendency of judges to use them for people who would have been sentenced to other, less restrictive community penalties and not in place of imprisonment. Many programs provided little treatment but subjected offenders to many technical conditions and close surveillance. Large proportions of participants, often majorities, breached conditions, had their community sentences revoked, and were then sentenced to confinement. The net effect was that the programs often increased both the use of imprisonment and corrections costs (Morris and Tonry 1990).

In retrospect, those results are not surprising. A vast increase in the number of people sentenced to probation and other community penalties paralleled the increases in imprisonment. This had two implications, one budgetary, one managerial. Prisons cost much more to create and operate than community programs. State budgets have been groaning under the burden for three decades. Prisons take political priority, and community corrections programs have long been seriously underfunded. Even with adequate funding, however, the challenges would have been enormous. The number of probationers and parolees increased by several times between 1970 and 1990, and the size of the already overburdened correctional apparatus grew substantially less. Private sector organizations with adequate funding have difficulty managing large-scale expansions successfully. Neither corrections managers nor corrections funding were up to it.

Those early programs also suffered from the times in which they were attempted. The era of law and order politics began in the 1970s and reached full force in the 1980s and early 1990s. Those were the years when severe mandatory minimum sentence, three-strikes, and truth-in-sentencing laws were enacted, when opinion surveys showed that Americans ranked crime and drugs as the nation's most pressing problems, and when Democrats and Republicans competed to show they were tougher on crime. Public attitudes toward crime and criminals became harsher. Prosecutors and judges became more severe independently of the passage of tougher sentencing laws. In retrospect, net-widening, strict enforcement of conditions, and large-scale revocations are not surprising. They reflected the temper of the times.

These are no longer those times. Almost everyone agrees that American punishment systems got out of control, that many sentencing laws are too harsh, and that there are too many people in prison. And this time other conditions are more promising. Many corrections programs have been shown to work. Correctional administration has been professionalized. And, not least importantly, there is wider understanding of the troubled lives of many offenders and of the damage to them, their families, and their communities that recent policies have produced.

B. Reducing the Current Prison Population

Reforming the flow of cases into court and developing effective sentencing guidelines systems will not by themselves resolve the prison population problem. Methods need to be developed to reduce the number of people already in prison. Two basic tools are available.

1. *Parole Release.* Almost every Western country has a system for selective release of prisoners. In some, for example, England and Wales, a parole board has authority to release prisoners after they have served a fixed percentage, usually half, of their sentences. That authority is limited to prisoners serving especially long sentences, which there means 4 or more years (actually 2, since prisoners receive a 50 percent credit for remission of sentence for good behavior; in the United States the term "good time" is used and the percentage is always lower). In other countries, like Germany, a special panel of appellate judges considers petitions for release. The release window is small: eligibility typically accrues after serving half the sentence, and remission rules require release after two-thirds. In Canada, parole boards handle most cases, and courts consider petitions for release from people convicted of murder.

Under indeterminate sentencing in the United States, every jurisdiction operated a parole release system, and the boards exercised broad discretion. Nearly two-thirds of states continue to operate parole release systems. Many, however, have enacted mandatory minimum sentence and truth-in-sentencing laws that trump the board's authority over most people convicted of serious crimes.

Reinvigoration and, where it was abandoned, reestablishment of parole boards' release authority could play an important part in addressing America's prison problem. Reasonable people disagree about the desirability of reviving parole release. The arguments against doing so are primarily three, one of which is obsolete. The first is that a public interest in transparency and accountability makes a system like Minnesota's presumptive sentencing guidelines preferable. Citizens know what's going on because it happens in public view, and judges must follow the guidelines or explain why not. The second is that the history of parole boards—often composed of political appointees lacking in relevant specialized knowledge, underfunded, poorly run, and risk-averse—gives little reason to suppose they'll do better in the future.

The third argument, influential in the 1970s and 1980s, is that knowledge of people's experiences in prison provides little or no additional information relevant to release decisions. In those years, however, researchers and many practitioners believed that treatment programs in prison were ineffective and that "nothing works." Since then we have learned that many well-designed, well-run, and well-targeted treatment programs can reduce reoffending. Successful participation in prison programs thus may provide new, relevant information to be taken into account in making release decisions.

The arguments in favor of reinvigorating parole release are stronger. Parole release systems can be professionally run and transparent. Research in the 1970s and 1980s showed that well-managed systems can develop guidelines for release decisions and operate administrative appeal systems that allow prisoners to contest the decisions. The first parole guidelines system, operated by the US Parole Board, worked as intended and, compared with prior practice, produced more consistent results. Parole boards in Minnesota, Oregon, and Washington established similar systems. A federally funded evaluation concluded that the federal and Minnesota systems improved consistency in release dates and time served (Gottfredson, Wilkins, and Hoffman 1978; Arthur D. Little, Inc. and Goldfarb and Singer, Esqs. 1981).

Parole guidelines have two important potential advantages and one major disadvantage. One advantage is that case-by-case parole decision making can be expeditious and economical—faster, less costly, and more easily appealed than decisions by judges. There is nothing inherently complicated about establishing an effective system of management controls. A second advantage is that parole boards can expeditiously address prison overcrowding problems by adjusting release dates. This commonly happened during the indeterminate sentencing era (Messinger, Berecochea, Rauma, and, Berk 1985).

The disadvantage is that parole boards have authority only over offenders sentenced to imprisonment. Parole guidelines can reduce disparities among people sentenced to imprisonment, but not between them and people sentenced to local jails or community punishments.

The solution to this last concern is for jurisdictions to develop both parole guidelines and presumptive sentencing guidelines. That would provide standards for nonprison sentences, increase consistency in release decisions, and diminish disparities in the sentences judges impose. Appellate sentence review is nearly nonexistent in most jurisdictions and is robust only in Minnesota and a few other states. Appellate judges tend to be highly deferential to trial judges' decisions. This is partly because appellate judges recognize, appropriately, that their familiarity with the case is limited. They know only what they read in lawyers' written submissions and what they sometimes hear in lawyers' short oral presentations. Perhaps less appropriately, appellate courts apply a tradition of comity in reviewing trial courts' decisions, much as states recognize other states' laws and countries those of other countries. Judges tend to respect other judges' autonomy.

This is not self-evidently desirable. Aristotle and Plato often had different views about what justice requires. Thurgood Marshall and Clarence Thomas undoubtedly would. Judges' personalities and beliefs influence how they react viscerally and intellectually. It is not obvious that idiosyncratic decisions about citizens' liberty deserve great deference.

2. *Safety Valve Systems.* Parole boards lack authority to release prisoners serving long minimum sentences and LWOPs. Sometimes almost every informed person in a particular case, including the sentencing judge, believes that mandatory minimum sentence or LWOP laws require a sentence that is unjustly severe. After-the-fact solutions like the petitions for resentencing some three-strikes cases that California's Propositions 36 and 47 authorized are rare and can affect only a tiny fraction of deserving cases. A better solution is for states and the federal government to establish safety valve systems that permit reconsideration of long sentences. The easy way to do this prospectively is to authorize parole boards or, as in Germany and some other European countries, specialized courts to consider the need for continued confinement of

any prisoner who has served more than a designated number of years. Three years for prisoners 35 and older and 5 years for all others would be appropriate. More than 150,000 people were serving life sentences in the United States in 2011, of whom 50,000 were serving LWOPs (Nellis 2013). Many hundreds of thousands more were serving sentences measured in decades.

If the emerging consensus that the American systems of sentencing and imprisonment are broken holds, the means to begin to repair them are available. Whether they are used remains to be seen.

2

Sentencing Fragments

WERE IT POSSIBLE FOR A group of time-traveling judges, lawyers, and corrections officials from 1970 to attend a national conference on sentencing in our time, they would be bewildered. The current system would be unrecognizable, and probably unimaginable.

American sentencing systems had changed very little since 1930. No one working within them in 1970 had ever known anything else. They must have seemed timeless. Every American state and the federal system had an indeterminate sentencing system premised on rehabilitation as its primary aim. Here is how Francis Allen, later the leading scholar of the subject, described the rehabilitative ideal in 1959:

> Measures employed to treat the convicted offender should serve a therapeutic function. . . . Such measures should be designed to affect changes in the behavior of the convicted person in the interests of his own happiness, health, and satisfactions and in the interest of social defense. (p. 226)

Sentences were to be individualized in every case to fit the offender's circumstances and needs (e.g., Rothman 1971).

Details varied, but the broad picture was everywhere the same. Sentencing was considered a professional matter requiring specialized expertise and best handled by knowledgeable officials working behind closed doors. Statutes defined crimes and set out wide ranges of authorized sentences—typically from probation or a fine to 10, 20, 30, or more years. Few laws mandated minimum sentences, and when they did they typically specified 1 or 2 years. Almost everyone disapproved of mandatory sentences.

Judges adjudicated cases; decided whether to impose prison, jail, probation, or monetary sentences; and set maximum and sometimes minimum prison terms. Sentence appeals were for all practical purposes unavailable. Judges had broad discretion to individualize sentences. No rules or standards existed that appellate judges could look to in deciding the rare cases in which appeals were filed. Parole boards decided who would be released and when, and subject to what conditions. Prison systems offered extensive time off for good behavior.

Punishments were mild by twenty-first-century standards. In 1960, for example, the mean times served nationally for murder, rape, and robbery were 121, 42, and 45 months (in 2009, the misleadingly low means were 175, 94, and 57 months).[1] In 1970, the incarceration rate for federal and state prisons had been fluctuating in a narrow band around 110 per 100,000 population since the 1920s. When jail inmates are added, the total rate was 150–60. Since 1961 the rate had been falling modestly but continuously (Cahalan 1986, table 3.23).

Indeterminate sentencing was not controversial. The Model Penal Code (American Law Institute 1962) endorsed it and contained numerous provisions meant to improve it. In 1972, the National Council on Crime and Delinquency's Advisory Council of Judges issued the second edition of its Model Sentencing Act; it too assumed the continuation of indeterminate sentencing. So did the President's Commission on Law Enforcement and Administration of Justice (1967), the National Commission on Reform of Federal Criminal Laws (1971), and the National Advisory Commission on Criminal Justice Standards and Goals (1973).

Indeterminate sentencing nonetheless imploded in the 1970s. All its premises and assumptions were attacked. Criticisms piled up. Judge

[1] Bonczar (2011). The 2009 means are misleadingly low because they are based on average times served of people released that year. One year's releases disproportionately include people serving short sentences—one-third of those serving 3 years are released, but only one-twentieth of those serving 20 years—and do not reflect the much longer sentences being served by people sentenced under recently enacted three-strikes, LWOPs, and similar laws. Those prisoners will never be released or will begin to be released only in coming years.

Marvin Frankel's *Criminal Sentences: Law without Order* (1973) referred to indeterminate sentencing as "lawless" because of the absence of standards for sentencing decisions and of opportunities for appeals. Unwarranted disparities were said to be common and risks of racial bias and arbitrariness to be high (e.g., American Friends Service Committee 1971). Legal scholars criticized the system's lack of procedural fairness, transparency, and predictability (e.g., Davis 1969; Dershowitz 1976). Researchers showed that the system did not keep its rehabilitative promises (e.g., Kassebaum, Ward, and Wilner 1971; Martinson 1974; Lipton, Martinson, and Wilks 1975). Others argued that parole release procedures were unfair and decisions were inconsistent (e.g., N. Morris 1974; von Hirsch and Hanrahan 1979).

Many but not all objections came from liberals. Conservatives complained that indeterminate sentencing allowed undue "leniency," thereby failing to honor retributive values (van den Haag 1975), and paid insufficient attention to punishment's deterrent and incapacitative effects (Fleming 1974; Wilson 1975). Policy histories of California's Uniform Determinate Sentencing Act of 1976 describe an alliance of liberals and conservatives, prisoners' rights groups and police unions, all favoring parole abolition and determinate sentencing, albeit for different reasons (Messinger and Johnson 1978; Parnas and Salerno 1978). The first set of sentencing guidelines developed by the Pennsylvania Sentencing Commission was rejected by the legislature for being too lenient (Martin 1984).

The criminal justice system in 2015 bore little resemblance to that of 1970. The combined incarceration rate for federal, state, and local facilities quintupled after 1973, rising continuously to more than 750 per 100,000 in 2007 before peaking (Carson and Sabol 2012; Minton 2012). Sentencing ceased being something handled behind closed doors but became instead for many years a central issue in partisan politics (Edsall and Edsall 1991; Anderson 1995). "Truth in sentencing," initially an expression of an aspiration for transparency, became a device for making punishments more severe (Alschuler 1993). One-third of states abandoned parole release altogether, and all abandoned it for some prisoners. A third of the states, the District of Columbia, and the federal system had established various types of sentencing guidelines. Sentencing appeals became possible. All states and the federal government enacted mandatory minimum sentence laws for drug and violent crimes, many requiring 5-, 10-, or 20-year or longer prison terms.

Complicating things further, a diverse set of new programs and policies in operation in 2015 sought to individualize sanctions. Many could have fit comfortably into indeterminate sentencing in its heyday. Most date from the mid-1990s. They include drug and other problem-solving courts, reentry programs aimed at reducing reoffending, many kinds of new treatment programs, and restorative and community justice programs.

In retrospect, four distinct periods are discernible. Indeterminate sentencing reigned through 1975. A short-lived "sentencing reform" period extended from 1975, when Maine abolished parole release and thereby became the first "determinate" sentencing state, to the mid-1980s. A primarily but not only liberal reform movement sought to make procedures fairer and sentences more predictable and consistent. Conservatives wanted greater certainty for political and crime control reasons, and liberals in order to increase consistency and fairness, but their conceptions of the problem and its solution were similar. The fundamental problem to be addressed was "racial and other unwarranted disparities," and the principal solution was to establish published standards for judges' and parole boards' decisions.

A "tough on crime" period extended from the mid-1980s through 1996. Conservative Republicans were the driving force, but their successful politics of law and order soon led Democrats to support harsher policies and compete to take the lead in proposing them, culminating in President Bill Clinton's avowal never to let the Republicans get to his right on crime. The focus on reducing disparities and making procedures fairer faded away. Policy changes sought primarily to make prison sentences longer and their imposition more certain. The principal mechanisms were mandatory minimum sentence, three-strikes, truth-in-sentencing, and life-without-possibility-of-parole laws (LWOPs). Three-strikes laws typically required minimum 25-year sentences for people convicted of a third felony. Mandatory sentence laws required 10- and 20-year and often life sentences. State truth-in-sentencing laws were enacted to obtain federal funds for prison construction under the Violent Crime Control and Law Enforcement Act of 1994. To qualify, states had to show that prisoners would serve at least 85 percent of their nominal sentences.

Few of the major innovations of the second and third periods—guidelines, mandatory minimums, three-strikes—would make sense to the time travelers. In 1970 it seemed obvious to informed people that judges and parole boards needed broad discretion in order to tailor sentences to individuals' circumstances. Many judges in later years for that reason strongly opposed guidelines, mandatory minimums, and other sentencing policy initiatives. Most in 1970 believed that sentencing was one of their most important and difficult responsibilities, and that sentences had to be individualized to be just. Lengthy prison terms were not in vogue—they violated a widely supported "least restrictive alternative" logic. The Model Penal Code accordingly established presumptions against imposition of prison sentences and in favor of parole release when a prisoner first became eligible. Mandatory punishments were seen as unwise and unjust. The US Congress, for example, in the Comprehensive Drug Abuse Prevention and Control Act of 1970 repealed most then-existing federal mandatory minimum sentence laws. Texas congressman George H. Bush was one of the most outspoken proponents of repeal. The Model Penal Code and the Model Sentencing Act disapproved of them.

Generalizing about the fourth, most recent period is harder. I call this the "equilibrium" period because few major changes were made to sentencing laws; growth in the prison population slowed and eventually stopped. It is easy to identify the principal aims of the first three periods: rehabilitation for the first, consistency for the second, and severity for the third. No single term encapsulates the fourth period. Some initiatives aim at greater severity, some at greater fairness, some at reduced recidivism, and some at reduced costs. Few laws enacted after 1996 were as severe and broad in scope as those that typified the third period, even though new sentencing laws increased penalties for firearms and immigration offenses, human trafficking, carjacking, and child pornography. Drug and other problem-solving courts, reentry programs, and diverse new treatment programs were established in many states. The goal was more often described as reduction in recidivism rather than rehabilitation of offenders, but the programs themselves would have fit comfortably into the indeterminate sentencing period.

After 2000, many state legislatures, generally in search of cost savings, enacted laws limiting the scope of some harsh sentencing provisions, narrowing grounds for revocations of parole and probation and authorizing earlier releases from prison for selected minor offenders. With few exceptions the statutory changes made only minor alterations to existing laws and nibbled at the edges of correctional budgets and imprisonment use (Austin et al. 2013).

The main elements of what we know about the effects of recent decades' sentencing policy changes can, in broad strokes, be summarized in comparatively few words. Parole guidelines and presumptive sentencing guidelines, when designed and implemented well, reduce unwarranted racial and other disparities, make decisions more consistent and predictable, and facilitate programmatic and budgetary planning. Statutory systems that specify sentences for typical offenses and voluntary systems of sentencing guidelines have few if any effects on sentencing patterns. Mandatory minimum and three-strikes laws have little or no effect on crime rates, shift sentencing power from judges to prosecutors, and often result in imposition of sentences that practitioners believe to be unjustly severe. Prosecutors and judges sometimes find ways to circumvent such laws but often feel their hands are tied. Mandatory minimum, three-strikes, truth-in-sentencing, and LWOP laws have greatly increased the lengths of prison terms in the United States and are a major cause of the fivefold increase in the imprisonment rate since 1973 and especially since 1990 (Raphael and Stoll 2013; Travis, Western, and Redburn 2014). A wide range of correctional treatment programs, when well designed, targeted, implemented, and managed, are capable of reducing offending (e.g., MacKenzie 2006; Welsh and Farrington 2006).

This chapter discusses the nature and effects of sentencing policy changes of the past four decades on convicted offenders, court processes, and the use of imprisonment. Effects on crime patterns and trends are discussed only concerning the tough on crime period, and only briefly. The innovations of the sentencing reform period did not generally aim to affect crime rates—that was seen as a police responsibility—but primarily to change sentencing patterns. Many proponents of policies adopted during the tough on crime period would say they were principally interested in reducing crime rates.

I. Forty Years of Sentencing Policy

Four features of sentencing systems warrant attention. The first, the simplest to describe, are the distinctive institutions and policies that characterize them. Parole release and individualization of decisions concerning individual offenders, for example, are emblematic of indeterminate sentencing, as three-strikes and truth-in-sentencing laws are of the tough on crime period.

The second feature, goals, is fuzzier. Most informed professional and scholarly observers would agree that rehabilitation and incapacitation were primary goals of indeterminate sentencing; regularity, consistency, and transparency, of the sentencing reform period; and severity, crime prevention, and public approval, of the tough on crime period.

The third feature, underlying values, is fuzzier still, because values are often implicit, but most informed observers would accept those I identify for each period. Few would disagree that values of compassion, acceptance of human weakness, and social integration underlay indeterminate sentencing, or that values of rationality, procedural fairness, and equality underlay the sentencing reform period. The tough on crime period came close to rejecting those values which center on the offender and his or her experience and prospects for a better life. The focus instead was primarily on society at large. The predominant underlying values included intolerance of deviance, denunciation of wrongdoing, and public safety. It is only a slight exaggeration, and for three-strikes, truth-in-sentencing, and LWOP laws not an exaggeration at all, to say that ostracism and banishment were also recurring themes, not unlike the medieval sanction of exile into a life of outlawry. In the equilibrium period, the values of the third period largely persist, but are augmented by concerns to reduce public expenditure and a revival of concerns for reintegration of offenders into the free community.

The fourth feature, empirical evidence about effectiveness, varies with the period and necessarily depends on what various innovations attempted, or purported to attempt, to accomplish. A few paragraphs back, I summarized the main conclusions that can be drawn from evaluation research and other systematic evidence.

Table 2.1 provides a summary of the four periods along the four dimensions. For each it identifies representative institutions, policy goals,

TABLE 2.1. Periods of American sentencing reform since 1930

	Representative institutions	Goals	Values	Evidence of effectiveness
Indeterminate sentencing (1930–75)	Broad judicial discretion Presentence reports (PSIs) Probation services Parole release Good time	Rehabilitation (Incapacitation) Least restrictive alternative	REHABILITATION Compassion Restraint Reintegration Crime reduction Social welfare	Rehabilitation—Little Prevention—Little Social welfare—Some Incapacitation—Some
Sentencing reform (1975–84)	Parole 1. Guidelines 2. Abolition Sentencing guidelines 1. Presumptive 2. Voluntary Determinate sentencing Sentence appeals	Consistency Transparency Proportionality Accountability Regularity	JUSTICE AS FAIRNESS Fairness Equality Proportionality Nondiscrimination	Disparity—Yes 1. Parole guidelines 2. Presumptive sent. guidelines Disparity—No 1. Determinate sentencing 2. Voluntary guidelines 3. Mandatory minimums Crime prevention—No Mandatory minimums

Tough on crime (1984–96)	Mandatory minimums Three strikes LWOPs Juvenile transfers "Sexual predator" laws Repeat offender laws	Crime prevention Political support Public confidence Severity	EXPULSION/ OUTLAWS Severity Populist democracy Denunciation Ostracism	Disparity—No 1. Mandatory minimums 2. Three strikes 3. Capital punishment Crime prevention—No 1. Mandatory minimums 2. Three strikes 3. Capital punishment 4. LWOPs
Equilibrium (1996–present)	All tough-on-crime policies Sentencing guidelines Risk prediction Treatment programs Reentry programs Drug courts Nibbling at the edges	Cost containment Reduced reoffending Reduced political risks Crime prevention	AMBIVALENCE Severity Bifurcation Reintegration Compassion	Tough on crime, as above Sentencing reform, as above Reduce recidivism—Yes Treatment programs Reduce recidivism—Mixed 1. Drug courts 2. Reentry programs

normative values or purposes, and such evidence as exists concerning whether the goals or purposes of each period were achieved.

A. *Indeterminate Sentencing*

From 1930 through 1975, the states and the federal government had broadly similar sentencing systems in which judges decided who went to prison and usually set minimum or maximum sentences. Parole boards decided who was released and when, and who was returned to prison for breach of release conditions. The system was essentially stable. The total imprisonment rate was stable at 150–160 per 100,000 population and declined slightly from 1960 to 1973, despite a substantial increase in crime rates.

Figure 2.1, the first of several similar figures, shows the number of stories published in the *New York Times* and the *Washington Post* between 1970 and 2011 that included the terms indeterminate or determinate sentencing. Although the first determinate sentencing laws were enacted in Maine in 1975 and California in 1976, the first national news stories on the subject appeared in 1979, when Minnesota's and Pennsylvania's

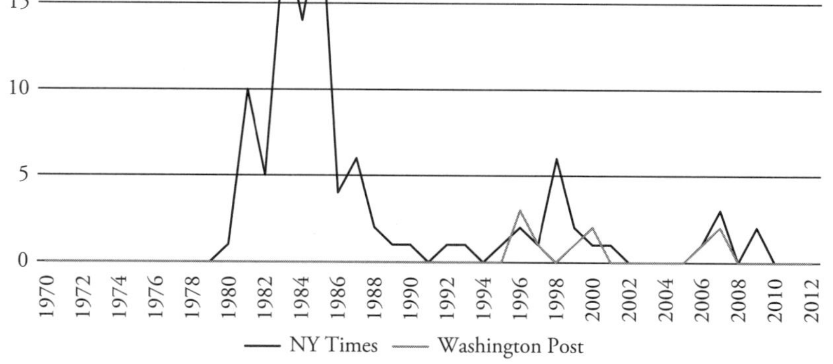

FIGURE 2.1. News stories, national newspapers, (in)determinate sentencing, 1970–2011

sentencing commissions set to work on the first presumptive sentencing guidelines. Coverage expanded during the 1980s, when many jurisdictions worked on or established guidelines, and basically ended in 1989. Almost all stories after that concerned political and other developments concerning the federal guidelines, which are best thought of as an expression of the tough on crime period. News coverage of sentencing initiatives designed primarily to make sentencing fairer and more consistent basically stopped, as policy makers' attention shifted to the goals and values of the tough on crime period.

The principal aim of indeterminate sentencing was to individualize treatment of offenders in order to rehabilitate most and incapacitate the rest. Policies sometimes referred to as "the least restrictive alternative" or "frugality" or "parsimony" created presumptions that punishments should be as unrestrictive as possible and that prisoners should ordinarily be released when they first became eligible.

The implicit underlying values are straightforward. They include a belief in rational, unemotional approaches to crime; compassion for offenders whose backgrounds, circumstances, or psychological characteristics shaped their criminality; the desirability of more fully integrating them into society; and the social welfare concern to deal with them in ways that enhanced their prospects for living successful, satisfying, law-abiding lives.

The origins of indeterminate sentencing lay in the perception than offending often resulted largely from the circumstances of peoples' lives, including social and economic disadvantage, lack of education or work skills, and mental health problems. Francis Allen put it this way: "Knowledge of the antecedents of human behavior makes possible an approach to the scientific control of human behavior" (1959, p. 226). Indeterminate sentencing was predicated on the idea that sentencing and parole release decisions should be based on assessments of offenders' prospects of living law-abiding lives and on efforts to enhance those prospects by means of correctional treatment programs (Rothman 1971). According to Enoch Wines (1880) and Zebulon Brockway (1912), the nineteenth century's leading American prison and parole reformers, the overriding objective was to individualize treatment in order to help offenders improve their lives and prospects. If that happened, they would be less likely to reoffend. Both they and society would benefit.

Leading American and European professionals and scholars from the 1890s through the early 1930s assumed that behavior is largely determined and that the criminal system should rehabilitate offenders when it can and incapacitate them when it cannot (Pifferi 2012). Most criminal justice professionals favored practical approaches. Exactly what should be done concerning a particular offender could be known only after considering all of his or her characteristics and circumstances.

Contemporaneous normative ideas lined up nicely with practice. Scholars and practitioners described indeterminate sentencing as utilitarian, and believed that retributive ideas were cruel and anachronistic.[2] Jeremy Bentham, the founding father of utilitarianism, argued that crime prevention should be the aim of punishment. Penalties should be individualized to fit offenders' "sensibilities," by which he meant their personal characteristics, but should never be more severe than necessary (Bentham 1970 [1789]). He regarded all inflictions of pain or suffering on anyone, including offenders, as "wicked." It should never be done except when some greater offsetting benefits would result.

Twentieth-century supporters of indeterminate sentencing were of like mind: infliction of pain or suffering on offenders simply because they had committed crimes was unacceptable. Herbert Wechsler, later the chief architect of the Model Penal Code, and coauthor Jerome Michael acknowledged that retribution may represent "the unstudied belief of most men" but averred that "no legal provision can be justified merely because it calls for the punishment of the morally guilty by penalties proportioned to their guilt, or criticized merely because it fails to do so" (Michael and Wechsler 1940, pp. 7, 11). Michael and philosopher Mortimer Adler explained that there are two incompatible theories of punishment: the "punitive" (retributive) and the "non-punitive" (consequentialist) and that "it can be shown that the punitive theory is a fallacious analysis and that the non-punitive theory is correct. . . . The infliction of pain is never justified merely on the ground that it visits

[2] Some more precisely described the foundations of indeterminate system as including both Benthamite utilitarianism, focused primarily on deterrence, and positivism, most famously associated at the time with Enrico Ferri (1917), with a focus on rehabilitation and incapacitation (Michael and Wechsler 1937; Wechsler and Michael 1937). Utilitarianism was the more commonly used term, loosely understood also to include positivist aims.

retributive punishment upon the offender. Punitive retribution is never justifiable in itself" (Michael and Adler 1933, pp. 341, 344).

The practical difficulty with indeterminate sentencing, despite the humane values it officially embodied, was that the technique of individualization necessarily gave enormous discretion to correctional officials. Until the prisoners' rights movement emerged in the 1960s and federal judges began to hear cases concerning prison conditions, correctional administrators were nearly immune from external review of what happened in prison (Turner 1971; Jacobs 1981). Nineteenth-century court decisions established a "hands-off" doctrine, in extreme cases explaining it on the rationale that prisoners were "slaves of the state" and had forfeited normal rights of citizenship. Until the due process movement emerged in the 1960s and 1970s, prisoners, parolees, and probationers were entitled to few legally recognized procedural protections concerning parole hearings or parole or probation revocations, nor to administrative or judicial review of decisions that affected them (Davis 1969).

Appellate review of sentencing decisions was also seldom available. Statutes and judicial decisions defined the elements of crimes, but specified only maximum sentences. No statutes, guidelines, court rules, or other standards provided criteria to guide judges' decisions. There were no bodies of case law developed by appellate courts in resolving sentencing appeals that gave guidance to trial judges, leading Norval Morris (1974) and many others later to propose the development of a "Common Law" of sentencing. This proved difficult concerning decisions for which there were no established legal criteria; there were no standards for appellate judges to apply in deciding whether particular decisions were reasonable or justifiable.

Systems of review of sentencing decisions were attempted in some states but were largely unsuccessful. An assessment of experiences in Connecticut and Massachusetts in the 1970s found that some sentences were overturned and modified in individual cases, but not in a way that gave rise to general standards. The reasons given for overturning sentences were typically that the sentence was "too severe" in general or "inappropriate" in light of the circumstances of the offense or the offender's personal characteristics. The offenders whose sentences were overturned or modified were no doubt delighted, but a series of essentially ad hoc decisions unsupported by reasoned explanations cannot produce a body of doctrine or a set of rules (Zeisel and Diamond 1977).

The ideas that individual judges should have broad discretion in setting sentences, that offenders should have no meaningful way to contest the judge's decision, and that parole boards should decide when prisoners are released have had three important long-term consequences that bedevil American sentencing law and policy in the twenty-first century. They are, first, that judges and parole boards may consider any information they deem relevant in deciding on a sentence or a release date; second, judges are bound by a low standard of proof, or none at all, in deciding whether the information is reliable; and, third, judges may give as great or greater weight to an offender's criminal history as to the offense of which he or she has been convicted. All three have frustrated efforts to achieve procedural fairness and substantive justice in all four periods. In those three characteristics, the US legal system is unique among Western countries.

1. *Relevant Evidence.* A judge may properly consider any information he or she deems relevant when deciding upon a sentence. A landmark Supreme Court decision, *Williams v. New York*, 337 U.S. 241 (1949), held that there are no effective limits. The court reasoned that rehabilitative purposes support the admission of all evidence that might possibly be relevant, notwithstanding that the appeal in *Williams* was from a death sentence and that the defendant claimed the contested evidence was prejudicial and unrelated to rehabilitative possibilities.

That logic and that case were invoked to uphold the constitutionality of the US Sentencing Commission's "relevant conduct" policy. When deciding the appropriate sentence under the federal guidelines, judges are directed to take into account not only the offense of which the defendant was convicted but also any other offense the judge believes occurred, whether or not a charge was filed or dismissed, and even if the defendant was acquitted. The US Supreme Court in *United States v. Watts*, 519 U.S. 148 (1997) and other decisions upheld the constitutionality of increasing punishments on the basis of crimes of which offenders had previously been acquitted.

2. *Burdens of Proof at Sentencing.* The second long-term consequence concerns the standard of proof that must be met before a judge may take information into account in imposing a sentence. The answer,

depending on the jurisdiction, is either that there is a low standard of proof or none at all.

Evidence relevant to whether the defendant committed the offense for which he will be sentenced must be evaluated under a "proof beyond a reasonable doubt" standard. By contrast, evidence relevant to an allegation of breach of contract or of negligence in an automobile accident must be evaluated under a civil law standard of "more probable than not" or "by a balance of probabilities." The reason for this centuries-old difference, one that exists in the jurisprudence of all Western countries, is straightforward. Any incorrect legal decision is regrettable, but it is especially regrettable when the stakes are especially high. In civil legal actions, the cost of a mistake is that someone suffers a loss that goes uncompensated or is wrongly ordered to pay damages. In a criminal case, life, liberty, reputation, and property are all at issue. Those are much higher stakes. That's why William Blackstone opined three centuries ago that it is better that 10 guilty men go free than that one innocent be convicted. In other noncriminal legal proceedings involving especially important or sensitive subjects, courts use an "intermediate scrutiny" standard—higher than the civil law standard but less exacting than the criminal law one.

No American jurisdiction requires that evidence germane to sentencing, often referred to as "sentencing facts," be proven by the criminal law or the intermediate standard. The US Supreme Court in *U.S. v. Blakely*, 542 U.S. 296 (2004), observed: "Sentencing courts have traditionally heard evidence and found facts without any prescribed burden of proof at all" (pp. 332–33). A majority of jurisdictions have no evidentiary standard at all in relation to sentencing decisions, not even the civil law "more probable than not." Judges may take into account any information they wish; most defendants have no legal basis for challenging the judge's inferences or conclusions.

I find this shocking, and do not understand why most people do not. It means that decisions about whether to send someone to prison, and for a longer or shorter term, are often made on the basis of information that is incorrect, misunderstood, or misinterpreted. Given the procedural informality and enormous volumes of cases in American criminal courts, there is no doubt that sentences are often based at least in part on inaccurate information. That problem is exacerbated by the ubiquity of plea bargaining. In more than 95 percent of cases, no one, including the prosecutor, is obligated to determine the key facts according to any established standard.

This legacy of indeterminate sentencing seems to have misshaped the thinking of American lawyers and judges. The absence of a meaningful standard for assessing evidence at sentencing and the injustices it produces nonetheless pass almost unnoted, as if they were something inevitable or inexorable.

Little has been written about the oddity that American law allows judges to choose between custodial and noncustodial punishments or between prison sentences of different lengths on the basis of factual conclusions they need not justify. Kevin Reitz, one of very few Americans who have written about it, assumes such an approach is unavoidable: "Practical reasons exist for the procedural differential between trial and sentencing. Sentencing proceedings occur in a much larger number of cases than full-blown trials—approaching 100 percent of all convictions. [A trial-like process at sentencing] . . . would be unsustainable. . . . Cumbersome rules of process are more expensive, and less workable, in an adjudicative milieu of complexities and shades of grey" (2011, p. 232). The American approach, however, is not inevitable. Other Western countries tightly limit the evidence that may be taken into account at sentencing.

In most continental European countries, indeterminate sentencing was rejected in the early decades of the twentieth century on the basis that giving judges so much discretion would contravene the "legality principle" requiring equal treatment of comparable cases and the moral principle that punishments should be proportionate to wrongdoing (Pifferi 2012). As a result, European judges have comparatively little discretion to increase punishments for aggravating reasons, though often they can reduce punishments for mitigating reasons (see, e.g., Hinkkanen and Lappi-Seppälä 2011). There is little latitude for aggravation of punishments.

In England and Wales and other common law countries, aggravating facts that might justify increasing a sentence must be proven beyond a reasonable doubt. The requirement in Canada is statutory. Case law in Australia and England establishes a reasonable doubt standard for aggravating factors and a "balance of probabilities" civil law standard for proof of mitigating factors (Ashworth 2011; Reitz 2011).

Other countries' approach to proof of aggravating circumstances is based on the view that findings of fact at the trial and sentencing stages are equally important and should be governed by the same restrictive standard. Andrew Ashworth explained about English law: "Bearing in mind the great effect on sentence which such issues may have, they ought properly to be resolved according to rules of evidence no less fair than those applicable at trial" (2010, pp. 375–76).

3. *Criminal History.* The third unfortunate long-term consequence of indeterminate sentencing concerns the influence of offenders' criminal histories on the sentences they receive. In contemporary American sentencing, an offender's prior record often matters more than the offense of which he was convicted. Under American guidelines systems, sentences for recidivist offenders are often two, three, or more times harsher than those for first offenders convicted of the same offense (Reitz 2010). Under "career criminal," "repeat offender," "habitual offender," and three-strikes laws, prior felony convictions can lead to decades-long and life sentences. In both these ways, previous convictions influence sentencing decisions much more heavily in the United States than in other Western countries.

This dubious distinction is another unfortunate legacy. In indeterminate sentencing systems, an offender's criminal history was simply one thing a judge might take into account. Even a judge's decision to increase a sentence because of an offender's criminal record had no necessary significant effect on how long he or she remained in prison. The parole board made release decisions. The judge's sentence mostly affected the maximum term, and few prisoners served anywhere near that long. Details varied between states. In some the judge could set a minimum sentence, but usually not more than a third of the maximum, and both were usually discounted by time off for good behavior. In other states, the minimum term before release eligibility was 1 year, irrespective of the maximum sentence set by the judge. The judge may have announced a harsher-sounding sentence because of prior convictions, and the parole board may have delayed release somewhat for the same reason, but the overall effects were usually modest. This is why in the 1970s critics often referred to "bark and bite sentencing"; the judge's bark was much harsher than the parole board's bite (Tonry 2001*a*, p. 29). This is also the origin of proposals for "truth in sentencing," offered as an alternative that would make the bark and the bite pretty much the same (Alschuler 1993).

The role of prior convictions in sentencing has received remarkably little attention, most of it precipitated by the English psychologist Julian Roberts (1997, 2008, 2010; Roberts and von Hirsch 2010). Most people in English-speaking countries, including judges, offenders, and the general public, appear in our time to believe that sentences should be harsher when an offender has previous convictions (Roberts 2008).

When indeterminate sentencing fell apart, the practical consequences of that widely shared intuition were vastly greater than anyone foresaw or most likely imagined. When sentencing commissions began to develop guidelines systems, most seem to have assumed almost automatically that criminal records should be part of the sentencing calculus. The development process almost always included research on past sentencing patterns and efforts to reflect those patterns in guidelines at least in part (Gottfredson, Wilkins, and Hoffman 1978; Parent 1988). That research showed that criminal histories affected the sentences judges imposed, so it seemed natural enough to early sentencing commissions to construct guidelines incorporating criminal history factors.

Criminal records had at most a diffuse and contingent effect on the lengths of prison sentences in indeterminate sentencing systems and the earliest sentencing guidelines. The prototypical guidelines systems in the 1970s were "voluntary," which meant that judges need not adhere to them. They were designed for use in indeterminate systems in which parole boards set release dates (Kress 1980). The sentencing guidelines might explicitly take criminal histories into account, but otherwise business could continue as usual. Since evaluations of the early voluntary guidelines nearly always found that they had no effect on judges' decisions, explicitly building criminal history into guidelines calculations had no necessarily important consequences. Since the parole board made the release decisions, in any case, the judge's handling of criminal history was not especially important.

The next generation of sentencing guidelines, however, was designed for jurisdictions without parole release. The result was that the criminal history dimensions of sentencing guidelines systems suddenly became crucial. If, in prototypical voluntary guidelines systems, a criminal record might result in a sentence twice as long as a first offender's, it didn't much matter. The judge could ignore the guidelines, and the parole board could largely ignore the judge's sentence.

When, however, Minnesota's and other early commissions developed "presumptive" guidelines, the weight given to criminal history mattered hugely. The new guidelines were not voluntary but were presumed to apply in every case, and judges' decisions to do something else could be appealed. Without parole release, the sentence the judge ordered became not something theoretical but the prison sentence the prisoner would serve, minus easily predicted reductions of time off for good behavior. And once state and federal guidelines systems began to establish presumptive and—in the federal case—so-called mandatory guidelines for sentences of 5, 10, and 20 years or more, it was a small step for legislators to do the same thing in mandatory minimum sentence, three-strikes, and truth-in-sentencing laws.

As a result, the United States has the longest prison sentences in the developed world for ordinary crimes as table 1.3 showed. Other than by referring to the widely shared intuition that prior convictions ought to make some difference in sentences for new offenses, however, no one has provided a convincing explanation for why in principle they should make a difference, especially a drastic one. The intuition by itself is not an explanation. Some intuitions are unworthy and should be resisted. Many people in earlier times assumed that women, blacks, and gay people should be treated differently from men, whites, and heterosexuals. Few today believe those intuitions should be respected or that it was ever right to take them into account. A few pages back I quoted major figures during the indeterminate sentencing period explaining why they believed it was obvious that the intuition that offenders deserve to suffer should be resisted.

Some people believe prior criminality is irrelevant to punishment for new crimes (Fletcher 1978; Singer 1979). Other people believe, for reasons that are seldom adequately explained, that prior crimes justify additional increments of deserved punishments. Ambitious, but tortured and unsuccessful, efforts have been made to develop retributive explanations. One argument is that a prior conviction places a special burden of law-abidingness on the individual (Lee 2010). Another is that the new crime constitutes a sign of disrespect of the state and a failure to act responsibly (Bennett 2010). All citizens, however, have a duty of law-abidingness, so that can't be why recidivists deserve greater punishment. And in democratic countries, disrespect and irresponsibility may be rude or unbecoming, but those qualities are not crimes. In a free society, citizens are entitled to be rude, eccentric, irresponsible, or "difficult." Offenders are not differently situated from other citizens in that respect, so disrespect and irresponsibility also cannot justify harsher punishment for recidivists (Tonry 2010).

One final explanation for the "recidivist premium" is that first offenders should be thought of as being punished less severely than they deserve, because their crime may have been out of character or the result of special, unlikely to be recreated, circumstances (von Hirsch 1981, 1985, 2010). For the second offense or perhaps the third, if offenders are given a bit more benefit of the doubt, they might receive a smaller discount. After that, it should be the deserved punishment, but no more, every time. However convincing that logic may be, and however accurately it describes what judges think they are doing when they sentence first- or second-time offenders, it can't explain why sentences become steadily harsher in the United States in direct relationship to the number of prior convictions. Nor can it explain why recidivists receive punishments two, three, or more times harsher than a first offender's.

As with the other unintended consequences of the demise of indeterminate sentencing, the United States is alone among Western countries in how prior convictions are handled. Other legal systems give criminal history a much smaller sentencing role. In Scandinavian countries, the role is very small. Judges and lawyers typically take the view that what is past is past. The earlier crime has already been punished; that is the end of the matter. Sentencing principles expressed in criminal codes authorize increments of additional punishment because of some prior crimes, but the increments are small and may be imposed only in narrowly defined circumstances (Asp 2010; Hinkkanen and Lappi-Seppälä 2011). In England, prior convictions are regarded as germane only when—in statutory language—they are "recent" and "relevant" (to the new offense, as when all the offenses are burglaries or all are sex offenses). Case law limits how large the increment can be (Baker and Ashworth 2010). In other common law countries, case law doctrines narrowly limit the influence of prior convictions. One standard formulation is that the maximum total sentence cannot exceed what would normally be imposed for a serious instance of the offense of conviction by itself (e.g., in Australia: Freiberg 2014).

Even during the indeterminate sentencing period, the discretion given to sentencing judges and parole boards to consider whatever evidence they deemed relevant, including prior convictions, is hard in retrospect to justify. If rehabilitation is a primary purpose of sentencing, as it nominally was, officials can be said to need broad discretion to consider the circumstances of the defendant's life and his or her prospects for rehabilitation. Conceivably, it could have been argued during the indeterminate sentencing period that good motives and animating rehabilitative and social welfare values justified informality.

In retrospect, it is clear that indeterminate sentencing seldom lived up to those purposes and values. Officials in many states tried, of course, and well-run correctional systems and facilities existed. Many American prisons, however, were terrible places, parole boards often were poorly run with unqualified patronage appointees as members, and treatment programs were often exiguous (Reitz 2012). The President's Commission on Law Enforcement and Administration of Justice in 1967 described things as they were then:

> For a great many offenders, then, corrections does not correct. Indeed, experts are increasingly coming to feel that the conditions under which many offenders are handled, particularly in institutions, are often a positive detriment to rehabilitation.
>
> Life in many institutions is at best barren and futile, at worst unspeakably brutal and degrading. To be sure, the offenders in such institutions are incapacitated from committing further crimes while serving their sentences, but the conditions in which they live are the poorest possible preparation for their successful reentry into society, and often merely reinforce in them a pattern of manipulation or destructiveness. (p. 159)

Historian David Rothman captured the dynamic in the title of his 1980 book *Conscience and Convenience.* "Conscience" expressed the rehabilitative ideal and, for many officials, genuine, well-meaning efforts to help offenders live better lives. "Convenience" expressed the corrupting effects of a system that gave prisoners almost no opportunity to challenge day-to-day conditions or fateful decisions about their lives, and that gave officials virtually unlimited control over their lives. Running a prison, probation service, or parole board is much easier when decisions need not be justified. Recall Lord Acton's axiom that power corrupts and absolute power corrupts absolutely.

From a twenty-first-century perspective, it seems surprising that indeterminate sentencing lasted as long as it did. Credible evidence of its rehabilitative effectiveness never existed. Problems with prison and parole systems had long been known and documented. Reports by the National Commission on Law Observance and Enforcement (1931) and the President's Commission on Law Enforcement and Administration of Justice (1967) describe strikingly similar failings and injustices four decades apart.

B. Sentencing Reform

From 1975 through 1986, many jurisdictions in one way or another—parole guidelines, voluntary and presumptive sentencing guidelines, determinate sentencing statutes, appellate review of sentencing—attempted to make sentencing fairer, more consistent, and more transparent. As in the preceding period, the prevailing views of theorists and of practitioners lined up nicely. Utilitarian ideas and aims were not entirely excluded (e.g., Hart 1968; N. Morris 1974), but the overall logic was retributive (e.g., Murphy 1973; von Hirsch 1976; H. Morris 1981). Crime prevention was seldom an explicit goal of major initiatives, or even an implicit one.[3] The focus was on the sentencing process and on individual sentences, not on their preventive effects. The underlying values were fairness, equality, equal treatment, and nondiscrimination. Evaluations showed that some initiatives were relatively successful and that others were not. With the exception of a handful of mandatory

[3] Crime prevention was sometimes the goal of narrowly focused sentencing law changes. During the 1970s and early 1980s every state but Wisconsin enacted one or more mandatory minimum sentence laws. With the conspicuous exception of the Rockefeller Drug Laws in New York, which mandated lengthy prison sentences (Joint Committee on New York Drug Law Evaluation 1978), those laws were typically much less severe than the minimum sentence laws enacted in the 1980s and 1990s. Most mandated short jail terms for driving while intoxicated or 1- or 2-year prison terms for offenses involving firearms (Shane-DuBow, Brown, and Olsen 1985).

minimum sentence laws, which I discuss below, evaluations did not attempt to measure crime prevention effects. The total incarceration rate including jail inmates rose rapidly, reaching 313 per 100,000 in 1986, principally because of increases in the number of cases being processed, the probability of imprisonment given a conviction, and the lengths of sentences imposed (Gilliard and Beck 1997; Blumstein and Beck 1999).

By the mid-1970s every major element of indeterminate sentencing was contested, and all of its underlying premises were challenged. Indeterminate sentencing was widely thought to be unjust (e.g., von Hirsch 1976) and to be predicated on a capacity to rehabilitate offenders that did not exist (e.g., Martinson 1974). Broad, unregulated discretions were said to permit idiosyncratic, arbitrary, and racist decisions (e.g., American Friends Service Committee 1971; Fogel 1979). Unwarranted sentencing disparities were said to be inherent in the system, the product of differences in judges' personalities and beliefs (Frankel 1973). Procedural informality was criticized as fundamentally unfair (Davis 1969).

The solutions seemed obvious: constrain judicial discretion, establish standards for sentencing, abolish or systematize parole release, and allow offenders to file appeals (N. Morris 1974; Dershowitz 1976). The primary aims were to make sentencing and parole fairer, more consistent, and more just: reduction in unwarranted sentencing disparities was the mantra.

Although law and order had begun to emerge as a partisan political issue in the late 1970s, the major goals of the early sentencing reform movement were fairness and consistency. This can be seen in the work of the National Academy of Sciences Panel on Sentencing Research. The primary emphases of its 1983 report and the literature reviews it commissioned were on the determinants of sentencing, disparity, and discrimination, and the effects on disparities and court operations of recent reform initiatives. Effects on crime rates, recidivism, and prevention received little attention (Blumstein et al. 1983, chaps. 1, 4).

The focus on procedural fairness and disparities can also be seen in the work of the earliest sentencing commissions. The Minnesota commission deliberated over two guidelines options—the "just deserts" and "modified just deserts" models—before selecting the latter. The Oregon guidelines enabling legislation unambiguously indicated that "punishment" was the purpose of sentencing (von Hirsch, Knapp, and Tonry 1987, chap. 4).

In the aftermath of the collapse of indeterminate sentencing and its primarily rehabilitative rationale, sentencing reform initiatives proliferated. The process was primarily technocratic—systematic, evidence-based, and cumulative. The earliest and most incremental initiatives sought to reduce disparities through development and use of parole guidelines and voluntary sentencing guidelines. These were followed by statutory determinate sentencing systems and presumptive sentencing guidelines.

1. *Parole Guidelines.* The early pilot projects for development of parole guidelines took place under the aegis of the US Parole Commission. The logic of the team headed by Leslie Wilkins and Don M. Gottfredson was that, using "salient factors" that predict recidivism, parole guidelines could be developed that would simultaneously reduce disparities in release dates and tie release decisions to predictions of parolees' prospects of living law-abiding lives. They reasoned that a well-run administrative agency could supervise parole examiners and operate a system of administrative appeals that would allow prisoners to contest their decisions. The US Parole Commission formally adopted a guideline system (Gottfredson, Wilkins, and Hoffman 1978). Parole boards in Minnesota, Oregon, and Washington did likewise. All sought to increase procedural fairness, reduce unwarranted disparities in time served, and make the release system more transparent and predictable. A major evaluation concluded that they succeeded (Blumstein et al. 1983).

If parole guidelines could reduce unwarranted disparities and increase consistency, the logical next step was to create comparable but more comprehensive guidelines for judges. That was attempted in all four of the pioneering jurisdictions. Parole guidelines in each jurisdiction were eventually succeeded by presumptive sentencing guidelines systems. I discuss them below but, in the interest of chronology, take a detour first to discuss an earlier generation of voluntary sentencing guidelines and a separate reform approach generally referred to as "statutory determinate sentencing."

2. *Voluntary Sentencing Guidelines.* The team of researchers who created the federal parole guidelines persuaded judges in Colorado and Vermont to collaborate with them in developing guidelines for sentencing.

They hypothesized that judges are less likely than parole examiners to support development of guidelines whose existence might give rise to appeals. As a consequence, the guidelines were voluntary and would not undermine judges' discretionary authority. Decisions were not appealable. The guidelines did not attempt to change existing practices or norms. Based on research on past sentencing practices in the jurisdiction, they did no more than indicate ranges of sentences that encompassed 80 percent of those previously imposed on people convicted of particular offenses and having similar records of prior convictions. The modest goal was to highlight past outliers and lessen their future frequency. The developers reasoned that judges would want to comply with local sentencing patterns once guidelines made them evident, and that over time compliance with the guidelines would become part of the local judicial culture and make outliers less common and disparities less pronounced (Gottfredson, Wilkins, and Hoffman 1978).

The underlying assumptions proved to be wrong. Judges were not much interested in knowing about past sentencing patterns, nor in taking them into account in making their own decisions.[4] An evaluation of the first federally funded pilot projects in Vermont and Colorado concluded that the guidelines had no effect on sentencing disparities or consistency (Rich et. al 1982). One possible reason was that the participating judges felt little sense of local ownership or commitment because the initiative for the guidelines had come from the research team. However, a subsequent evaluation of statewide voluntary guidelines developed at the initiative of the state judiciaries in Florida and Maryland reached the same conclusions (Carrow et al. 1985).

Those evaluations were not finished or published until the 1980s. In the meantime, voluntary guidelines had been established at state or local levels in every state (Blumstein et al. 1983; Tonry 1996, chap. 3).

---

[4] A parallel initiative in the Canadian provinces of British Columbia, Manitoba, Newfoundland, and Saskatchewan was no more successful. "Sentencing information systems" were created that informed judges of patterns of sentences previously imposed for particular offenses in their courts (Doob and Park 1987; Doob 1989, 1990). The initiative was terminated after several years of pilot projects. The key premise—that judges would want to know what sentences other judges had imposed in similar cases—proved to be faulty. In the project's final report, the director, Anthony N. Doob, observed, "Judges do not, as a rule, care to know what sentences other judges are handing down in comparable cases" (Doob 1989, p. 6).

Nearly all of those early voluntary guidelines systems were abandoned or fell into desuetude.

Even so, a number of states established voluntary guidelines systems in the 1980s and 1990s, despite a continuing absence of evidence from credible evaluations or other research showing that they reduced the extent of unwarranted sentencing disparities. American judges commonly opposed proposals to develop presumptive guidelines that might limit their discretion (e.g., Griset 1991). They were usually successful. Rather than abandon efforts to reduce sentencing disparities, reformers in many states promoted as a fallback the development of voluntary guidelines (von Hirsch, Knapp, and Tonry 1987). Prison population increases in two especially well-known voluntary guidelines systems, in Delaware and Virginia, have been smaller than elsewhere, and their proponents claim and believe they have improved consistency and reduced disparity. If that is true, Gottfredson, Wilkins, and Hoffman (1978) may in the long term be validated in their belief that compliance with guidelines would eventually become part of local judicial culture and part of what judges believe is a component of doing their work responsibly.

Voluntary guidelines have attracted renewed interest in recent years because of two US Supreme Court decisions (*U.S. v. Booker*, 543 U.S. 220 [2005], and *Blakely v. Washington*, 542 U.S. 296 [2004]), which created new procedural requirements for presumptive sentencing guidelines systems. Presumptive guidelines, discussed below, have been shown to be capable of reducing disparities and achieving other sought-after goals. Nonetheless, in response to *Blakely*, Ohio in 2006 converted its presumptive guidelines system into a voluntary one.

3. *Statutory Determinate Sentencing.* Some states followed another path, although to a dead end. The most influential reform proposals called for abolition of parole release and creation of enforceable standards to guide judges' decisions in individual cases (e.g., N. Morris 1974; von Hirsch 1976). Policy makers in some states responded by building standards into their criminal codes. Maine in 1975 went partway, abolishing parole release and thereby becoming the first modern "determinate" sentencing state in the sense that the length of time to be served under a prison sentence could be known, that is, determined, when it was imposed. Maine, however, did not establish standards for

sentencing. California did. It enacted the Uniform Determinate Sentencing Act of 1976, abolishing parole release and specifying normal, aggravated, and mitigated sentences for most offenses in statutes. Other states—including Arizona, Indiana, Illinois, and North Carolina—quickly followed California's lead, though in somewhat different ways. Evaluations concluded, however, that such laws had little if any effect on sentencing disparities or patterns (Blumstein et al. 1983, pp. 353–411; Tonry 1987). No additional states since the mid-1980s have created statutory determinate sentencing systems.

4. *Presumptive Sentencing Guidelines.* Acting on Judge Marvin Frankel's proposal in *Criminal Sentences: Law without Order* (1973), Minnesota in 1978 established a specialized administrative agency, a sentencing commission, with authority to promulgate presumptive sentencing guidelines. They were to be presumptive in the sense that judges were required to provide reasons for imposing sentences that were not authorized in the guidelines; the adequacy of those reasons could be reviewed by appellate courts. Judge Frankel argued that permanent administrative agencies would be better situated than legislatures—afflicted by high turnover, short attention spans, and tendencies to react impulsively to short-term emotions and political concerns—to develop rational, evidence-based policies. An independent sentencing commission, he hoped, would be somewhat insulated from political pressures. Because of its permanence, a commission over time would develop specialized expertise and an institutional memory, and could revise and amend the guidelines to respond to changing priorities and conditions.

Minnesota's guidelines took effect in 1980. The Minnesota commission made a number of unprecedented decisions. It sought—the first time a jurisdiction did so explicitly—to base its guidelines on an agreed normative framework, which it called "modified just deserts." It developed comprehensive guidelines for all felony offenses, classifying them into groups on the basis of assessments of each offense category's seriousness, and not on the basis of statutory maximum sentences, which were highly inconsistent. It interpreted ambiguous language in its enabling legislation to require that a "capacity constraint" guide its decisions. It decided that its guidelines should not produce a prison population exceeding 95 percent of the rated capacity of Minnesota's existing or planned prisons. This was done through use of statistical models that predicted the sentencing patterns likely to result from application of draft guidelines being considered.

The commission forced itself to make trade-offs. If the commission wanted to increase sentence lengths for particular offenses, offsetting reductions had to be made for others. In order to monitor compliance with the guidelines, the commission required judges, or clerks working for them, to prepare a report on each sentence imposed. A staff member, or, if that proved ineffective, the commission chair, Supreme Court Chief Justice Judge Douglas Amdahl, telephoned laggards to obtain the reports. This meant that for the first time a state could develop comprehensive data on statewide sentencing patterns. The statute authorized defense and prosecution appeals of sentences. Judges who imposed a sentence inconsistent with the guidelines were required to offer "substantial and compelling" reasons for doing so (Knapp 1984; Parent 1988).

The guidelines worked. Judges complied with the guidelines in most cases and gave reasons when they did not. Sentencing disparities declined, including in relation to race and gender. Plea bargaining continued, but occurred in the shadows of the guidelines, which meant that it too became more consistent. The commission from time to time in later years revised the guidelines to change presumptive sentences for particular offenses and altered sentences for other offenses to comply with the capacity constraint. Minnesota prisons operated within their capacities, during a period when prison populations were rising rapidly in most states and prisons in most states were overcrowded. The prison population increased during the 1980s, but in line with increased capacity resulting from construction of new prisons. The appellate courts created a sentencing appeal jurisprudence (Reitz 1997; Frase 2005). The long sought "common law of sentencing" began to emerge.

Pennsylvania, Oregon, and Washington created similar systems in the 1980s, and Florida, Kansas, North Carolina, and Ohio in the 1990s. Their experiences differed, but Washington (Boerner and Lieb 2001), Oregon (Bogan and Factor 1997), and North Carolina (Wright 2002) had successes comparable to Minnesota's.

Evaluations showed that well-designed and well-implemented presumptive guidelines systems can make sentencing more predictable, reduce racial and other unwarranted disparities, facilitate systems planning, and control correctional spending. "Population constraint" policies in Minnesota, Washington, and North Carolina worked. During the periods when they were in effect, prison systems in all three states operated within capacity and kept prison population growth well below national and regional averages (Tonry 1996).

North Carolina has been the most successful. In 1970, North Carolina had the highest incarceration rate in the country but it had fallen to 31st by 1999 (Wright 2002). It ranked 30th or 31st for the following 10 years and was 32nd in 2013 (Carson 2014). From 1994, when the guidelines took effect, through 2013, the North Carolina imprisonment rate was essentially flat.

A handful of studies have concluded that presumptive guidelines, especially with population constraint policies, help control prison population size (Marvell 1995; Nicholson-Crotty 2004; Reitz 2006; Stemens, Rengifo, and Wilson 2006). Marvell (1995) examined prison population growth from 1976 to 1993 in nine guidelines states, compared with the national average, and concluded that guidelines based on population constraints produced lower rates of increase. Nicholson-Crotty (2004), using 1975–98 prison data in a 50-state analysis, concluded that guidelines incorporating capacity constraints moderate imprisonment growth and that those not based on constraints exacerbate it. Stemens, Rengifo, and Wilson (2006) analyzed state sentencing patterns in 1975–2002 and concluded that states that adopted presumptive guidelines and abolished parole release had lower incarceration rates and lower rates of prison population growth than other states. Spelman (2009, p. 59), in an analysis of the causes of state prison population changes from 1977 to 2005, concluded that presumptive guidelines "reduce prison populations in both the short run and the long run."

Notwithstanding those positive findings, things quickly changed. The successes of presumptive sentencing guidelines proved much less important to policy makers after the early 1990s than in earlier years. Presumptive sentencing guidelines fell from favor. The three most recent presumptive systems, in Kansas, North Carolina, and Ohio, were established in 1993–96. A few voluntary or advisory systems have been developed since then. In Oregon, the committee that drafted and monitored the guidelines was closed down (Bogan and Factor 1997). Sentencing commissions in Florida, Louisiana, Tennessee, and Wisconsin were abolished, and Washington's lost its staff and budget in

2011 (Frase 2013). The Pennsylvania Commission on Sentencing survived, but Pennsylvania Supreme Court decisions effectively converted the nominally presumptive guidelines into voluntary ones (Reitz 1997; Kramer and Ulmer 2008).

Policy making ceased to be greatly concerned about evidence, fairness, and consistency. In Minnesota, the legislature in 1989 instructed the commission to give much less weight to its population constraint policy (Frase 2005). The Washington commission gave up the policy on its own (Boerner and Lieb 2001). In Oregon, a broad-based mandatory minimum sentence law was enacted that trumped the guidelines (Merritt, Fain, and Turner 2006). The Ohio guidelines were converted from presumptive to voluntary in 2006. The North Carolina and Minnesota commissions, however, continue to develop correctional impact projections of proposed new sentencing laws; the projections are commonly believed to have slowed the enactment of laws that would require additional prison space (Frase 2013).

The presumptive guidelines systems in the 1980s were developed in a period before American crime control policy became highly politicized and when the primary policy goal was to reduce disparities and unfairness. Those commissions focused primarily on developing systems for achieving greater fairness and consistency and on the use of population projection methods for financial and facilities planning. Population constraint policies made obvious sense to the early guidelines commissions and to the legislatures that established them. Concern for managing prison population growth and corrections budgets, not reduction of sentencing disparities, was the primary policy goal underlying creation of the North Carolina, Kansas, and Ohio commissions in the 1990s.

The promulgation of federal sentencing guidelines, which took effect in 1987, coincided with the beginning of the end of the sentencing reform period that targeted disparities and the beginning of the tough on crime period that sought increased certainty and severity. The Sentencing Reform Act of 1984 created the US Commission on Sentencing and directed it to develop guidelines to reduce disparities, to provide for use of nonincarcerative punishments for most first offenders, and to develop population-constraint-based guidelines that would not result in larger numbers of prisoners than federal prisons could accommodate. The commission ignored the directives concerning first offenders and

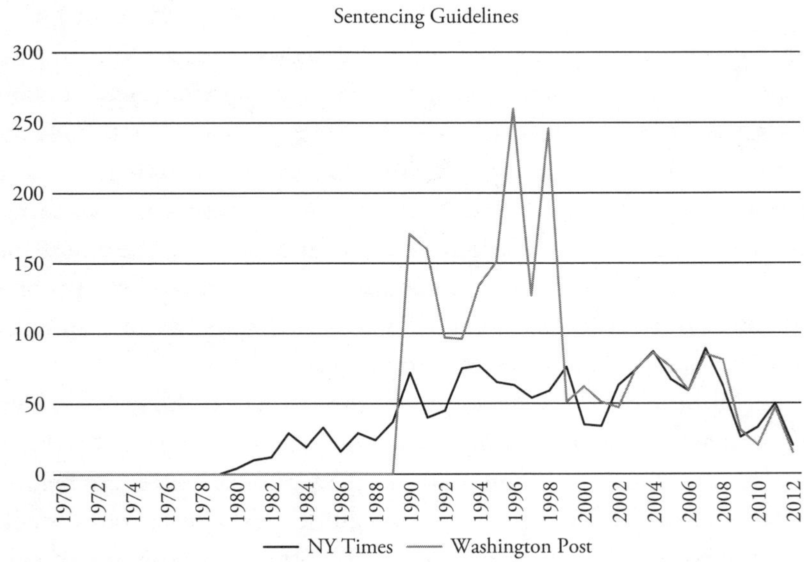

FIGURE 2.2. News stories, national newspapers, sentencing guidelines, 1970–2012

the prison population constraint and instead promulgated "mandatory" guidelines (Tonry 1996, chap. 3; Stith and Cabranes 1998). The federal guidelines were made voluntary by the US Supreme Court in *U.S. v. Booker*, 543 U.S. 220 (2005).

The major initiatives of the sentencing reform period, like those of indeterminate and determinate sentencing, also received only short-lived national attention. Most media attention since 1989 has concerned the federal sentencing guidelines, which are better classified as a product of the tough on crime period. Figure 2.2 shows mentions of sentencing guidelines in *Times* and *Post* stories from 1970 to 2011. From 1979 through 1988, when only states operated guidelines systems, the *Times* published 25 or 30 stories a year. The *Post* had none. Beginning in 1979, the *Post* began covering guidelines, and the *Times* picked up its pace.

Most of that subsequent coverage concerned the federal guidelines. They, however, unlike the earlier state guidelines, were not focused on consistency and fairness. The guidelines "mandated" sentences much more severe than had been common in federal courts and reduced imposition of probationary sentences from half of all cases before guidelines took effect to less than 10 percent afterwards. The term "mandated" is in quotes because that is how the US Sentencing Commission chose to describe the guidelines. The 1984 Sentencing Reform Act, however, does not refer to mandatory guidelines; it directed the commission to develop presumptive guidelines like those in Minnesota and Washington. The commission's guidelines were controversial from the outset and were the subject of continuous amendments and a series of high-profile Supreme Court decisions. They thus provided subjects for numerous news stories, especially in Washington, DC.

Federal developments attract much more attention than what happens in states, even though more than 95 percent of sentences are imposed in the states, and more than 90 percent of prisoners are held in state prisons and local jails. The federal guidelines were so controversial and disliked that state policy makers, who often had no knowledge of the successful state systems, typically opposed development of guidelines on the assumption that they would be like the federal guidelines (Reitz and Reitz 1993).

The sentencing reform period basically ended by the late 1980s, even though a few states later established guidelines systems aimed primarily at controlling prison populations and costs. Nominally, the tough on crime initiatives aimed at crime prevention through deterrence and incapacitation. Partisan political considerations and a fundamental diminution in empathy for individual defendants were at least as important (Windlesham 1998; Gest 2001).

In retrospect, some of the policy initiatives of the sentencing reform period were strikingly successful. Policy makers and researchers through an evidence-based process of trial and error successively attempted a series of innovations that sought to address the shortcomings of indeterminate sentencing. Some, including statutory determinate sentencing schemes, voluntary sentencing guidelines, and—in Canada—sentencing information systems had little influence on judges' sentencing decisions and quickly lost momentum. Others, notably presumptive sentencing guidelines, parole guidelines, and appellate sentence appeals, were shown in some jurisdictions to achieve their goals. Few new jurisdictions adopted them during the tough on crime period.

C. Tough on Crime

During the tough on crime period, from the mid-1980s through 1996, most American jurisdictions enacted some or all of mandatory minimum sentence, truth-in-sentencing, "sexual predator," "career criminal," three-strikes, and LWOP laws (Sabol et al. 2002; Stemens, Rengifo, and Wilson 2006). Most policy initiatives sought to make sentences harsher and more certain and, implicitly or explicitly, to prevent crime through deterrence and incapacitation. The primary focus shifted from fairness to offenders to harshness, crime prevention, and symbolic denunciation of crime and criminals.

Unlike during the preceding two periods, prevailing normative ideas about punishment among philosophers and other theorists were not reconcilable with the logic of policy making. Theorists remained mostly retributivist (e.g., Duff 1986; Robinson 1987*b*; M. S. Moore 1993), but sentencing policies were hard to reconcile with ideas about proportionality and parsimony. Sentencing policies also found little support in research findings. Severe punishments have little if any effect on crime rates (see, e.g., Travis, Western, and Redburn 2014, chap. 5) and often result in circumvention by practitioners in some cases and in imposition of sentences everyone directly involved believes to be unjust in others (Tonry 2009*a*). The imprisonment rate continued to increase rapidly, reaching 615 per 100,000 in 1996, principally because of increases in sentence lengths and sharply increased arrest and imprisonment rates for drug offenders (Blumstein and Beck 1999; Raphael and Stoll 2013).

Federal developments during this period were typical of those in most states. Between the passage of the federal Sentencing Reform Act of 1984 and the October 1, 1987 implementation of federal sentencing guidelines, the US Congress enacted the Anti-Drug Abuse Act of 1986. That law created a new set of mandatory minimum sentences for drug and violent crimes, including the federal 100-to-1 law that mandated sentence lengths for crack offenses that were the same as those for powder cocaine offenses involving quantities 100 times larger (e.g., 5 grams of crack compared with 500 grams of powder). By mandating minimum sentences for many drug crimes, the 1986 Anti-Drug Abuse Act made development of a comprehensive set of proportionate sentencing standards more difficult (Stith and Cabranes 1998). Most people believe violence is more serious than drug possession or sales of small amounts, but the 1986 law required, counterintuitively, that drug offenses be punished more severely than many violent crimes.

The US Congress continued to enact severe sentencing laws for another decade, many of which trumped the guidelines. In the Omnibus Anti-Drug Abuse Act of 1988, the Congress enacted a more comprehensive and severe set of mandatory minimums. In 1994, the Violent Crime Control and Law Enforcement Act of 1994 authorized federal funding for prison construction to states that enacted truth-in-sentencing laws requiring prisoners to serve 85 percent of their nominal prison terms. Congress also enacted additional mandatory minimum laws, including the federal three-strikes law. The federal laws paralleled, presaged, and encouraged passage of three-strikes and truth-in-sentencing laws in slightly different majorities of the states.

The policy initiatives of the tough on crime period undermined pursuit of the aims of the preceding period. Three centuries of experience have shown that mandatory punishments foster circumvention by prosecutors, juries, and judges and thereby produce inconsistency and unfairness between cases. Historian Douglas Hay (1975) showed how in eighteenth-century England juries in their findings of fact, judges in their evidentiary and legal rulings, and government ministers in their clemency decisions managed to reduce the number of executions substantially during a period when the Parliament made many more crimes punishable by death. American Bar Foundation researchers in the 1950s documented comparable ways that judges avoided imposing mandatory minimum sentences they believed to be too severe (Dawson 1969; Remington 1969). All major studies of the operation of mandatory minimum sentence laws since the early 1970s have documented comparable patterns of circumvention in some but not in most or all cases (Tonry 2009*a*).

Mandatory minimum sentence, three-strikes, and truth-in-sentencing laws also transfer dispositive discretion about the handling of cases from judges, who are expected to be nonpartisan and dispassionate, to prosecutors, who are much more vulnerable than judges to being influenced by political considerations and public emotion (Tonry 2004). Many American prosecutors pride themselves on their responsiveness to public opinion (see, e.g., Miller and Caplinger 2012; Wright 2012).

This transfer of power from judges to prosecutors did not trouble legislators, David Boerner (1995), a former Seattle deputy chief prosecutor explained, because they trusted prosecutors to be tough on crime and insist on severe sentences, but were much less trustful of judges to do these things.

Providing a comprehensive summary of the numbers of states that adopted particular policies might seem necessary if recent developments are to be isolated and understood. This is not as easy as might be assumed, because some laws that in outline look similar to modern laws were enacted before 1975, sometimes long before. Because state laws vary substantially, writers and evaluators define initiatives in different ways. For example, a Vera Institute of Justice analysis of the effects of sentencing law changes since 1975 combined into a single category three-strikes laws enacted under that name in the 1990s with "habitual offender" laws dating from the 1920s onwards (Stemen, Rengifo, and Wilson 2006). In most states, such laws long ago largely fell into disuse and in any case were usually applied to chronic property offenders, not to the violent and drug offenders targeted by most modern three-strikes laws. Likewise, an Urban Institute analysis of the effects of truth-in-sentencing laws included within that category any law that limited parole release for specific categories of offenders. By that measure, 42 states had truth-in-sentencing laws, although many were not characterized that way when they were enacted, and only 28 (plus the District of Columbia) satisfied criteria for federal prison construction funding (Sabol et al. 2002).

Table 2.2 shows which states enacted three-strikes and truth-in-sentencing laws and when. Laws are characterized in their modern forms, partly because I am interested in trying to understand contemporary developments, and partly because recently enacted laws reflect the distinctive temper of our time. Thus I regard as truth-in-sentencing states the 28 that qualified for federal prison construction funds under the Violent Crime Control and Law Enforcement Act of 1994. I classify as three-strikes states the 27 that enacted laws under that name. Very few were enacted after 1996, but every one that was enacted remained in force in 2015.

All but three of the 27 three-strikes laws were enacted between 1993 and 1995, and 21 of the 28 state truth-in-sentencing laws that qualified

TABLE 2.2. Dates of enactment: Three-strikes and truth-in-sentencing laws

Type of law	Pre-1993	1993–94	1995–96	1997–98	Since 1999
Three-strikes	NONE	14 (**CA**, CO, **CT**, **GA**, IN, **KS**, **LA**, MD, **NC**, NM, **TN**, **VA**, **WA**, WI)	10 (AR, **FL**, MT, **ND**, NV, **NJ**, **PA**, **SC**, **UT**, VT)	NONE	3 (AL–2006, **AZ–2006**, MA–2012)
Truth-in-sentencing	5 (DE—1989, MN—1992, **PA—1911**, **UT—1985**, **WA—1990**)	7 (**AZ**, **GA**, MI, MO, **NC**, OR, **VA**)	14 (**CA**, **CT**, **FL**, IL, IA, **KS**, **LA**, ME, MS, **ND**, NY, OH, **SC**, **TN**)	3 (DC, **NJ**, OK)	NONE

Sources: Chen 2008 (three-strikes); Sabol et al. 2002 (truth-in-sentencing: qualifying for federal prison construction funds); current media; States shown in bold type enacted both kinds of statute.

for federal prison construction finds were enacted between 1993 and 1996. None of them has been repealed, and they continue to mandate lengthy prison sentences. They have, however, almost entirely fallen from view, as figures 2.3 and 2.4 show. Both the *New York Times* and the *Washington Post* devoted many stories to three-strikes and truth-in-sentencing laws from 1993–94 through 1998, and relatively few since. That the media pay little attention to them does not mean they are not used. Prosecutors continue to use the threat of their application to induce guilty pleas and related waivers of trial and appeal rights. Judges have little choice but to send people affected by them to prisons for very long times.

1. *Truth-in-Sentencing Laws.* The term was invented in the 1980s. It plays on the name of the federal "truth-in-lending" laws of the 1970s that sought to lessen deceptive lending practices by requiring lenders and merchants to disclose interest rates and other key financial terms to consumers. The implication is that indeterminate sentencing, like consumer lending fraud, is fundamentally dishonest and wrongful.

That was, and remains, a bad rap. Discretionary parole release was meant to allow for sentence lengths to be tailored to the rehabilitative prospects and other circumstances of individual offenders. Most laws

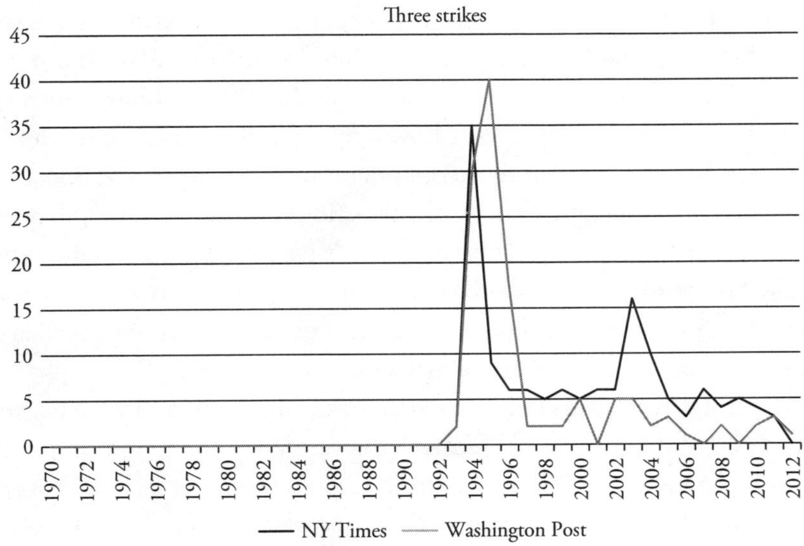

FIGURE 2.3. News stories, national newspapers, three-strikes laws, 1970–2012

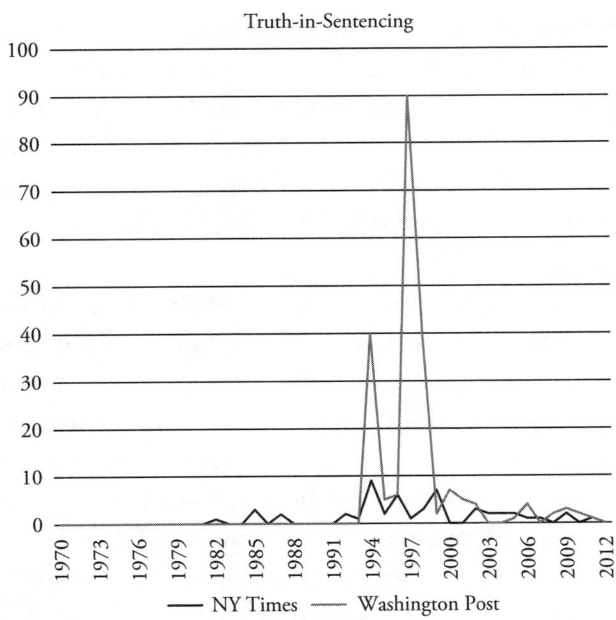

FIGURE 2.4. News stories, national newspapers, truth in sentencing, 1970–2012

establishing maximum prison sentences for particular crimes were enacted before 1980, often many years earlier. In American law and practice they were traditionally meant not to indicate how long a sentence in a particular case should be or how long an individual should remain in prison but to set an absolute final date by which a prisoner must be released. Any judge, prosecutor, or corrections official working in an indeterminate sentencing jurisdiction knew this, as did any legislator who worked on criminal justice subjects. Many lay people may not have understood exactly how things worked, but most knew that parole existed and that most prisoners were released onto it.

The real drivers of truth in sentencing were different, and were part of the ideological and political ferment that underlay the tough on crime period. One was that it was easy to misrepresent parole release in ways that could make ordinary people believe something deceptive was going on. Lay people were understandably confused when they read or heard media reports that an offender sentenced to, say, 30 years was released after 3. Criminal justice officials understood that the real time to be served was vastly shorter than 30 years, and so did any experienced reporter. Reporters and editors sensitive to the ethics of "truth in reporting" would presumably not knowingly mislead citizens, but most chose nonetheless to dramatize crime stories. The old saw "If it bleeds, it leads" explains why. Sensational stories attract readers and viewers. The result was to create a general public susceptible to claims that indeterminate sentencing was deceptive. Demagogic politicians manipulated that susceptibility.

The other drivers, and the real forces behind truth in sentencing, were political and ideological. Republicans in the 1980s and 1990s successfully made crime a major issue in American politics and repeatedly promoted ever harsher laws to show their commitment (Windlesham 1998; Gottschalk 2015). Republicans and conservatives generally, as they had during the sentencing reform period, wanted punishments to be made more severe. So did many judges, who were often frustrated that prisoners were released sooner than they would have wanted. Solely to make a symbolic point, judges sometimes imposed sentences expressed in decades or centuries even though they knew the maxima had little or no practical or legal significance. Attacking parole release in favor of fixed, "truthful" sentences simultaneously demonstrated seriousness about crime as an issue and provided a mechanism for making prison sentences longer.

Conservative policy advocates in the tough on crime period worked hard to define the differences between the sentences judges announced and the times prisoners served as a problem that needed fixing. Republican George F. Allen's 1993 campaign for governor of Virginia, for example, focused heavily on his opposition to parole release and his promise to abolish it if elected. He was, and he did.

The Case for More Incarceration, a US Department of Justice report promoted by US Attorney General William Barr (1992), for example, argued that "prison works," urged that more people be sent there, proposed a major national program of prison construction, and called for abolition of parole release. Barr's proposals were embodied in proposed legislation that became the Violent Crime Control and Law Enforcement Act of 1994, as amended in 1996. The law unambiguously sought to increase the number of people in prison and the periods they spent there. To qualify for federal for prison construction funds, a state had to demonstrate that it

> (A) has increased the percentage of convicted violent offenders sentenced to prison; (B) has increased the average prison time which will be served in prison by convicted violent offenders sentenced to prison; (C) has increased the percentage of sentence which will be served in prison by violent offenders sentenced to prison.

States had to demonstrate that affected prisoners would be required to serve at least 85 percent of their nominal sentences (or, in indeterminate sentencing states, a mean average of at least 85 percent).

Evaluators at the Urban Institute sought to determine the effects of truth-in-sentencing laws on sentencing patterns and prison populations. They concluded that truth-in-sentencing laws had large projected effects in the seven states they examined closely. When implemented as part of a comprehensive change to the sentencing system, "truth-in-sentencing laws were associated with large changes in prison populations" (Sabol et al. 2002, p. vii). In one such state, "the increase in the percentage of sentences required to be served before release led to larger increases in length of stay and consequently a larger effect of length of stay on the expected number of prisoners" (p. vii).

TABLE 2.3. Estimated percentage of sentence served prior to enactment of truth-in-sentencing compared with projected future percentages

State	Percentage sentence served by offenders released during 1993	Estimated percentage served for offenders entering prison during 1991	Expected percentage under truth in sentencing
Georgia	42	51	100
Washington	76	76	85
Illinois	44	43	85
Ohio	26	83*	97
New Jersey	39	37	85
Pennsylvania	46	108*	100*
Utah	36	32	Indeterminate

Sources: Ditton and Wilson 1999; Sabol et al. 2002, table 3.3.

*Minimum sentences in jurisdictions retaining parole release; other items refer to maximum sentences.

Table 2.3 shows that the percentages of sentences projected to be served in the seven states under truth-in-sentencing were much higher than for those released in 1991 and 1993. In most states they at least doubled. The evaluators observed that the effects were much less than if violent crime rates had not begun a substantial decline after 1991: "Were the sentencing practices of 1996 to persist during a time when the number of violent offenses increases, the impacts on prison populations and corrections management could be dramatic" (p. 31).

A Vera Institute of Justice study looked at the effects on prison populations of a wider range of sentencing policy changes in all 50 states between 1975 and 2002 (Stemen, Rengifo, and Wilson 2006). Truth-in-sentencing laws were included. The authors concluded: "States with separate time served requirements for violent offenders had higher incarceration rates than other states" (p. iii).

The RAND Corporation also carried out a federally funded evaluation of the effects of the federal truth-in-sentencing initiative (Turner et al. 2001). It concluded: "Nationwide, the imposed maximum sentence length, the average length of prison term, and the percent of term served for violent offenses have increased for TIS [truth-in-sentencing]

TABLE 2.4. Adoption of life without parole, US states, by decades through 2009

	Pre-1950	1950–59	1960–69	1970–79	1980–89	1990–99	2000–2009
Northeast	PA (1941)	MA (1951)		NH (1974), ME (1976)	VT (1982), RI (1984), CT (1985)	NJ (1995), NY (1995)	
Midwest	SD (1939)	MI (1953)		IL (1973), IA (1976)	MO (1984), WI (1984)	IN (1993), ND (1995), OH (1997), MN (1998)	NE (2002) KS (2006)
South	MS (1848)		WV (1966)	AR (1976), LA (1976), SC (1976)	AL (1981), DC (1981), MD (1987), OK (1987)	DE (1990), GA (1993, 2009), TN (1993), FL (1994), NC (1994), VA (1994), KY (1998)	TX (2005)
West			MT (1967)	ID (1972), WA (1975), NV (1977), CA (1978), NM (1979)	HI (1986), OR (1989)	CO (1990), UT (1992), WY (1996)	AZ (2006)

Source: Ogletree and Sarat (2012)

states between 1993 and 1997. For non-TIS states, sentence lengths have been dropping, and months served have dropped slightly" (p. 134).

The Urban Institute study defined any state that had eliminated the possibility of parole release for some or all prisoners as a "truth-in-sentencing state." Marvell and Moody (1996) examined prison population effects of parole abolition and, using 1971–93 state prison data, found that only one of 10 abolition states experienced a higher rate of increase than the 50-state average. The lowest rates of growth were in Minnesota and Washington. The states included in that study, however, abolished parole release during the sentencing reform period; none of them then had a truth-in-sentencing 85-percent-to-be-served requirement. Several abolition states had adopted presumptive sentencing guidelines that incorporated prison capacity constraints.

Findings that the early abolitions of parole release restrained prison population growth are thus not inconsistent with the Urban Institute, Vera, and RAND findings that truth-in-sentencing laws, which effectively abolished parole release for affected prisoners, increased it. Unlike the truth-in-sentencing initiatives, the earlier abolitions of parole were not meant to increase the lengths of prison sentences.[5]

William Spelman, in the conclusion of an especially comprehensive analysis of the causes of state prison population increases since 1977, observed:

> Truth-in-sentencing laws have little immediate effect but a substantial long-run effect. This analysis makes sense: Truth-in-sentencing laws increase time served and reduce the number of offenders released in future years; the full effect would only be observed after prisoners sentenced under the old regime are replaced by those sentenced under the new law. (2009, p. 59)

The Urban Institute, Vera, and RAND studies inevitably underestimate the effects of truth-in-sentencing laws on prison population growth because their data cover periods ending, respectively, in 1996–98, 2002,

[5] The earlier abolition proposals were meant to reduce disparities and enhance consistency and proportionality (N. Morris 1974; von Hirsch and Hanrahan 1979). The overriding aim was greater fairness, not harsher punishment.

and 1997. The ultimate effects of truth-in-sentencing legislation remain unknown, because comparatively few of the people sentenced under them have yet been released. This is true of all laws enacted during the tough on crime period that mandated sentences of historically unprecedented lengths.

California's and other states' three-strikes laws mandated 25-year minimum sentences. Under an 85 percent rule, a prisoner serving a 25-year sentence is not eligible for release before 21 years and 3 months. The first person sentenced to prison under California's law or any other three-strikes law enacted in 1994–96 will not be released because his or her sentence has expired until late in 2015 or early in 2016. Each year's entry cohort so far has been a net addition to the states' prison populations. Only after the passage of several more years will prisoners newly admitted begin to be offset by the release of prisoners sentenced under three-strikes laws two decades earlier. Generalized to encompass all three-strikes, truth-in sentencing, and mandatory minimum laws, this is the principal reason why American imprisonment rates rose until 2007 even though American crime rates fell continuously after 1991 (Travis, Western, and Redburn 2014, chaps. 2, 3).

2. *Life without the Possibility of Parole.* Nearly 50,000 people were serving LWOPs in 2011 (Nellis 2013). There were many more when this book was published. They were authorized in the District of Columbia and every state except Alaska. Seven states had such laws before 1970. Compared with other Western countries, these numbers are astonishing. Most do not authorize LWOPs, and where they are authorized they affect only handfuls of prisoners. LWOPs are unconstitutional in European countries under both European and national laws (van Zyl Smit and Snacken 2009). In 2013, the European Court of Human Rights in *Case of Vintner and Others v. The United Kingdom* declared them unlawful in EU and other signatory countries as a violation of the European Convention of Human Rights.

Enactment of LWOP laws in recent decades was catalyzed by the revival of capital punishment in the United States following the Supreme Court's decision in *Gregg v. Georgia*, 428 U.S. 153 (1976) upholding its constitutionality if specific conditions were met. Many states enacted LWOP laws in the 1980s through the mid-1990s in part at the urging of death penalty opponents who believed them strategically important as a politically credible alternative to capital punishment. In explaining why section 6.06 of the Model Penal Code's revised sentencing provisions does not forbid LWOPs, the draftsmen explained:

> The increasing use of whole-life sentences in this country has been driven largely by their role in the death-penalty debate. In many jurisdictions, life without parole serves as the chief alternative to capital punishment for the most aggravated homicides. In states without capital punishment, legislative authorization of natural-life sentences is sometimes thought essential to public acceptance of a system with no death penalty. (American Law Institute 2011, p. 13)

However, as table 2.4 shows, the large majority of new LWOP laws were enacted during the tough on crime period and are at least in part attributable to the same social and political forces that supported enactment of three-strikes and truth-in-sentencing laws.

Astonishingly little research has been done on sentences of life without the possibility of parole (Ogletree and Sarat 2012). A recent National Academy of Sciences panel on the deterrent effects of the death penalty concluded that there is no convincing evidence that capital punishment has greater deterrent effects than life without parole (Nagin and Pepper 2012). However, there is no research on the deterrent effects of LWOPs compared with parolable life sentences or shorter fixed sentences. They received heavy media attention only for a few years in the 1990s, as figure 2.5 shows, but remain in place almost everywhere.

3. *Mandatory Minimum Sentence and Three-strikes Laws.* Between 1975 and 1996, mandatory minimums were America's most frequently enacted sentencing law changes. By 1983, 49 of the 50 states had adopted them for offenses other than murder or drunk driving (Shane-DuBow, Brown, and Olsen 1985, table 30). By 1994, every state had adopted mandatory penalties; most had many (Austin et al. 1994). Most apply to drug offenses, murder, aggravated rape, firearms felonies, or felonies committed by people with previous felony convictions. Between 1985 and mid-1991, the US Congress enacted at least 20 new mandatory penalty provisions; by 1991, more than 60 federal statutes subjected more than 100 crimes to mandatory penalties (US Sentencing Commission 1991*b*, pp. 8–10). More followed. Since the mid-1990s, most new federal

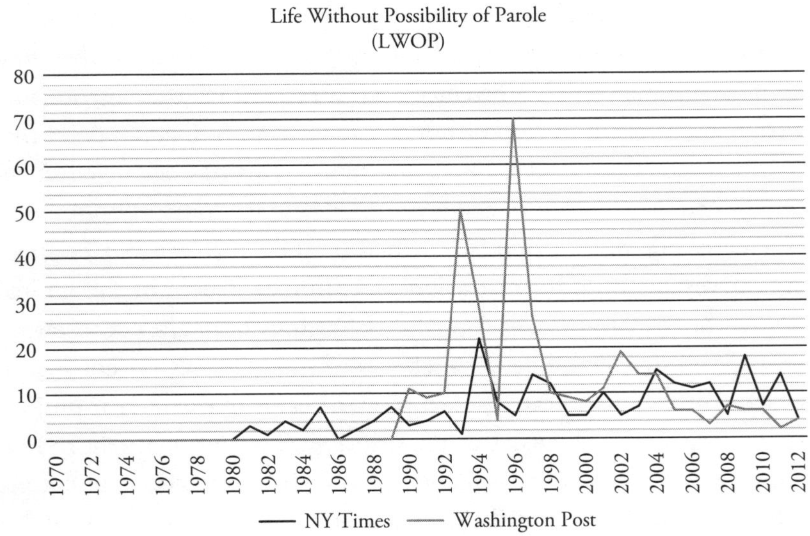

FIGURE 2.5. News stories, national newspapers, LWOPs, 1970–2012

and state mandatory minimums have concerned sexual offenses, child pornography, and gun crimes. Three-strikes laws are a subcategory of mandatory minimums—conviction of a designated offense triggers a statutory mandate that the judge impose a prison sentence of at least a specified minimum length.

Knowledge about mandatory minimum sentences has changed remarkably little in the past 30 years. What we knew in 1983 is what we know now (Blumstein et al. 1983; Travis, Western, and Redburn 2014). Their ostensible primary rationale is deterrence. It is not unreasonable for someone new to the subject to assume that the threat of a mandatory prison sentence deters would-be offenders. After all, nearly everyone is careful to avoid overstaying a parking meter when a tow truck or traffic officer is nearby, and slows down when seeing a police car. Nonetheless, the overwhelming weight of the evidence is that they have few if any deterrent effects in relation to serious crimes (Durlauf and Nagin 2011; Travis, Western, and Redburn 2014, chap. 5). A few authoritative surveys of the evidence conclude that deterrent effects can sometimes be demonstrated, but also conclude that existing knowledge is too fragmentary or the estimated effects are so small as to have no practical relevance for policy making (Pratt et al. 2006; Nagin 2013).

The evidence is equally overwhelming that practitioners often evade or circumvent mandatory penalties, that they create stark disparities between cases in which they are circumvented and cases in which they are not, and that they often result in imposition of sentences in individual cases that everyone directly involved believes are unjust. This has been well documented since the eighteenth century (e.g., Hay 1975; Tonry 2009*a*).

The classic demonstration is provided by the American Bar Foundation's Survey of the Administration of Criminal Justice in the United States in the 1950s. I present some of its findings in detail because they vividly demonstrate the perverse effects of mandatories on court processes and sentencing. Frank Remington, director of the 18-year project, observed at its end, "Legislative prescription of a high mandatory sentence for certain offenders is likely to result in a reduction in charges at the prosecution stage, or if this is not done, by a refusal of the judge to convict at the adjudication stage. The issue . . . thus is not solely whether certain offenders should be dealt with severely, but also how the criminal justice system will accommodate to the legislative charge" (Remington 1969, p. xvii).

Donald Newman described how Michigan judges dealt with a lengthy mandatory minimum for drug sales:

> Mandatory minimums are almost universally disliked by trial judges. . . . The clearest illustration of routine reductions is provided by reduction of sale of narcotics to possession or addiction. . . . Judges . . . actively participated in the charge reduction process to the extent of refusing to accept guilty pleas to sale and liberally assigning counsel to work out reduced charges. . . . [Between May 8, 1952, and June 30, 1956], only 12 sale-of-narcotics convictions were recorded in Detroit out of 476 defendants originally charged with sale. The remainder (except a handful acquitted altogether) pleaded guilty to reduced charges. (Newman 1966, p. 179)

Newman described how prosecutors sidestepped 15-year mandatory maximum sentences for breaking and entering and armed robbery:

> In Michigan conviction of armed robbery or breaking and entering in the nighttime (15-year maximum compared to 5 years for daytime

> breaking) is rare. The pattern of downgrading is such that it becomes virtually routine. . . . Armed robbery is so often downgraded that the Michigan parole board tends to treat a conviction for unarmed robbery as prima facie proof that the defendant had a weapon. And the frequency of altering nighttime burglary to breaking and entering in the daytime led one prosecutor to remark: "You'd think all our burglaries occur at high noon." (1966, p. 182)

Robert O. Dawson described "very strong" judicial resistance to a 20-year mandatory minimum for sale of narcotics:

> All of the judges of Recorder's Court, in registering their dislike for the provision, cited the hypothetical case of a young man having no criminal record being given a 20-year minimum sentence for selling a single marijuana cigarette. Charge reductions to possession or use are routine. Indeed, in some cases, judges have refused to accept guilty pleas to sale of narcotics, but have continued the case and appointed counsel with instructions to negotiate a charge reduction. (1969, p. 201)

More recent evidence on implementation of mandatory sentencing laws is entirely consistent. It comes primarily from six major studies of state laws. One is an evaluation of New York's Rockefeller Drug Laws, which required lengthy mandatory minimum sentences for a wide range of drug offenses (Joint Committee on New York Drug Law Evaluation 1978). One concerns a Michigan law requiring imposition of a 2-year mandatory prison sentence on persons convicted of possession of a gun during commission of a felony (Loftin and McDowall 1981; Loftin, Heumann, and McDowall 1983). Two concern Massachusetts's Bartley-Fox Amendment, which required a 1-year prison sentence for persons convicted of carrying a firearm unlawfully (Beha 1977; Rossman et al. 1979). One concerns a 1994 Oregon law that established lengthy minimum sentences for 16 offenses (Merritt, Fain, and Turner 2006). The last is an evaluation of the effects of a truth-in-sentencing law in New Jersey (McCoy and McManimon 2004). They all found that case-by-case differences in prosecutorial charging and bargaining decisions produced massive disparities between comparable cases, that prosecutors and judges (and sometimes police) often changed their practices to avoid imposition of the harsh punishments, that the sentences were imposed in the remaining cases, and that overall there were few or no effects on conviction rates.

Vigorous and highly publicized efforts were made to make the newly enacted laws effective. New York's Rockefeller Drug Laws attracted massive media attention of which prospective drug dealers could not have been unaware. The legislature authorized and funded 31 new courts to handle drug cases, and forbade some kinds of plea bargaining to assure the mandatory sentences were imposed. Massachusetts's Bartley-Fox Amendment forbade use of procedural devices commonly used to dispose of cases informally. In Michigan, the prosecutor in Wayne County (where Detroit is) established a ban on plea bargaining and launched a major publicity campaign that promised "One with a Gun Gets You Two."

> *Rockefeller Drug Laws.* Practitioners tried to circumvent mandatory sentences and often succeeded; the remaining cases were dealt with as the law dictated (Blumstein et al. 1983, pp. 188–89). Drug felony arrests, indictment rates, and conviction rates all declined after the law took effect. The likelihood that a person arrested for a drug felony was imprisoned was the same after the law took effect—11 percent—as before (Joint Committee on New York Drug Law Evaluation 1978). For those who were convicted, the likelihood of being imprisoned and the average length of prison term increased substantially.
>
> *Massachusetts's Bartley-Fox Amendment.* Massachusetts's Bartley-Fox Amendment required a 1-year mandatory minimum prison sentence, without suspension, furlough, or parole, for anyone convicted of unlawful carrying of an unlicensed firearm. The primary findings of two major evaluations and a reassessment of their data were that police became more selective about whom to frisk, decreased the number of arrests, and seized many more weapons without making an arrest. Charge dismissals and acquittals increased significantly. The percentage of defendants who entirely avoided a conviction rose from 53.5 to 80 percent. Of the comparatively few vulnerable defendants who were finally convicted, the probability of receiving an incarcerative sentence increased from 23 to 100 percent (Beha 1977; Rossman et al. 1979; Carlson 1982).

The Michigan Felony Firearms Statute. This law specified a 2-year mandatory prison sentence for possession of a firearm while engaging in a felony. The findings paralleled those in the earlier studies. There were many more dismissals. Conviction probabilities declined. The probability of imprisonment did not increase, but lengths of sentences increased for those sent to prison. The percentage of defendants incarcerated among those potentially vulnerable did not change markedly (Heumann and Loftin 1979; Loftin, Heumann, and McDowall 1983).

Trial rates increased from 16 to 41 percent for felonious assaults because of an adaptive response, the "waiver trial." The judge would convict the defendant of a misdemeanor rather than the charged felony (only felonies were covered) or, with the prosecutor's acquiescence, acquit the defendant on the firearms charge. In another routine circumvention, the sentence that otherwise would have been imposed was decreased by 2 years, and the mandatory 2-year increment was then added (Heumann and Loftin 1979, pp. 416–24).

Oregon's Measure 11. Adopted by referendum in 1994, the law required mandatory minimum sentences from 70 to 300 months for anyone convicted of 16 (later 21) designated crimes. RAND Corporation evaluators hypothesized that judges and lawyers would alter previous ways of doing business in order to achieve results that seemed to them sensible and just. They expected that changes in charging and plea bargaining would result in fewer people being convicted of Measure 11 offenses and more of non–Measure 11 offenses. They also expected that those convicted would receive harsher sentences. The research confirmed the hypotheses. Changed sentencing patterns resulted primarily from changes in charging (fewer Measure 11 crimes, more lesser crimes) and plea bargaining (fewer pleas to initially charged offenses, more to lesser included offenses) (Merritt, Fain, and Turner 2006).

New Jersey Truth in Sentencing. Candace McCoy and Patrick McManimon (2004) examined sentencing patterns and case processing in New Jersey following enactment of a truth-in-sentencing law requiring people convicted of designated offenses to serve 85 percent of the announced sentence. This was not a mandatory minimum sentence law, but similar hypotheses apply: that charging and bargaining patterns would change to shelter some defendants from the new law, and that sentences would be harsher for those not sheltered. Both hypotheses were confirmed.

Federal sentencing. Mandatory penalties loom large in the federal system. Drug prosecutions make up a major portion of the federal case load; a large percentage are affected by mandatory minimum sentence laws, including the 100-to-1 crack/powder sentencing law through 2010 and the 18-to-1 law since. In addition, however, until *Booker* was decided in 2005, the US Sentencing Commission regarded the federal guidelines overall as mandatory.

The main findings of a sizable number of federal studies parallel those from the states: mandatory penalties increase the power of the prosecutor; they foster widespread circumvention, and increase disparities in sentences received by comparable offenders (e.g., Hofer 1990; Schulhofer and Nagel 1997; Hofer 2012).

Because of their almost unreviewable constitutional authority, federal prosecutors have inherent power to protect defendants from mandatories when they wish to do so. Before *Booker* was decided, circumvention of the guidelines and statutory minimums by judges was mostly done surreptitiously. Since *Booker*, and especially since *Kimbrough v. United States*, 552 U.S. 85 (2007), held that a judge's disagreement with omission policy decisions is a valid reason for a departure from the guidelines, judges have been openly disregarding the guidelines (e.g., Kaiser and Spohn 2014).

As a consequence of the interplay of mandatory minimum sentence laws and mandatory guidelines, prosecutors' plea negotiation leverage was substantially enhanced, so much that federal court of appeals judge Gerald Lynch (2003) described prosecutors as the primary federal sentencers. That is an extraordinary admission for a judge to make, but from the outset this was an almost inevitable consequence of the federal guidelines. An early commission-sponsored study acknowledged that in many cases the "sentencing decision is not being made by the judge" (Nagel and Schulhofer 1992, p. 553).

When prosecutors are determined that defendants receive very long sentences, defendants are in a weak bargaining position, especially in drug cases, because only the prosecutor has authority to decide what charges will be filed and what charges, if any, will be dismissed. When, however, prosecutors are sympathetic to a particular defendant, or believe mandatory penalties are too severe, they can easily manipulate federal sentencing laws and guidelines. This happened often, as a long series of analyses has consistently shown (e.g., Schulhofer and Nagel 1989, 1997; Hofer 1990, 2012; Johnson 2014).

The major initiatives of the tough on crime period were failures by all plausible criteria. As many policy makers intended, however, they did send more people to prison for longer times. Their inflexibility and severity require imposition of punishments that often violate ideas about proportionality and parsimony that have long been ubiquitous in Western countries and, except for the last 30 years, in the United States. They produced unprecedented imprisonment rates that public officials of almost every ideological caste, scholars, and human rights advocates now decry. Newt Gingrich, for example, observed on CNN's *Crossfire* program on May 21, 2014, "It would be hard to overstate the scale of this tragedy" (Gingrich and Jones 2014).

D. Equilibrium

A huge amount of state and federal sentencing legislation was enacted after 1996, and many new community-level initiatives were begun, but generalizations are difficult to offer. The late University of Chicago Law School professor Norval Morris often quoted a probably apocryphal Chinese proverb: "When much noise on stairs, nobody comes." There has been an enormous amount of state sentencing legislation since 2000. National Conference of State Legislatures records document more than 1,100 new laws. Many hundreds have slightly narrowed the scope of severe existing laws, made limited categories of low-risk prisoners newly eligible for release, and reduced the frequency of parole and probation revocations. However, like the noise on Morris's stairs, the changes have not added up to much (Austin et al. 2013).

Few new laws characteristic of the tough on crime period were enacted. The most notable exceptions were adoptions of three-strikes laws in Arizona and Alaska (for sex offenders) in 2006 and in Massachusetts in 2012. The Alaska and Massachusetts laws were precipitated by recent notorious cases. New federal mandatory minimum sentence laws were enacted for child pornography, carjacking, and human smuggling, and a few similar laws in states, but they typically lacked the breadth and severity of the preceding generation of mandatories.

No major laws from the tough on crime period have been repealed except in Michigan in 2002, but a few have been revised in significant ways. New York's Rockefeller Drug Law was moderated, though exceedingly long sentences are still mandated for some offenders (New York State 2012). The US Congress replaced the 100-to-1 crack/powder cocaine ratio with an 18-to-1 ratio. California voters in 2012 and 2014 narrowed the scope of the three-strikes law, but it still requires minimum 25-year sentences for the cases it continues to cover.

Drug and other problem-solving courts proliferated beginning in the early 1990s, as did prisoner reentry programs in the early 2000s. Steadily accumulating evidence that well-designed, managed, and targeted treatment programs can reduce reoffending has catalyzed development of large numbers of programs in prisons and in communities (Cullen 2013; Jonson and Cullen 2015).

Identifying aims and underlying values of the equilibrium period is not easy. Institutions, laws, and practices from each of the three preceding periods coexist with newer community and restorative justice programs, and each carries a set of aims and values with it. Two-thirds of states retain parole release authority over many prisoners. Almost all of the severe laws of the tough on crime period endure, as do voluntary and presumptive sentencing guidelines and parole guidelines.

Various recent initiatives, including drug courts, prisoner reentry programs, and new treatment programs, seek to reduce reoffending through individualization of programs to address offenders' needs and deficits. Mandatory minimum, three-strikes, truth-in-sentencing, and LWOP laws seek to assure that offenders are punished severely. Guidelines systems seek to provide fair procedures, reduce disparities, and make the process open and understandable. Restorative and community justice programs aim to heal relationships among offenders, victims, and communities.

No general theoretical logic is discernible in the crazy quilt of diverging policies; some are best described as retributive, some as deterrent or incapacitative, some as rehabilitative, some as restorative, some simply as vindictive and vengeful. Within the theory class, retributivism remains predominant (von Hirsch and Ashworth 2005; Robinson 2008, 2013).

Almost the full possible range of practical aims can be inferred from current institutions and policies—rehabilitation, reintegration, crime reduction, banishment, exemplary punishment. The same is true of implicit values: depending on the institution or policy in issue, they might be described as humane or inhumane, rehabilitative or destructive, restorative or iatrogenic, proportionate or disproportionate. In 2015, pretty much anything goes.

The imprisonment rate continued to increase rapidly for a few years after the tough on crime period ended, then slowly, until it peaked at 756 per 100,000 in 2007. It fell slightly thereafter (Carson 2014).

During the equilibrium period, as the name suggests, sentencing matters have been in a holding pattern. Almost all the policy initiatives undertaken since 1975 remain in place. The transitions from indeterminate sentencing into the sentencing reform period, and from it into tough on crime, were marked by decisive changes in direction, by creation of new policies and practices, and by rejection of earlier ones. Nothing so decisive happened during the equilibrium period. Not everything works, but everything remains in place.

II. What Next?

The equilibrium period may be ending. The preferable directions of change should be self-evident: away from rigidity, severity, and insensitivity to the causes of human failings, and toward flexibility, moderation, and compassion. The quotations from Newt Gingrich, William Bennett, and other Right on Crime spokesmen in chapter 1 make it clear that conservative American political figures are no longer monolithically committed to toughness, no matter what the human and financial costs. Support by voters for referenda permitting medical use of marijuana, legalizing marijuana, requiring diversion of first- and second-time nonviolent drug offenders into treatment programs, and pruning some of the worst excesses of California's three-strikes law show that American citizens are willing to consider new ways of doing business. The question whose answer will determine the future is what elected politicians can be persuaded to do. The indications so far are at best promising.

The lessons of the past 40 years are straightforward and relatively uncontroversial. Indeterminate sentencing could not keep its rehabilitative promises or justify the injustices that resulted from individualization without rules, standards, accountability, or transparency. It had pernicious effects on legal standards for admission of evidence, burdens of proof, and consideration of criminal history at sentencing. None of those deficiencies should be accepted or allowed to continue.

That does not mean that all of the features of indeterminate sentencing should be rejected. Parole boards with release authority have potentially important roles to play in evening out disparities in judges' sentences, taking account of individual differences in setting prison release dates, and regulating prison population numbers. Individualization of sentences within bounds and under general rules is inevitable and essential if sentencing is to take account sensibly and justly of the circumstances, characteristics, and situations of individual offenders. Attempting to address the causes of offending in individual cases and to improve offenders' prospects for living satisfying, law-abiding lives should be primary objectives of just sentencing systems.

The legacy of the sentencing reform period is also mixed. There are two primary lessons to be learned. Sentencing standards that lack meaningful presumptive authority are unlikely to be effective either as management tools or as means to reduce sentencing disparities. Well-designed and implemented parole and presumptive sentencing guidelines can be used to minimize disparities, establish and effectuate policies, and plan facilities and budgets. Presumptive guidelines of either sort, or both, should be a component of every American jurisdiction's efforts to bring justice, fairness, predictability, and rationality to the sentencing of convicted offenders.

The policies and institutions of the tough on crime period have fared less well. Mandatory minimum, three-strikes, and truth in sentencing laws failed to prevent crime significantly, as many of their proponents insisted they would, and at unacceptable cost in human suffering, collateral effects, and state spending. They produced massive prison populations.

They also produced innumerable injustices in one-size-fits-all rigidity and severity, and in the widespread but inconsistent circumventions they provoked. The moral is clear. All of these laws should be repealed and replaced with sentencing systems that allow judges to punish deeply culpable wrongdoers appropriately while retaining authority, under established standards and subject to appeal, to punish others less severely or in different ways.

3

Federal Sentencing

"WRONG TIME, WRONG PLACE" WOULD be a fitting epitaph for the US Sentencing Commission and its guidelines. The initiative was conceived in a kinder, gentler time, as the first President George Bush might have put it, before sentencing policy became highly politicized and when the principal aims of sentencing reform were fair procedures, just punishments, and reduced disparities.

Senate Bill 2699, the first proposal to establish a federal sentencing commission, was introduced by Senator Edward Kennedy in 1975. It was ahead of its time. It was the first legislative proposal anywhere for a sentencing commission, proposed the same year as enactment of the first modern determinate sentencing law in Maine, three years before enactment of the first state sentencing commission legislation in Minnesota and Pennsylvania, and nine years before the US Congress enacted the Sentencing Reform Act of 1984.

The legislation was enacted, the commission was appointed, and the guidelines took effect, however, just as the tough on crime period hit its stride. The archetypal symbol is the federal Anti-Drug Abuse Act of 1986, which contained a host of lengthy mandatory minimum sentence laws including the 100-to-1 crack cocaine provisions. That act was passed between the appointment in 1985 of the initial commissioners and the implementation in 1987 of the federal guidelines.

What began as a modest, technocratic reform proposal, which by 1984 had been adopted and was working well in several states, resulted in the most radical, controversial, and disliked sentencing system in

American history. The initial guidelines were criticized on normative grounds (because they were too harsh), on fairness grounds (because they forbade consideration of offender characteristics most judges believe to be important), on outcome grounds (because they would not reduce sentencing disparities), on technocratic grounds (because they were too complex), on operational grounds (because their complexity made calculation errors inevitable), on policy grounds (because they narrowed judicial discretion and increased prosecutorial power), and on process grounds (because they foreseeably led practitioners to circumvent them) (Stith and Cabranes 1998).

All these problems were apparent by the late 1980s, but successive commissions have refused to address them, generally digging in their heels instead. Gradually, beginning in the mid-1990s and culminating in 2005, the US Supreme Court in *Booker v. U.S.*, 543 U.S. 220 (2005), loosened the guidelines and reined in the commission. The "mandatory" guidelines were made "advisory." Before that happened, though, the quality of justice in federal courts suffered grievously. Tens of thousands of people received sentences much more severe than could be justified by the crimes they committed or of any imaginable salutary effects of their punishments. The federal example became a major impediment to reform of state sentencing. The drafters of the American Bar Association's 1994 Standards for Sentencing Procedures and Alternatives explained that their work used the clumsy phrase "sentencing structures" instead of the more familiar "sentencing guidelines" because of the federal guidelines' fearsome reputation. Mere mention of guidelines proposals in the states led to kneejerk hostility and opposition (Reitz and Reitz 1993).

Recent incarnations of the federal commission have in some ways tried to make the guidelines more rational and less severe, especially in relation to mandatory minimum sentences and crack cocaine, and have regularly sought advice from outsiders. The commission has become slightly bolder and in July 2014 proposed lowering guideline ranges for many drug offenses, with retroactive application to potentially more than 46,000 federal inmates (US Sentencing Commission 2014*c*). The Congress accepted the proposal (US Sentencing Commission 2015).

The commission has, however, consistently failed to propose or make major changes to the guidelines' most controversial features. Those include their complexity, their rigidity, their severity, their aversion to use of community-based punishments, and their "relevant conduct" provision that directs judges to increase sentences on the basis of alleged crimes for which the defendant was not charged or convicted, and even of which he or she was acquitted. The only full-blown commission-related proposal for a major overhaul came from a former commission chairman, Federal District Court judge William K. Sessions III (2011). Under that proposal, the guidelines would again become largely mandatory, judges would not be allowed to take offenders' personal backgrounds and characteristics into account, and other than for alleged crimes of which a defendant was acquitted the relevant conduct rule would endure. Those proposals would have retained all the worst features of the failed mandatory guidelines (Baron-Evans and Stith 2012).

The current commission chair, Federal District Court judge Patti B. Saris (2011, 2013), has repeatedly decried what she describes as growing disparities in application of the guidelines, and urged Congress to enact legislation to reinvigorate them. She does not acknowledge that most practitioners and outside observers believe federal sentencing is more just under the advisory guidelines. A 2010 survey of federal district court judges demonstrates how far out of step the commission is. Only 3 percent of the judges thought that the mandatory guidelines in effect in 2005 "best achieve the purposes of sentencing." Seventy-five percent said the then-current advisory guidelines did. Seventy-six percent of judges said that commission policies on individualization of sentences did not provide appropriate grounds for departures and 65 percent said the departure policies were "too restrictive" (US Sentencing Commission 2010, tables 14, 17). Those figures are striking because the vast majority of federal judges were appointed after the guidelines took effect. They have known nothing else and could have been expected to be socialized into the values of the system as it existed when they took office. The vast majority of district court judges in 1990 held similar views (Federal Courts Study Committee 1990).

This chapter tells that story. It is an important story. The federal sentencing guidelines' notoriety significantly set back constructive sentencing policy change in the states. American political culture may, however, soon be as receptive to fundamental rethinking of sentencing as it was 40 years ago. If that happens, presumptive guidelines of the sort Federal

District Court judge Marvin Frankel first proposed are the best means Americans have identified for establishing sentencing systems that are reasonably fair, just, and consistent (Frankel 1972, 1973; Frase 2013).

The problems of the federal guidelines were not inevitable. They resulted from the tough-on-crime politics of the 1980s and the personalities and political ambitions of the original members of the US Sentencing Commission. Even now the guidelines could be reformulated in ways that offer reasonable prospects for achieving their original aims. At the end of this chapter, I describe how that can be done.

Two not unimportant questions are whether federal sentencing is more or less just than before the guidelines took effect on October 1, 1987, and whether "unwarranted" disparities are more or less common. Federal sentencing for sure is less just. For many offenses, sentences are much too severe both absolutely and compared with lesser punishments commonly received for more serious crimes. Judges are forbidden to take into account circumstances of offenders' lives that would justify less harsh punishment. Judges are strongly discouraged from imposing community punishments in cases in which that is the most appropriate thing to do. The relevant conduct policy of punishing people for crimes of which they have not been convicted is fundamentally unfair. It is unimaginable in the legal system of any other Western democracy.[1]

Federal sentencing disparities are undoubtedly worse than they were before October 1, 1987, and are worse than they would have been in the counterfactual world in which the Sentencing Reform Act of 1984 was not enacted. There are two reasons to be confident this is true. The first is that nearly half of convicted federal offenders received community punishments in 1985, compared with fewer than 10 percent in 2014; by definition many fewer people were at risk of disparities in prison sentences. Unwarranted disparities in community penalties are, of course, also undesirable. As a practical matter, however, the stakes are much higher when prison is involved. Disparities in who is sent there and for

[1] The list could go on. Reduced punishments are authorized, for example, for offenders who give "substantial assistance" to the prosecution of other people. High-level drug and organized crime offenders, who have information to share, often receive less severe punishments than low-level offenders. Prosecutors have unilateral authority to decide to charge or insist on guilty pleas to offenses subject to lengthy mandatory minimum sentences; all else equal, targeted defendants receive dramatically longer sentences (US Sentencing Commission 2004; Hofer 2012).

how long are what really matter. The mere fact of conviction is stigmatizing and has detrimental effects on offenders' employment prospects, reputations, and community standing. A community punishment is seldom likely to worsen those effects. Prison sentences, however, ruin lives, break up families, and damage offenders' children in ways that community punishments do not (Murray et al. 2014; Jacobs 2015).

The second is that the federal Parole Commission's guidelines for release from prison were impressively successful at reducing disparities in prison sentences (Gottfredson, Wilkins, and Hoffman 1978; Arthur D. Little, Inc. and Goldfarb and Singer, Esqs., 1981). The Sentencing Reform Act eliminated parole release and replaced it with "truth-in-sentencing" that requires prisoners to serve at least 85 percent of their sentences. Federal sentencing was fairer in 1985 for those who were sent to prison and for those who were not.

It is impossible to know what federal sentencing would have looked like had the guidelines not been adopted. Had the 1984 indeterminate system continued without major changes, disparities would have been less. Had another guidelines commission been established later, it is reasonable to believe that it would not have made the radical policy decisions made by the original commission. No other sentencing commission preceding (Minnesota, Pennsylvania, Washington), contemporaneous with (Oregon), or following the federal commission (North Carolina, Ohio, Kansas) established a system of comparable severity, rigidity, and complexity. It is plausible to suppose that another later commission would have followed the paths pioneered by the states.

I say a bit more about those answers in the conclusion. First, I tell the federal story in more detail. Section I provides a capsule history of the conception, design, implementation, and ultimate emasculation of the federal guidelines. In section II, I sketch what the federal sentencing system looked like in the years immediately before the guidelines took effect, and compare that to the years since.

Section III describes critical decisions made by the initial commission in the development of the guidelines, and their implications. This is not only of historical interest and importance. Many critical decisions were not required by the Sentencing Reform Act. Some statutory provisions—for example, those creating a presumption that nonviolent first offenders should normally not be sentenced to imprisonment and directing that the guidelines be formulated to minimize the likelihood that the federal prison population would exceed the capacity of the federal prisons—were flatly ignored. Much that the initial commission did could have been, and still could be, done differently under the terms of the enabling legislation.

Section IV describes the guidelines development process and why they took the shape they did. Former commission member and now Supreme Court associate justice Stephen Breyer at the time painted a picture of earnest, hardworking commissioners struggling against overwhelming complexities and making difficult technocratic decisions in order to devise a workable system that would reduce disparities. Critics didn't understand this, Justice Breyer wrote, and made the best the enemy of the good. The true story is of a poorly managed agency that made fateful but fundamental early mistakes, many politically motivated, compounded by arrogance and an unwillingness to reconsider that eventually led to *Booker* and its progeny.

Section V sets out what needs to be done to create a system of federal sentencing that does less harm and more good. The Supreme Court's decision in *Blakely v. Washington*, 542 U.S. 296 (2004), points the way forward.

I. The Rise and Fall of the Federal Sentencing Guidelines

The federal commission and guidelines can be traced directly to Judge Frankel's 1972 proposal in the *University of Cincinnati Law Review* for the creation of specialized administrative agencies charged with developing rational sentencing policies. Frankel elaborated the proposal in *Criminal Sentences: Law without Order* (1973).[2] He wrote that American sentencing was "lawless" because, uniquely in American law, no standards governed judges' sentencing decisions or provided criteria for appellate courts to apply in reviewing them. Presumptive sentencing rules developed by an independent, expert, politically semi-insulated administrative agency could, he wrote, provide those standards.

[2] According to Google Scholar, Frankel's book is by far the most frequently cited book or article on sentencing. As of July 23, 2015, it had been cited 1,312 times, far ahead of the 835 and 689 of the next most cited works.

Frankel's ideas were explored in a series of workshops run by Professor Daniel J. Freed at Yale Law School. Participants drafted model enabling legislation (O'Donnell, Curtis, and Churgin 1977).[3] Senate Bill 2699 was based on the Yale model.

A. The Sentencing Reform Act of 1984

Senator Kennedy reintroduced versions of the sentencing commission legislation in every subsequent Congress until it passed, both while he was chair of the Senate Judiciary Committee and later when Republican senator Strom Thurmond replaced him. After a few iterations as a stand-alone, the sentencing proposals were merged into omnibus bills to enact a federal criminal code based on the recommendations of the National Commission on Reform of Federal Criminal Laws (1971). The code bills, designated as Senate Bill 1 in several congresses as a symbol of the importance congressional leaders attached to them, were eventually abandoned in the face of mostly conservative opposition to expansion of federal authority in criminal justice matters, traditionally a state and local sphere.[4] Finally, once again a stand-alone measure, supported by Senators Kennedy and Thurmond, the Sentencing Reform Act of 1984 became law.

In retrospect, too much time had passed. Washington, DC, had become the wrong place for an overhaul of sentencing policy. Part of the problem was that the proposals had become encrusted with provisions added at different times, reflecting diverse ideological and political beliefs, and sometimes pointing in different policy directions. Some reflected the essentially liberal and proceduralist values of the sentencing reform period

---

[3] The late University of Chicago law professor Norval Morris and I, with others including Judge Frankel, Deputy Attorney General Harold Tyler, Bureau of Prisons director Norman Carlson, US Parole Commission research director Peter B. Hoffman, and the US Department of Justice's criminal code specialist Ronald Gainer, in 1977 created a simulated commission that attempted to develop model guidelines (Tonry 2009*c*). Personal (e.g., clashing egos, eccentric personalities), political (e.g., larger ambitions), and policy (e.g., control of prosecutorial discretion) problems that bedeviled the federal commission arose in the simulation.

[4] This is a tad ironic. Republican senators and congressmen in the 1980s and 1990s were the principal proponents of a wide range of laws that federalized criminal law. This was notably true of drug crimes, carjacking, child pornography, firearms offenses, domestic violence, sex offender registration and notification laws, and truth-in-sentencing laws.

in which Frankel's ideas took shape. They expressed the influence and attitudes of Judge Frankel, Senator Kennedy, and those around them:

> *Diversion of Non-violent First Offenders.* Section 994(j) reflected the premises of the "National Moratorium on Prison Construction" and "alternatives to imprisonment" movements of the 1970s and early 1980s that imprisonment is harmful, should be used only as a last resort, and should seldom be used for first offenders (Platt and Takagi 1977, p. 11; Austin and Krisberg 1982). The commission was directed "to *insure* that the guidelines reflect the *general appropriateness* of imposing a sentence other than imprisonment in cases in which the defendant is a first offender who has not been convicted of a crime of violence *or an otherwise serious offense*" (emphasis added for reasons explained below).
>
> *Tailoring Guidelines to Prison Capacity.* Section 994(g) drew on the Minnesota Sentencing Commission's successful use of a "capacity constraint" policy to prevent prison overcrowding. That commission assumed for humanitarian and operational reasons that the number of inmates in a prison should never exceed 95 percent of its design capacity. If the projected numbers were larger, the legislature could authorize and fund construction of additional capacity, or the commission could revise the guidelines to reduce the numbers (Parent 1988). Accordingly, section 994(g) provided that the "sentencing guidelines prescribed under this chapter shall be formulated to minimize the likelihood that the Federal prison population will exceed the capacity of the Federal prisons."
>
> *Coercive Rehabilitation Programs.* Section 994(k) reflected contemporaneous skepticism about the ethical justifications and effectiveness of rehabilitative programs associated with the "nothing works" movement that took shape in the mid-1970s (Martinson 1974; N. Morris 1974; Cullen 2013). It specified that the guidelines should "reflect the inappropriateness of imposing a sentence to a term of imprisonment for the purpose of rehabilitating the defendant or providing the defendant with needed . . . correctional treatment."

However, other provisions reflected the essentially conservative and punitive values of the tough on crime period, and expressed the influence and attitudes of Senator Thurmond, Attorney General Ed Meese, and those around them:

> *Anticipating Three Strikes.* Section 994(h), anticipating the three-strikes laws enacted in many states and by the Congress in 1993–96, charged the commission to "assure that the guidelines specify a sentence to a term of imprisonment at or near the maximum term authorized for categories of defendants" convicted of a violent or drug offense and having two prior violent or drug felony convictions.
>
> *Chronic Offenders.* Section 994(i) directed the commission to "assure that the guidelines specify a sentence to a substantial term of imprisonment for categories of defendants" who had two or more prior felony convictions, or derived substantial income from crime, or committed the offense in furtherance of certain conspiracies, or committed a violent felony while on release pending trial, sentence, or appeal, or committed certain drug felonies.
>
> *Serious Violent Injury.* Section 994(j) directed the commission "to *insure* that the guidelines reflect . . . the *general appropriateness* of imposing a term of imprisonment on a person convicted of a crime of violence that results in *serious* bodily injury" (emphasis added).

Senators Kennedy and Thurmond reconciled their differences in co-sponsoring the legislation. The commission could likewise easily have reconciled the "liberal" and "conservative" directives. Guidelines could have been drafted that prescribed community punishments for most nonviolent first offenders, specified significant prison terms for people convicted of unusually violent crimes or who had serious and extensive criminal records, and set presumptive sentence lengths so that projected numbers of prisoners could have been accommodated in available and planned prison capacity. Minnesota had shown that these things are doable, including making explicit policy trade-offs by reducing sentences for some offenses in order to increase them for others. This was done both in designing the initial Minnesota guidelines and in revising them over time (Knapp 1984). Washington, Oregon, and North Carolina later also demonstrated the effectiveness and rationality of guidelines that included prison capacity constraints (Tonry 2013; Frase 2013).

The optimal federal strategy would have been to increase punishments for people convicted of violent crimes and decrease them for the much larger number of people convicted of nonviolent and drug crimes. Then and now known as "bifurcation," that is how most countries' governments responded to the trebling of crime rates throughout the Western world in the 1970s and 1980s (Bottoms 1977; Tonry 2007). New prosecutorial diversion and community sanction programs proliferated in other Western countries, and prison space was increasingly reserved for violent offenders (Albrecht 2001; Tonry 2001*b*). In the United States, North Carolina's sentencing commission in the early 1990s, also in the heat of the tough on crime period, received enormous attention, including a public sector innovation award from Harvard's Kennedy School of Government, for doing exactly that. New guidelines made prison sentences for serious crimes harsher than those previously served, but also vastly increased the proportion of people convicted of lesser crimes who received community punishments (Wright 2002).

The founding members of the US Sentencing Commission, however, vigorously carried out only the "conservative" statutory directives. Politics and political ideology were the explanation. Republicans were hammering away at law and order and welfare fraud as wedge issues meant to separate working-class voters from their traditional Democratic leanings (Edsall and Edsall 1991). The Reagan administration was in power. The commission's seven members were appointed by President Ronald Reagan, three of them judges proposed by Supreme Court chief justice Warren Burger. Six of the seven members were openly identified as conservatives, and the seventh, Stephen Breyer, then a federal circuit court judge, was well known as a pragmatist who as a legislative assistant to Senator Kennedy had shown he could work with conservative Republicans. One indication is that he was nominated for appointment to the Federal First Circuit Court of Appeals in the fall of 1980, after Republicans had made it clear that they would block President Jimmy Carter's judicial nominees pending the presidential election. Breyer was nonetheless confirmed before the election, a man conservatives believed they could trust.

The federal commission ignored the "liberal" directives in the 1984 act, followed the conservative directives, and developed guidelines that together with California's three-strikes law and the federal 100-to-1 crack cocaine law became the emblems of the excesses of the tough on crime period (Travis, Western, and Redburn 2014, chap. 3). Below, I describe the major junctions at which the commission repeatedly made right turns when the statute would have permitted, and sometimes prescribed, policy moves in other directions. One I describe here as illustrative and discuss in more detail below involves the commission's interpretation of section 994(j)'s directive calling for diversion from imprisonment of nonviolent first offenders.

In quoting from the statute, I twice italicized the word "insure." That is because the Congress directed the commission "to insure" only two things: that the guidelines reflect the general appropriateness, first, "of imposing a sentence other than imprisonment in cases in which the defendant is a first offender who has not been convicted of a crime of violence or an otherwise serious offense," and, second, "of imposing a term of imprisonment on a person convicted of a crime of violence that results in serious bodily injury." No informed person would disagree that the commission did the second. As to the first, the commission ignored the symmetrical phrasing "violence or an otherwise serious offense" and defined "otherwise serious" to include almost all federal offenses. Before the guidelines took effect, the commission's own data showed, nearly half of sentenced offenders were sentenced to fines or probation, without prison time; afterward the commission projected that many fewer would receive straight probation. The probation percentages were projected to decline from 60 to 33 percent for property offenders, from 64 to 43 percent for burglars, from 21 to 5 percent for drug offenders, and from 31 to 15 percent for violent offenders (US Sentencing Commission 1987*c*, p. 68).

The results of that single low-visibility choice to nullify a clear congressional directive contributed significantly to the ensuing rapid increase in federal imprisonment rates, and to the guidelines' intense unpopularity among federal practitioners. The presumption against imprisonment of most nonviolent first offenders disappeared. Judges were directed to send to prison many people whose later lives would be fundamentally damaged. Below, I discuss a considerable number of comparable low-visibility choices that made federal sentencing more inflexible, mechanical, and severe. First, though, I discuss the guidelines' reception in their early years.

B. Early Reactions to Federal Sentencing Guidelines

The federal guidelines were not foreordained to have much influence. Many changes in sentencing laws and policies have relatively little effect. Evaluations of "voluntary" (now called "advisory") sentencing guidelines in the 1970s and early 1980s, for example, concluded that they had little or no effect on sentencing patterns (Blumstein et al. 1983). Evaluations of mandatory minimum sentence laws over a half century concluded that, depending on the prevailing policy climate, they are always or often circumvented (Tonry 2009*a*; Travis, Western, and Redburn 2014, chap. 3). Evaluations showed that intermediate sanctions programs established in the 1980s to serve as alternatives to imprisonment were typically used instead as alternatives to probation (Morris and Tonry 1990).

The federal guidelines potentially faced two major challenges. The first was that practitioners would nullify them. They could simply ignore the guidelines, as happened with the early voluntary sentencing guidelines (Rich et al. 1982; Carrow et al. 1985). Or practitioners could change how cases were processed in order to circumvent the guidelines and continue doing business as usual, as happened with many mandatory minimum sentence laws (Joint Committee on New York Drug Law Evaluation 1978; Heumann and Loftin 1979).

The commission attempted to compel judicial compliance in a variety of ways. One, not based on the enabling legislation, which describes a system of presumptive guidelines akin to Minnesota's or Washington's, was to describe the federal guidelines as "mandatory" (e.g., US Sentencing Commission 1991*b*). The aim was presumably to give the guidelines greater psychological or moral force. Judges might be expected to be more uncomfortable disregarding a "mandatory" than a "presumptive" guideline.

A second effort to elicit compliance was to draft guidelines and policy statements in exceedingly close detail. Drug offenses, for example, were defined in terms of quantities and property offenses in terms of amounts in much greater detail than in federal statutes. Separate guideline ranges were provided for robbery on the basis of the amount; whether a weapon was present, brandished, or used; what type of weapon; whether injury resulted, and if so of what type and degree. Most state guidelines systems by contrast recognize two or three main categories of major offenses; judges take account of other factors in deciding whether to depart.

Still another effort to compel compliance was to forbid or disapprove many offender characteristics that most judges believe to be appropriate and ethically relevant as bases for departures from otherwise applicable guidelines ranges.[5] Section 3553(b) authorized departures concerning factors "not adequately taken into consideration" by the commission. In order to minimize departures that would survive appellate scrutiny, the commission sought to show that it had adequately considered all factors that judges commonly consider important. It forbade many things most people would consider obviously appropriate considerations in many cases. Declared "not ordinarily relevant" were age, physical condition, drug or alcohol dependence or abuse, education, vocational skills, employment record, and family ties and responsibilities.

The second major challenge to successful implementation of the guidelines, especially acute because many commission decisions alienated judges, was that the courts would declare them unconstitutional. Most who considered the matter did so: "More than 200 district judges invalidated the guidelines and all or part of the Sentencing Reform Act" (US Sentencing Commission 1990*a*, p. 11).[6] Those decisions were explained in constitutional terms, but the number of cases and their vehemence suggested that the underlying problem was antipathy to the guidelines.

The US Supreme Court, in a decision many of its members likely later regretted,[7] upheld the constitutionality of the commission, the guidelines, and the Sentencing Reform Act. *Mistretta v. United States*, 488 U.S. 361 (1989), rejected constitutional arguments that district and appellate court judges had accepted. One was that Congress delegated

[5] The commission has recently preferred that the term "departure" be reserved for decisions expressly permitted under guidelines policy statements and that other sentences not consistent with guidelines be referred to as "variances" (Saris 2011, p. 58). "Departure" is a term of art long used to refer to sentences not within applicable guidelines ranges, including by state sentencing commissions. I use the term "departure" in that broader, conventional way.

[6] That was more than a third of the 541 sitting district court judges in 1990 (US Courts 2014, table 1.1).

[7] *U.S. v. Booker*, 543 U.S. 220 (2005), the culmination of a series of Supreme Court decisions that progressively undermined the guidelines and restored discretion to district court judges, made the guidelines advisory. Several *Mistretta* justices were still on the court.

excessively broad rule-making authority to the commission. A second was that separation-of-powers doctrines were violated when the commission, a rule-making administrative agency of a type usually located in the executive branch of government, was placed in the judicial branch. A third often-made argument on which the court did not rule was that the guidelines violated defendants' constitutional due process rights to individualized consideration of offense and offender characteristics.

The federal dice were cast, but the controversies did not go away. The Federal Courts Study Committee, appointed by Chief Justice William Rehnquist to assess the guidelines' early operation, observed, "It became obvious from our earliest requests for comment and information from federal judges and others who work daily in the system . . . that there is a pervasive concern that the Commission's guidelines are producing fundamental and deleterious changes in the way federal courts process criminal cases" (Federal Courts Study Committee 1990, p. 135).

The Study Committee received testimony from 270 people, including judges, probation officers, prosecutors, defense lawyers, representatives of organized groups such as the American Bar Association, and members of the US Sentencing Commission. Only three commission members and Attorney General Richard Thornburgh spoke in favor of the guidelines. No other witness opposed the following proposal:

> Congress should amend the Sentencing Reform Act to state clearly that the guidelines promulgated by the Sentencing Commission are general standards regarding the appropriate sentence in the typical case, not compulsory rules. Although the guidelines should identify the presumptive sentence, the trial judge should have general authority to select a sentence outside the range prescribed by the guidelines, subject to appellate review for abuse of discretion. The exercise of this discretion may be based upon factors such as an appropriate plea bargain or the defendant's personal history. (Federal Courts Study Committee 1990, p. 142)

The Study Committee proposed not the abandonment of guidelines but replacement of the "mandatory" federal guidelines with presumptive guidelines like those in Minnesota, Washington, and Oregon. All had proven effective by 1990 at reducing disparities while permitting judges flexibility to take account of the distinctive circumstances of individual offenses and offenders (Tonry 1996).

The committee noted a series of practical problems. Sentencing proceedings had become much more time-consuming. The guidelines were inflexible and arbitrary. They disrupted plea bargaining, threatened to increase demands for trials, and distorted the role of the probation officer. Most disturbingly to judges, "the rigidity of the guidelines is causing a massive, though unintended, transfer of discretion and authority from the court to the prosecutor. . . . The result, it appears, is that some prosecutors (and some defense counsel) have evaded and manipulated the guidelines" (Federal Courts Study Committee 1990, p. 138).

A short time later, Judge William W. Schwartzer, director of the Federal Judicial Center (FJC), the research and training agency of the federal courts, wrote: "We are paying a high price for the present sentencing system, and not only in dollars. It is a high price in terms of the integrity of the criminal justice process, in terms of human life and the moral capital of the system. The elimination of unwarranted disparities is a worthy objective but it has not been achieved. Instead a system conducive to producing arbitrary results has been created" (Schwartzer 1991, p. 341).

Schwartzer took a risk saying that. Earlier, under pressure from sentencing commission chairman William Wilkins, the FJC embargoed a research report by staffer Paul Hofer (1990) that documented manipulation and evasion of the guidelines by prosecutors and judges.[8] The research, based on interviews and analyses of case files in six districts, had been approved for publication by the FJC's board. It was the first time in the FJC's history that an approved report was later withdrawn.[9]

[8] The project, "Sentencing Procedures under the 1984 Sentencing Reform Act," was one of two on sentencing announced in the center's 1989 annual report: "This study [Hofer 1990], based on field research in six districts, will analyze the operation of different procedures adopted by courts to accommodate the demands of guideline sentencing. It will address procedures that seem to work well and, of the procedures that have been tried, those that seem not to" (Federal Judicial Center 1989, p. 21). The other project is described in the 1990 annual report as completed. The field study is never again mentioned in an annual report.

[9] Two commission-sponsored studies of the guidelines' early implementation reported the same results (Schulhofer and Nagel 1989; Nagel and Schulhofer 1992). So did the commission's congressionally mandated self-evaluation (US Sentencing Commission 1991*a*). Hofer (1990), despite Judge Wilkins's displeasure, was made available to the Federal Courts Study Committee and was relied upon: "Both the FJC Study and the Schulhofer and Nagel Study found that the Guidelines are being manipulated and evaded on a widespread basis" (Beale 1989, pp. 14–15).

Judge Gerald W. Heaney, a senior judge of the Eighth Circuit Court of Appeals, in one of the first empirical evaluations of the guidelines' operation, examined experiences in four district courts. Here are his main conclusions: "The roles of the prosecutor and the probation officer in the sentencing process have been enhanced and that of the district judge diminished. While district judges are required to devote more time to sentencing, their discretion has been severely limited. . . . There is little evidence to suggest that the congressional objective of reducing unwarranted sentencing disparity has been achieved. . . . Voluminous anecdotal evidence and case law show the unfairness of the guidelines and the disparities created through their application" (Heaney 1991, pp. 163–64, 167).

The federal guidelines' reputation was set. At the founding meeting of the National Association of Sentencing Commissions in Boulder, Colorado, in 1993, directors of state commissions emphasized that the federal example created huge problems: "No state commission representative, in more than three hours of conversation, mentioned the federal sentencing guidelines except to emphasize that their state had taken pains to avoid association with the federal model" (Orland and Reitz 1993, p. 838). Kay A. Knapp, the first executive director of the federal commission, ruefully later observed: "No matter how misguided otherwise, no state commission has been so foolish as to adopt the highly complex and mechanistic federal sentencing policy that has so incurred the wrath of the legal community" (Knapp 1993, pp. 678–80). Knapp and the federal commission's first general counsel, Denis J. Hauptly, had earlier described the federal guidelines' failures in detail and advised states how to avoid them (Knapp and Hauptly 1992).

The federal guidelines' reputation presented serious challenges to subsequent efforts to develop presumptive guidelines in American states. Why this was so is illustrated by figure 2.1, which shows articles about state or federal guidelines published in American law reviews from 1970 to 2012. Even though federal courts sentence only a tiny percentage of convicted criminal offenders, federal developments receive so much more attention than what happens in states that the federal experience becomes the standard reference point. Two articles on state guidelines were published before 1989, the period during which the most successful systems were established, and usually only two or three—if any—in most subsequent years. There were more than 40 articles per year on federal guidelines between 1989 and 2005, when *Booker v. U.S.*, 543 U.S.

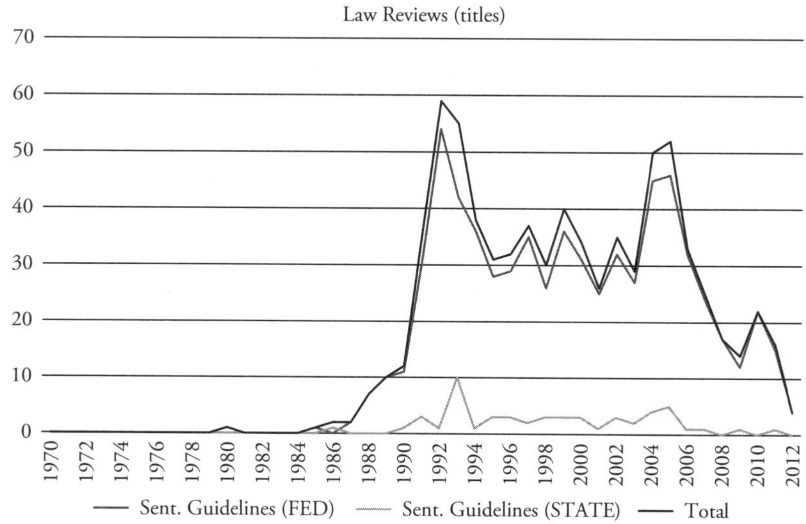

FIGURE 3.1. Sentencing guidelines articles, US law reviews, 1970–2012

220 (2005), was decided. A state policy maker might easily assume that the federal experience and excesses were the norm. Figures 2.1–2.4 in chapter 2 showed similar imbalances in coverage of state and federal sentencing policy developments in 1970–2012 in the *New York Times* and the *Washington Post.*

The federal example bedeviled the work of the committee drafting the American Bar Association's 1994 Standards for Sentencing Procedures and Alternatives. The principal draftsmen, father and son Curtis and Kevin Reitz, observed: "The widespread unpopularity of the federal guidelines" was "a major stumbling block." The ABA standards refer to "sentencing structures" to make its proposals: the word "guidelines," they wrote, "was excised from the standards to avoid any appearance of approval of federal law." They elaborated: "At every stage of the drafting process, detailed presentations were made to explain the ways in which the proposed standards were substantially different than the federal system, and were borrowed instead from more promising state innovations" (Reitz and Reitz 1993, pp. 170–71).

Except as a model to be repudiated, the federal guidelines have had no significant influence on subsequent development of American sentencing policy. This can be seen in the reports issued to date from the American Law Institute's ongoing effort to develop a Model Penal Code—Sentencing to serve as a resource for state and federal policy makers The federal commission and guidelines are mentioned only a handful of times, usually only as a bibliographical reference (American Law Institute 2007, 2011). This is the only textual mention: "The revised Code discourages commissions from following the early practice of the United States Sentencing Commission, which has been much criticized for its failure in its early years to borrow from the experiences of preexisting state commissions and, indeed, for its failure adequately to investigate those experiences" (American Law Institute 2007, p. 58).

C. The Commission since Mistretta

From their inception until 2005, when the US Supreme Court decided *U.S. v. Booker*, 543 U.S. 220, the federal guidelines were widely disliked and resented by judges and other practitioners. The commission paid little attention, but eventually the US Supreme Court did. In *Koons v. United States*, 518 U.S. 81 (1996), the court broadened judges' discretion to depart. In *Booker*, the court decided that the guidelines suffered from fundamental constitutional problems and that the only way to preserve them was to make them advisory. In *Gall v. United States*, 522 U.S. 38 (2007), the court directed appellate courts to use a deferential "abuse of discretion" standard when assessing the adequacy of reasons given by sentencing judges for departing from the guidelines. A series of cases, including *Kimbrough v. United States*, 552 U.S. 85 (2007), and *Spears v. United States*, 555 U.S. 261 (2009), authorized judges to depart from guidelines when they disagreed with commission policy decisions. This ended the obligatory effects of the commission's effort to declare particular considerations "not relevant" or "not ordinarily relevant." The commission nonetheless continues to insist that trial judges' decisions should be governed by those provisions (Saris 2011, 2013; US Sentencing Commission 2012*b*).

U.S. v. Booker also nullified much of the 2003 Feeney Amendment, which attempted to make the guidelines even more rigid. In Justice Breyer's words, the amendment was thereafter "not relevant." The Feeney Amendment sought to limit sentencing judges' discretion to depart downward from the guidelines, provided tighter standards for appellate sentence review, and directed the commission to amend the guidelines in particular ways and "ensure that the incidence of downward departures are [*sic*] substantially reduced." Part of the Prosecutorial Remedies and Tools against the Exploitation of Children Today ("PROTECT") Act of 2003,[10] it was motivated by Republican representative Tom Feeney's real or feigned belief that federal judges too often departed downward to impose "lenient" sentences. Its provisions on judicial discretion were in effect only a bit more than a year but caused a furor (e.g., Bibas 2004; Mason 2004). The Feeney Amendment is primarily only of historical interest, but while it lasted it substantially affected federal sentencing, reducing downward departures by 5 percent and increasing average prison sentences by 2 months (Freeborn and Hartmann 2010).

The commission never seriously considered making fundamental changes to the guidelines during the 18 years before *Booker* was decided. It devoted much of its energy to trying to make the guidelines more prescriptive. In the period since the appointment in 1994 of Judge Richard P. Conaboy as the commission's second chair, however, it has sometimes done or tried to do admirable things aiming to make federal sentencing somewhat more just in relation to mandatory minimums and drug crimes. In 1991 and repeatedly subsequently the commission has shown the injustice and distorting effects of mandatory minimum sentence laws and urged their repeal or modification (e.g., US Sentencing Commission 1991*b*, 2011; Saris 2013).[11] In 1995, and repeatedly thereafter, the commission urged the Congress to revise or repeal the 100-to-1 crack cocaine sentencing law (1995*a*, 1997*a*, 2002, 2007). In 2007, the commission amended the guidelines to correct one of its most egregious earlier errors. The guidelines ceased directing judges to impose prison sentences on drug offenders that were longer than were required by applicable mandatory minimum sentence laws.

The commission examined use of nonincarcerative punishments several times, but never made any significant changes to its policy of limiting their use to a tiny percentage of sentenced offenders. Table 3.1 summarizes commission policy statements on permitted, discouraged, and forbidden reasons to depart from the guidelines. The changes are few and modest. An effort led by commissioner Helen Corrothers, whose earlier career involved correctional work, proposed that the commission

---

[10] Public Law No. 108–21, 117 Stat. 650 (2003).

[11] In this and the following paragraphs, citations showing only dates refer to US Sentencing Commission publications.

TABLE 3.1. Departure provisions, federal sentencing guidelines, 1987, 2014

Section	Subject	1987	2014
5H1.1	Age	NOT ordinarily relevant	MAY be relevant*
5H1.2	Education and vocational skills	NOT ordinarily relevant	NOT ordinarily relevant
5H1.3	Mental and emotional conditions	NOT ordinarily relevant	MAY be relevant*
5H1.4	Physical condition or appearance	NOT ordinarily relevant	MAY be relevant*
5H1.4	Drug or alcohol dependence or abuse	NOT a reason for downward departure	ORDINARILY NOT a basis for downward departure
5H1.4	Gambling addiction	[no provision]	NOT a basis for downward departure
5H1.5	Employment record	NOT ordinarily relevant	NOT ordinarily relevant
5H1.6	Family ties and responsibilities	NOT ordinarily relevant	NOT ordinarily relevant
5H1.11	Military service	[no provision]	MAY be relevant*
5H1.11	Civic, charitable, and public service, etc.	[no provision]	NOT ordinarily relevant
5H1.12	Lack of guidance as a youth	[no provision]	NOT relevant in determining whether to depart
5H1.12	Disadvantaged upbringing	[no provision]	NOT relevant in determining whether to depart

Notes: *" . . . [if] present to an unusual degree and distinguish[es] the case from the typical case covered by the guidelines." This wording varies slightly between provisions but is substantively similar in all.

Sources: US Sentencing Commission 1987*a*, 2014*b*, sections 5H1.1–5H1.12. Explanations for changes are set out in appendix C to the 2014 manual (amendments 386, 466, 475, 569, 649, 651, 674, 739).

broaden use of intermediate sanctions (1990*b*). A simplification project launched by commission chairman Richard Conaboy in 1995–96 included a working group on alternatives (1996*e*). A recent examination of intermediate punishments in the federal system noted their important potential roles but recommended no meaningful policy changes (2009). None of these undertakings resulted in significant changes.

Table 3.2 shows the issues given primary emphasis in the commission's annual reports to Congress since 1991. Mandatory minimums

TABLE 3.2. US Sentencing Commission, priority topics, 1990–2014

Year	Business	Drugs	Mandatories	Other	Sex	Simplification
1990				Plea negotiation, alternatives		
1991			Mandatories			
1992		Quantity guidelines				
1993	Computer	100:1		Corruption		
1994						
1995	Elder fraud	100:1			Rape, HIV	Simplification
1996	Computer				Child victims	Simplification
1997	Money laundering	100:1				
1998	Telemarketing					
1999	Fraud	Methamphetamine				
2000		Drugs	Mandatories			
2001	Money laundering	Ecstasy, methamphetamine				
2002		100:1		Native Americans		
2003	Cybercrime, fraud			Departures, campaign finance		

2004				Departures, recidivism, *Blakely*	
2005	Antitrust			*Booker*, recidivism	
2006		Steroids		*Booker*	
2007		Cocaine			
2008	Disaster fraud	100:1		*Gall*, *Kimbrough*	
2009			Mandatories		
2010			Mandatories	Alternatives	
2011	Iran sanctions	100:1	Mandatories		
2012			Mandatories	*Booker*	Child pornography
2013	Economic crimes			*Booker*	Child pornography
2014	Fraud		Mandatories		

Sources: US Sentencing Commission, Annual Reports—various years; US Sentencing Commission 2014*b*.

and sentencing for cocaine offenses recur. Other subjects come and go, usually in response to new legislation or to heightened congressional attention to particular offenses. For a short time in the mid-1990s "simplification" was a prominent issue, though it never happened (1996*d*). In recent years, the commission has been preoccupied with the effects of *Booker* and efforts to reinvigorate the guidelines in its aftermath.

The commission has submitted reports to Congress on many other subjects urging guideline and statutory changes. Proposals never involved changes to the guidelines' basic structures or features. Topics included campaign finance (2003*a*), computer crime (1996*a*, 2003*b*), disaster relief (2008), money laundering (1997*b*), sexual offenses (1995*b*, 1995*c*, 1996*b*, 2012*a*), and corporate crime (1995*d*, 1998, 2003*c*). Not surprisingly the reports correspond to the changing emphases shown in table 3.2.[12]

In some minor ways, the commission over time slightly humanized the guidelines. The original version provided that age, education and vocational skills, mental and emotional conditions, physical condition including drug dependence and alcohol abuse, employment records, family ties and responsibilities, and community ties are "not ordinarily relevant in determining whether a sentence should be outside the applicable guideline range" (1987*a*, Part H, §§5H1.1–5H1.6). To this the commission later added that "lack of guidance as a youth and similar circumstances indicating a disadvantaged upbringing" are "not relevant" and that "civic, charitable, or public service . . . and similar prior good works" are not ordinarily relevant. Those latter changes aimed to undo the effects of federal appellate court decisions that had approved judges' departures from the guidelines for reasons of extraordinary disadvantage or public service.

Many of the offender characteristics the commission ruled out of bounds concern subjects that most judges and other practitioners (and most people) believe are often germane to deciding what a just and appropriate sentence might be. In more recent years the commission has allowed judges somewhat greater authority. Education and vocational skills, employment record, and family ties and responsibilities in 2013 continued to be "not ordinarily relevant." However, age and mental,

[12] Each annual report, of course, also discusses amendments proposed for congressional consideration.

emotional, and physical conditions have been shifted into a "may be relevant" category and drug and alcohol abuse have been shifted from "not" to "not ordinarily" relevant; these changes are less significant than appears from the words used.[13] Moving in the other direction, the commission has declared that gambling addiction is not a valid reason for mitigating a sentence. Anyone familiar with criminal courts, however, knows that alcoholism, drug dependence, and gambling addiction are often primary causes of offending (2014*e*).

In 2015, despite commission proposals for legislation to reinvigorate its authority, the guidelines limped along. Judges are still directed by the commission to follow a "three-step" process of first calculating sentences according to guideline provisions, then consulting the Guidelines Manual concerning commission policies and determine whether they authorize a "departure," and finally considering whether a "variance" is appropriate even though a "departure" is not authorized (Saris 2011, pp. 57–58).[14] In principle, departure decisions are subject to appeal by the aggrieved party under the criteria set out in the Sentencing Reform Act of 1984, as amended, but as a practical matter recent Supreme Court decisions give judges broad discretion. An "abuse of discretion" review standard effectively requires appellate judges to rule that no reasonable judge would have imposed a challenged sentence. That is not often likely to happen. Not surprisingly, rates of downward departures have steadily increased since *Booker* was decided.

Table 3.3 shows patterns of compliance for selected years since 1996. The overwhelming picture is of judges and prosecutors increasingly mitigating the guidelines' severity, with short-lived hiccups in 2004 while the Feeney Amendment was in effect. Striking patterns appear for sentences imposed from within applicable guideline ranges, downward departures, and departures requested by prosecutors. The percentage of within-guideline sentences fell almost continuously from 70 percent

[13] Baron-Evans and Stith (2012, p. 1723) point out that despite the changes of a few characteristics from "not ordinarily relevant" to "may be relevant," commission policy statements specify that they must be "present to an unusual degree and distinguish the case from the typical cases covered by the guidelines." This, they observe, is "essentially the same standard for characteristics deemed 'not ordinarily relevant.'"

[14] Departure and variance are in quotation marks to signify the commission's distinctive use of those terms.

Table 3.3. Within-guidelines sentences and departures, federal courts, selected years, 1996–2013, percentages

Disposition	1996	2000	2004*	2004#	2006!	2008	2010	2012	2013
A. Within range	69.6	64.5	72.2	71.8	61.7	59.4	55.0	52.4	51.2
B. Departure down	10.3	17.0	11.6	13.2	12.0	13.4	17.8	17.8	18.7
C. Government requests, of which	19.2	17.9	15.5	14.4	24.6	25.6	25.4	27.8	27.9
Substantial assistance	19.2	17.9	15.5	14.4	13.4	13.3	11.6	11.7	11.7
Early disposition					7.4	7.9	9.9	11.2	10.6
Other					2.8	2.4	3.9	4.9	5.2

Source: US Sentencing Commission, Annual Reports, various years.

*Pre-*Blakely* (October 1, 2003–June 24, 2004).

#Post-*Blakely* (June 25–September 30, 2004). Data for 2004 are divided to take account of *Blakely v. Washington*, 542 U.S. 296 (2004), a decision concerning the Washington State guidelines that raised doubts about the federal guidelines' constitutionality. Many federal judges construed *Blakely* to apply in principle to federal sentencing and altered their practices accordingly (US Sentencing Commission 2005). Departure rates rose immediately.

!Beginning in 2006, "Government Requests" includes "Early Dispositions" and "Other" Government-sponsored Downward Departures.

to a bit more than half. The latter rate, however, is attributable more to the effects of mandatory minimum sentence laws than to discretionary judicial decisions to comply with the guidelines. The percentage of downward departures nearly doubled in absolute terms, but by more than that for cases in which the judge took the initiative without a prosecutorial request. Prosecutors also increasingly requested mitigated sentences, some for defendants who provided substantial assistance to the government in other cases and some under a 2003 law that authorized reductions, mostly in immigration cases, for defendants who agreed to fast-track dispositions that involve simplified court procedures.

The federal guidelines were controversial and disliked mostly because of critical decisions the commission made. Although a few of the resulting policies have been tinkered with, most remain fully or largely in effect. Only if most of them are eventually changed is there much chance that federal guidelines will someday work as Judge Frankel hoped and expected they would. In sections III and V, I discuss those critical choices and the changes that need to be made. The stage needs to be set first, though, by describing the federal sentencing system before the guidelines took effect and shortly afterward.

II. Federal Sentencing before and under Guidelines

The federal sentencing system in the mid-1980s was, along with the guidelines systems in Minnesota and Washington, among the best run and least unjust of any in the United States. There were two reasons why that was so. First, the US Parole Commission had been successfully operating and continuously refining and revalidating its prison release guidelines for more than a decade (Hoffman 1976, 1983, 1995). They incorporated evidence-based policy decisions about prediction of reoffending and reduction of disparities in prison terms (Gottfredson, Wilkins, and Hoffman 1978). Presumptive sentencing guidelines in Minnesota and Washington were reducing disparities in sentence lengths in those states. The federal system was the one other jurisdiction that was doing that reasonably effectively.

Second, federal judges had discretion for almost all offenses and offenders to fine-tune sentences to individual offenders' circumstances. If imprisonment seemed unwarranted, it need not be imposed. Only 50.3 percent of federal sentences in 1985 were to imprisonment, including split sentences (Bureau of Justice Statistics 1990, table 4.1 and p. 47). Thirty-seven percent were "straight" probation. Eleven percent were stand-alone fines. By 1990, still a turbulent year because *Mistretta* had just been decided, 60.4 percent of sentences were to imprisonment and 37.5 percent were to straight probation (McDonald and Carlson 1992, tables 1, 5).

In 1995, however, post-*Mistretta*, 78.7 percent of sentences were to imprisonment, and only 13.6 percent were to straight probation (US Sentencing Commission 1996*c*, table 18). In 2013, only 7.1 percent of sentenced offenders received straight probation; 5.4 percent received split sentences including some confinement. The remaining 87.3 percent were sentenced solely to prison (US Sentencing Commission 2013, fig. D).

The reduction in use of straight probation was the result of an explicit commission policy choice. It required prison sentences for many cases that previously in the federal system and typically in state systems resulted in community punishments. This is because the federal guidelines apply to all federal convictions, including both felonies and misdemeanors. In Minnesota, by contrast, the sentencing guidelines apply only to felonies, which are much less than half of all convictions. The guidelines create a presumption in favor of a prison sentence only for about 20 percent of felonies. Minnesota judges then had and still have complete discretion over the vast majority of cases they sentence.

There was another important contextual consideration when the US Sentencing Commission set to work. America in the late 1980s, like America today, was socially, economically, and politically diverse. This is manifested within individual states in substantially different sentencing norms in different areas. The classic pattern is that sentences are most severe in rural areas and least in large cities, with suburbs and towns falling in between. Effective guidelines can ameliorate those differences, but only a little. Attitudes and beliefs about crime and punishment vary geographically. Judges and prosecutors almost inevitably are influenced by the prevailing views in the communities in which they live. Many prosecutors passionately believe that as elected officials in a democratic society they should take account of and reflect local beliefs (Boerner 2012; Wright 2012).

What is true of a single state in the nature of things is even truer in a large, federal country characterized by major regional differences in cultural traditions and political beliefs. It would be astonishing if attitudes toward crime and punishment were the same in California, Louisiana, Maine, and Texas, or in "red" and "blue" states generally. Table 3.4 shows familiar data on differences in state imprisonment rates in 1987 and 2011. There were distinctive state and regional patterns in 1987. They were much the same in 2011. The US Sentencing Commission, in its research on past sentencing practices, like every other sentencing commission, learned that there were major differences in sentencing patterns in different district courts and either naively or in willful denial acted as if guidelines can substantially alleviate them.

The continuities over a quarter century shown in table 3.4 are stunning. The average ranking in the Northeast, the lowest, was 38 in 1987 and 41 in 2011. The Midwest was 31 and 30, the West 24 and 27, and the South 16 and 13. Five states, Louisiana, Alabama, Oklahoma, Georgia, and Arizona, ranked in the top ten in both years. Eight states were among the ten lowest ranked in both years (Minnesota, North Dakota, Maine, Massachusetts, New Hampshire, Rhode Island, Vermont, and Utah). Some states changed relative rankings significantly, but most only slightly. Minnesota was 49th both years, and New Hampshire was 47th. Louisiana was ranked second in 1987 and first in 2011.

Federal judicial districts are organized within states. States with small populations constitute a single district. Populous states are divided into several. Judges and US Attorneys mostly are selected from within the states in which courts are located. Many assistant US attorneys, defense lawyers, and probation staff also come from the states where they work. Those who do not are quickly socialized into prevailing local norms and practices. It would be remarkable if their work in federal courts were not powerfully influenced by local standards. Sentencing standards will inevitably be resisted and circumvented if they vary substantially from the beliefs about just punishments of the people who must apply them.

No system of sentencing guidelines can substantially reduce disparities across an entire continent, as table 3.5 illustrates. It shows patterns

TABLE 3.4. Imprisonment rates per 100,000 population and national rank, by region and state, 1987 and 2011

	1987	2011
Northeast		
Northeast total	169	296*
Connecticut[a]	144 (35)	350 (34)
Maine	106 (42)	147 (50)
Massachusetts[f]	106 (43)	206 (45)
New Hampshire	81 (47)	198 (47)
New Jersey[e]	177 (26)	270 (40)
New York	229 (18)	283 (39)
Pennsylvania	136 (37)	402 (23)
Rhode Island[a, d]	100 (45)	196 (48)
Vermont[a]	91 (46)	255 (42)
Average region rank	37.7	40.9
Midwest		
Midwest total	185	389*
Illinois[e]	171 (27)	376 (28)
Indiana	192 (25)	442 (17)
Iowa	101 (44)	295 (37)
Kansas	237 (15)	324 (36)
Michigan	259 (12)	434 (20)
Minnesota	60 (49)	183 (49)
Missouri	222 (21)	512 (10)
Nebraska	123 (40)	244 (43)
North Dakota	57 (50)	206 (46)
Ohio[c]	224 (20)	441 (18)
South Dakota	154 (30)	426 (22)
Wisconsin	124 (39)	359 (33)
Average region rank	31	29.9

TABLE 3.4. (*continued*)

South		
South total	254	552*
Alabama	307 (6)	650 (3)
Arkansas	227 (19)	544 (8)
Delaware[a, b]	327 (5)	440 (19)
Florida	265 (11)	538 (9)
Georgia	274 (10)	547 (7)
Kentucky	147 (32)	478 (12)
Louisiana	346 (2)	865 (1)
Maryland	282 (9)	380 (27)
Mississippi	254 (13)	690 (2)
North Carolina	250 (14)	362 (32)
Oklahoma	296 (8)	631 (5)
South Carolina	344 (3)	473 (13)
Tennessee	156 (29)	443 (16)
Texas	231 (17)	632 (4)
Virginia[e]	217 (22)	469 (14)
West Virginia	77 (48)	366 (31)
Average region rank	15.5	12.7
West		
West total	214	418*
Alaska[a]	339 (4)	400 (24)
Arizona[b]	307 (7)	589 (6)
California	231 (16)	394 (25)
Colorado[c]	145 (34)	427 (21)
Hawaii[a, d]	141 (36)	283 (38)
Idaho	149 (31)	486 (11)
Montana	147 (33)	367 (30)
Nevada	432 (1)	463 (15)
New Mexico	169 (28)	328 (35)

TABLE 3.4. *(continued)*

West		
Oregon	200 (23)	372 (29)
Utah	111 (41)	242 (44)
Washington[c]	134 (38)	259 (41)
Wyoming	195 (24)	383 (26)
Average region rank	24.3	26.5

Notes: 2011 counts are based on prisoners with sentences of more than 1 year, under the jurisdiction of correctional officials. The imprisonment rate is the number of prisoners with a sentence of more than 1 year per 100,000 residents. Resident population estimates are for January 1 of following year. [a]2011 prisons and jails form one integrated system. Data include total jail and prison populations. [b]2011 prison jurisdiction population based on custody counts. [c]2011 includes some prisoners sentenced to 1 year or less. [d]2011 counts include dual jurisdiction cases where the inmate is currently housed in another jurisdiction's facilities. [e]2011 includes some prisoners sentenced to 1 year. [f]The 2010–11 imprisonment rates include prisoners sentenced to more than 1 year but held in local jail or houses of correction in Massachusetts. *Rates shown are for 2010.

Sources: 1987 data, Greenfeld 1988; 2011 data, Carson and Sabol 2012; 2011 regional rates, Guerino, Harrison, and Sabol 2011.

of compliance with the federal guidelines in six federal district courts in 1991, 2000, and 2010. Two of the districts were selected because they had especially low departure rates in 1991, two because they had especially high departure rates, and two because their departure rates reflected national averages. Reflecting the guidelines' increasing flexibility over time, the percentages of sentences imposed from within applicable guideline ranges fell continuously in five of the six districts. The continuities, however, are much more striking. Each district has its own distinctive pattern. Virginia and Oklahoma judges most often sentenced from within guidelines ranges and Arizona and Pennsylvania judges least often. North Carolina and Maryland judges fell in between. The differences are robust over two decades.

Patterns are shown for the three most common dispositions: within-range sentences, downward departures following prosecutorial "substantial assistance" motions, and other discretionary downward departures. The latter two are shown separately and combined.

There were dramatic differences in formal guidelines compliance in 1991 in terms of percentages of cases falling within guidelines ranges—above 95 percent in Oklahoma and Virginia, around 80 percent in

TABLE 3.5. Compliance with federal sentencing guidelines, six districts, 1991, 2000, 2010

Dist.	Within Range			Substantial Assistance			Downward, Discretionary			All Down		
	1991	2000	2010	1991	2000	2010	1991	2000	2010	1991	2000	2010
OK, East	96.8	67.7	63.7	0	03.1	22.1	03.2	29.2	13.3	03.2	32.3	35.4
VA, East	94.5	89.0	73.7	03.1	07.4	04.1	01.3	03.5	20.3	04.4	10.9	24.4
MD	80.6	57.7	46.2	14.3	28.2	22.3	04.2	13.3	27.3	18.5	41.5	49.6
NC, Mid	80.3	81.2	73.2	15.8	13.9	10.2	02.9	03.0	13.0	18.7	16.9	25.2
AZ	55.7	28.6	43.5	10.9	07.2	02.8	32.0	63.5	52.3	42.9	70.7	55.1
PA, East	54.0	52.2	37.3	41.0	36.6	32.0	04.0	10.2	29.8	45.0	46.8	61.8

Source: US Sentencing Commission, 2010 Datafile, OPAFY10.

Maryland and North Carolina, and about 55 percent in Arizona and Pennsylvania. In 2010, the rankings were the same. Oklahoma and Virginia judges were nearly twice as likely as Arizona and Pennsylvania judges to impose sentences within applicable guideline ranges. North Carolina and Maryland judges again fell in between.

There were also major differences between districts in the kinds of departures judges made and how often they made them:

> In Virginia, substantial assistance departures were at all times rare, ranging between 3 and 7 percent of cases. In Pennsylvania they were at all times common, ranging between 32 and 41 percent.
>
> In North Carolina, discretionary downward departures were at all times rare, ranging between 3 and 13 percent of cases. In Arizona, they were at all times common, ranging between 32 and 64 percent.
>
> In Virginia and North Carolina, downward departures of either kind were comparatively rare, never exceeding 25 percent combined, and were usually much less frequent. In Arizona and Pennsylvania, downward departures were the norm, ranging between 43 and 71 percent of cases.

Each of the six districts continues to follow its own distinctive practices and, relative to the others, is recognizably the same place in post-*Mistretta* 1991, post-*Koons* 2000, and post-*Booker* 2010. No system of federal guidelines could have produced similar sentencing patterns in those six districts or in Louisiana, Maine, and California. It was foolhardy for anyone to think that rigid, detailed guidelines, covering all felonies and misdemeanors, would be applied in the same way across a vast continent.

III. The Critical Choices

The commission, for reasons no outsider will presumably ever fully understand, promulgated a system of detailed, mechanistic guidelines. Justice Breyer twice offered unpersuasive behind-the-scenes accounts that emphasize technocratic problems to be solved and an idealistic commitment to reducing sentencing disparities and insisted that ideological and political considerations had little influence (Breyer 1988, 1999). Former commissioner Ilene Nagel offered a similar though less closely argued apologia (I. Nagel 1990). The introduction to the federal Guidelines Manual attributes their main features to a determination to reduce the prevalence of unwarranted disparities. There was, however, never any convincing evidence that the initial guidelines reduced disparities compared with sentencing or imprisonment patterns before the guidelines took effect, despite a congressionally mandated commission self-evaluation that declared victory (US Sentencing Commission 1991*a*).

Most empirically savvy sentencing specialists found the commission evaluation so flawed methodologically and conceptually that no conclusions could be reached (Rhodes 1992; Tonry 1992*a*; Weisburd 1992; Doob 1995). The US General Accounting Office in an independent, congressionally mandated evaluation concluded that it is "impossible to determine how effective the sentencing guidelines have been in reducing overall sentencing disparity" (US General Accounting Office 1992, p. 10).

A commission assessment of the guidelines' first 15 years concluded that, relative to the guidelines' offense severity and criminal history categories, an important qualification, disparities significantly declined under the guidelines in comparison with earlier periods (US Sentencing Commission 2004). However, Paul Hofer, the commission's longtime special projects director and lead author of its 15-year self-evaluation, more recently observed:

> While reduction of disparity was the most important goal of sentencing reform, there is little doubt that total unwarranted disparity was greater under the mandatory guidelines than it was prior to their implementation. Unwarranted disparity must be defined in relation to the purposes of sentencing and assessed in the system as a whole and not merely at one stage or decision. By this measure, disparity from other sources increased even as disparities among judges due to philosophical differences were modestly reduced. Disparities were created by prosecutors' charging and plea-bargaining decisions. (Hofer 2011, p. 680)

In other words, analyses of cases as they appear in court suggested that disparities decreased. Analyses of cases as prosecutors received them would have shown increased disparities. The guidelines increased prosecutors' capacity to influence sentences through charging and dismissal decisions, especially for offenses potentially subject to mandatory minimums. Johnson (2014) concluded that on average, controlling for case characteristics, prosecutorial charge dismissals reduced lengths of federal prison sentences by 17 percent. Shermer and Johnson (2009) earlier found that federal prison terms were about 20 percent shorter for offenders who received charge reductions. Neither the commission report nor Hofer attempted to compare disparities before and under guidelines relative to the broader but more appropriate criteria of offense characteristics, criminal history, and morally relevant offender characteristics. Nor to my knowledge has anyone else. There the matter rests.[15]

---

[15] Commission staff and outside researchers have continued to study sentencing disparities. There are two types of studies. One attempts to model sentencing to determine the respective influence of interjudge (or interdistrict) differences, guideline offense severity levels, and criminal history scores (e.g., Scott 2010). Interjudge and interdistrict differences are always found, but they are usually less significant than offense severity and criminal history variables. This is not surprising, given the guidelines' rigidity and their vigorous enforcement for many years by appellate courts. Selection bias is the Achilles heel of these studies. They use offense level and criminal history scores as they appear in the court record, and cannot take account of presentencing differences between cases in

The federal guidelines cover all federal crimes. These include many federal regulatory and white-collar crimes but also drug crimes, common law crimes coming within federal jurisdiction, and, in recent years, large numbers of immigration offenses. Discretionary parole release was abolished. The sentence announced, less mechanically determined 15 percent time off for good behavior, is the sentence that is served.

Judges in setting sentences are first supposed to consult a schedule that specifies a "base offense level" for the offense of which the defendant was convicted. Then, on the basis of various offense characteristics, the offense level is adjusted upward or downward (almost always upward). Next, the judge is directed to determine the offender's criminal history score. Finally, the judge is to consult a two-dimensional grid to determine the prescribed sentence.

To this point, the federal guidelines differ from state systems in Minnesota, Washington, Oregon, North Carolina, and Kansas only in their ornateness. The federal guidelines divide offenses into 43 categories rather than, at that time, ten (Minnesota), eleven (Oregon), or fourteen (Washington) and are considerably more detailed in differentiating offenses. These might be described as differences in degree rather than in kind, but there are other, much more fundamental, differences.

Many features of the federal guidelines that judges found most objectionable resulted not from the requirements of the Sentencing Reform

charges and dismissals, offense characteristics, and sometimes criminal history which prosecutors and defense counsel may have chosen not to mention at all or in full in an agreed stipulation of facts (Hofer 2011).The other develops models for a sample of recent cases and a sample of cases in the commission's original preguidelines database and assesses comparative "consistency." They typically show reduced disparities under guidelines. They suffer from a larger selection bias problem since it is impossible to control for presentencing differences in case processing in the two periods. There are two other insurmountable problems. First, apples and oranges: preguidelines prison sentences were premised on parole release eligibility and cannot be directly compared with guidelines prison sentences (and estimations of times served before parole release are too crude to be credible). Second, the analyses measure consistency in relation to guidelines' offense severity and criminal history variables. This was long ago shown to be premised on a non sequitur (Doob 1995). It would be astonishing if consistency with variables used in the guidelines were not greater under guidelines amidst vigorous commission and appellate court efforts to enforce them than in a period when they did not exist as formal criteria. Doob pointed out, hypothetically, that preguidelines sentencing could have been perfectly consistent but according to a set of criteria different from those the commission chose. Using guidelines criteria as the measure of consistency would completely miss the prior pattern.

Act of 1984 but from the commission's policy choices. This section discusses nine critical choices that could have been made otherwise:

First, nullifying the statutory directive (section 994[j]) against imprisonment of first offenders "not convicted of a crime of violence or an otherwise serious offense" by defining as "serious" many offenses that typically received probation before the guidelines took effect;

Second, ignoring section 994(g)'s directive that the guidelines "shall be formulated to minimize the likelihood that the Federal prison population will exceed the capacity of the Federal prisons";

Third, treating sentences to probation as "zero months imprisonment" and thereby triggering statutory section 994(b)(2)'s provision that "if a sentence specified by the guidelines includes a term of imprisonment," the top of the guideline range may not exceed the bottom by the greater of 25 percent or 6 months; the effect was to reduce the use of probation as a stand-alone punishment in the federal courts by 80 percent;

Fourth, interpreting a statutory directive to consider the relevance to sentencing of a list of personal characteristics in such a way as to declare that almost all were either "not relevant" or "not ordinarily relevant," thereby depriving sentencing judges of authority to take account of characteristics in individual cases that many believed to be highly germane;

Fifth, giving the prosecutor sole discretion to decide when defendants are eligible for sentence reductions for providing substantial assistance to the government;

Sixth, adopting "relevant conduct" rather than the offense of conviction as the basis for applying guidelines;

Seventh, providing guidelines only for imprisonment and, to a much lesser extent than before the guidelines took effect, probation; there are no guidelines for fines as stand-alone sanctions for individual offenders or for any other nonincarcerative punishments;

Eighth, raising sentencing severity generally, in order to incorporate mandatory penalty provisions into the grid, rather than having the mandatories operate as trumps; and

Ninth, adopting a 43-level sentencing grid that looks and is arbitrary, impersonal, and mechanical and reduces the credibility of the guidelines in the eyes of judges and others.

None of these decisions was required by the Sentencing Reform Act of 1984. They all could have been made otherwise. The first five involve statutory interpretations; the rest involve commission policy decisions about guidelines architecture.

A. Nullifying the Directive to Divert Nonviolent First Offenders from Imprisonment

The commission largely overrode the statutory directive in section 994(j) to "insure" that nonviolent first offenders should ordinarily receive non-incarcerative sentences. Confronted by its own empirical research showing that many first offenders were sentenced to probation before the guidelines took effect, the commission devised its own broad definition of "serious" (US Sentencing Commission 1987*b*).

Here is how the commission described what it did: "The Commission's solution to this problem has been to write guidelines that classify as serious many offenses for which probation previously was given and provide for at least a short period of imprisonment in such cases" (US Sentencing Commission 1987*b*, section 4[c]). The rationale was that the courts had in the past ordered probation for "inappropriately high percentages" of white-collar offenders, including such crimes as "theft, tax evasion, antitrust offenses, insider trading, fraud, and embezzlement."

White-collar crimes such as antitrust offenses, insider trading, and tax evasion represent only a tiny percentage of offenders who received probation before the guidelines took effect.[16] The people who were swept into the commission's "white-collar" net were mostly not investment

[16] Justice Breyer likewise disingenuously referred to "white-collar offenders, including tax, insider-trading, and antitrust offenders who previously would have likely only received probation" as the group affected. The justification for disregarding the congressional "insure" was that the "Commission considered present sentencing practices, where white-collar criminals receive probation more often than other offenders who committed crimes of comparable severity, to be unfair" (Breyer 1988, p. 22). Concerning section 994(j)'s parallel directive to "insure" long sentences for repeat offenders, Breyer indicated the commission felt obliged to obey. "In this area, where the Commission had little legal room to set sentences, prison sentences will increase" (1988, p. 25).

bankers, business executives, and wealthy tax evaders but ordinary people convicted of immigration offenses, minor postal thefts, drug offenses, and property crimes, as well as low-level bank-teller embezzlers. As I noted above, 37 percent of sentenced offenders in 1985 received straight probation, and only 7.1 percent in 2013. Most of the difference involves minor offenders. For nondrug offenses, the commission claimed that it set prison sentence lengths largely on the basis of research on past practice (Breyer 1999). Had it done the same for community penalties, the guidelines would have required imprisonment of many fewer minor offenders and fostered less prosecutorial evasion and judicial agonizing.

B. Ignoring the Prison Population Constraint Directive

Section 994(g)'s statutory directive to formulate guidelines that "minimize the likelihood that the Federal prison population will exceed the capacity of the Federal prisons" is straightforward. Minnesota's experience since 1980 had demonstrated that a population constraint policy could be effective. Complying required only that the commission make adjustments concerning use of prison sentences for particular categories of offenders and sentence lengths for offenders on whom imprisonment should be imposed.

The commission ignored the directive.[17] The clearest example was its nullification of the presumption that many first offenders should not be sentenced to prison. That inevitably increased the prison population.

A second policy decision that affected prison populations concerned sentence lengths. The commission "analyzed data drawn from 10,000 presentence investigations, crimes as distinguished in substantive criminal statutes, the United States Parole Commission's guidelines and resulting statistics, and data from other relevant sources." The commission indicated that while it did not consider itself "bound by existing sentencing practice, it has not tried to develop an entirely new system of sentencing on the basis of theory alone. Guideline sentences in many

[17] Justice Breyer snidely observed, "Minnesotans may agree, for example, that building new prisons is undesirable or impractical; they may be willing to tailor prison sentences to create a total prison population of roughly constant size. There is no such consensus, however, throughout the nation as a whole" (1988, p. 4). That, however, is precisely what section 994(g) directed the commission to do.

instances will approximate existing practice" (US Sentencing Commission 1987*a*, pp. 1–4, 10–11).

Justice Breyer's explanation of the commission's policy choices was more explicit: "It decided to base the guidelines primarily upon typical, or average, actual past practice. The distinctions that the guidelines make in terms of punishment are primarily those which past practice has shown were actually important factors in pre-guideline sentencing. The numbers used and the punishments imposed would come fairly close to replicating the average pre-guidelines sentence handed down to particular categories of criminals" (Breyer 1988, p. 17). The commission, following Minnesota's example, could have shortened prison terms relative to practices before the guidelines took effect in order to offset the decision largely to eliminate use of probation as a stand-alone punishment.[18] It declined to do so.

A third policy decision concerning mandatory minimum sentences, discussed in subsection H below, also defied the prison population constraint directive. The Anti-Drug Abuse Act of 1986, creating a series of mandatory minimum sentences for drug crimes, was enacted after the commission was appointed and before it submitted draft guidelines to Congress. It pegged minimum sentences to quantities, often 500 (5 years) and 5,000 grams (10). Thus any offense involving 500–4,999 grams triggered a minimum 5-year sentence. Rather than build that into the guidelines, the commission chose to establish longer sentences for intermediate quantities. Congress did not mandate those increased sentence lengths. They substantially exacerbated federal prison

[18] In combination with the near elimination of probation, this inevitably caused a substantial increase in prison numbers for mathematical reasons. For many minor offenses, only small percentages of convicted offenders received prison sentences before the guidelines took effect. By definition, those sent to prison on average committed relatively more serious versions of those offenses. The mean average prison sentence length thus represented exceptional cases, but under the guidelines was prescribed for all cases. Here is an example. In 1985, the year used as the basis of projections, only 24 percent of low-level ($1,500) embezzlers received prison time. The original guidelines specified a prison sentence of 2–8 months. The commission assumed an average of 5 months under the guidelines. Because so few minor embezzlers previously received prison sentences, the commission observed, "The average time served by all first-time embezzlers convicted at trial of stealing $1500 is actually about 1 month (rather than 2–8 months)" (US Sentencing Commission 1987*c*, p. 24). The commission could have calculated past sentence lengths for all cases by counting as "zero months" those that previously received probation. The effect would have been to reduce sentence lengths under the guidelines and respect the prison capacity constraint.

population growth. In reporting to Congress on projected prison population growth under the guidelines, the commission claimed its policies would cause only modest growth but that the mandatories would cause substantial growth. The commission disingenuously attributed growth resulting from its gratuitous higher sentences for intermediate drug quantities not to its own policy choices but to the mandatory minimum sentence laws (US Sentencing Commission 1987*b*, 1987*c*).[19]

C. Probation as a Form of Imprisonment

A critical low-visibility choice with major consequences concerned the almost metaphysical question of whether probation is a generically distinct punishment or a term of "zero months imprisonment." The commission took the second position and thereby nearly eliminated probation as a stand-alone sentence. In so doing, the commission also greatly reduced scope for the use of other community punishments, because they were authorized only as conditions of straight probation or of the probation component of a split sentence. This obscure conceptual point was made important by statute section 994(b)(2), which provided: "If a sentence specified by the guidelines includes a term of imprisonment, the maximum of the range established for such a term shall not exceed the minimum of that range by more than the greater of 25 percent or 6 months."

If probation had been treated as a stand-alone punishment, section 994(b)(2) would have been irrelevant. A guideline could have specified sentences for specific offense/criminal history combinations that included probation or, in the alternative, a range of prison sentences that satisfied the 25 percent/6 months requirement (for example, probation or a sentence of 12 months to 18 months). Several states do something

[19] Justice Breyer, likewise ignoring prison population increases attributable to the commission's handling of mandatory minimums, made the same claim: "Accordingly, the Commission propounded guidelines that, by themselves, do not deviate enormously from average prior practice. . . . [The commission] predicts that the effect of the guidelines on prison population is somewhere between −2 percent and 10 percent in comparison to what would have occurred had they not been put into effect" (1988, p. 24). Paul Hofer (2012) has observed that the current commission in its 2011 report on mandatory minimum sentences continues to attribute the effects of its incremental drug quantity steps to the mandatory sentence laws without acknowledging the effects of its own discretionary decisions.

similar. Minnesota's guidelines contain many provisions in which the presumptive sentence is not to a prison term, but in which a range of sentence lengths is prescribed for cases in which judges decide to impose a state prison sentence. When, however, the federal commission defined probation as zero months' imprisonment, section 994(b)(2) applied and a maximum range of "0 to 6 months" was the result.

Before the federal guidelines took effect, probation sentences were ordered for 64 percent of burglars, 60 percent of property offenders, 59 percent of fraud offenders, and 57 percent of income tax offenders in the sample of cases used to project the guidelines' effects. The corresponding figures under the guidelines were projected, respectively, to be 43 percent, 33 percent, 24 percent, and 3 percent (US Sentencing Commission 1987*c*, pp. 60–61 and table 2).

Little can be said in favor of the commission's decision. It required a tortured interpretation of words whose common-language meaning is clear. Probation is and has always been a distinct form of punishment, an alternative to imprisonment and not ordinarily a supplement. Split sentences that combine the different punishments have always been a hybrid.

The commission's interpretation is conceptually muddled. The guidelines authorize fines as stand-alone punishments for individuals on the same basis as straight probation. In effect, the commission also characterized fines as zero months' incarceration and limited their use to cases otherwise potentially subject to not more than 6 months imprisonment.

Prison in most jurisdictions serves as a backup for both fines and probation, to be used sometimes when offenders fail to meet their obligations. When obligations are met, offenders are entitled to absolute discharges. The commission's decision to define probation as a form of imprisonment was a major part of its near nullification of the first-offender nonimprisonment presumption.

D. Departures

Booker and its progeny provided much broader latitude within which sentencing judges may operate than the commission was initially prepared to allow. The original guidelines and, with some minor modifications, the guidelines in effect in 2015, aggressively sought to limit departures. The statute allowed but did not require the commission to do this. Section 994(d) directed the commission in classifying offenders to consider the relevance of a number of factors: (1) age; (2) education; (3) vocational skills; (4) mental and emotional condition to the extent that such condition mitigates the defendant's culpability or to the extent that such condition is otherwise plainly relevant; (5) physical condition, including drug dependence; (6) previous employment record; (7) family ties and responsibilities; (8) community ties; (9) role in the offense; (10) criminal history; and (11) degree of dependence upon criminal activity for a livelihood.

The commission decided that numbers 9–11 were relevant, principally as bases for increasing sentence severity. Numbers 1–8 were determined to be "not ordinarily relevant in determining whether a sentence should be outside the applicable guideline range" (US Sentencing Commission 1987*a*, Part H, §§5H1.1–5H1.6).

Section 3553(b), as initially enacted, describing the sentencing judge's considerations at sentencing, is deferential to the commission's discretionary choices. It directed the court to "impose a sentence of the kind, and within the range" indicated by the applicable guideline and policy statements, unless it found "that there exists an aggravating or mitigating circumstance of a kind, or to a degree, not adequately taken into consideration by the Sentencing Commission in formulating the guidelines that should result in a sentence different from that described." Those provisions mesh and meant that sentencing judges had very little authority to depart from the guidelines. Before *Booker* was decided, it was not easy to convince appellate courts that the sentencing commission had not "adequately" considered particular offender circumstances.

The commission claimed that its policies concerning offenders' personal characteristics were rooted in concern to prevent preferment of privileged white-collar offenders. In practice those policies mostly damaged poor and minority offenders. Kate Stith and Steve Yoh long ago observed that "denying judges the opportunity to mitigate sentences on the basis of social disadvantage has worked *against* poor and minority defendants" (1993, p. 287; emphasis in original). Except for white-collar and regulatory offense defendants, most criminal defendants in federal courts, as in state courts, come from socially and economically disadvantaged backgrounds. Such considerations as education, employment record, family ties, and overcoming severe childhood diversity do not ordinarily distinguish privileged defendants from others but differentiate among unprivileged defendants.

That this is so can be seen in two instances in which the commission closed 'loopholes," as the commission saw them, that appellate courts opened. In *U.S. v. Big Crow*, 898 F. 2d 1326 (1990), the Eighth Circuit Court of Appeals approved a downward departure for a Native American defendant who overcame severe childhood adversity and achieved an exemplary work record. In response, the commission forbade mitigated sentences for "contributions related to employment and similar prior good works." When the Ninth Circuit in *U.S. v. Lopez*, 945 F. 2d 1096 (1991), approved a sentence reduction because of a defendant's troubled childhood and lack of guidance as a youth, the commission responded by forbidding reductions for "lack of guidance as a youth and similar circumstances indicating a disadvantaged upbringing."

E. Substantial Assistance Motions

Much the most common basis for open reduction of sentences below guideline ranges has been that the defendant provided "substantial assistance to the government." The prosecution must request the reduction before the judge may grant it. If the motion is made, the judge may impose sentences less severe than is otherwise specified in guidelines.

The commission, not the Congress, conditioned sentence reductions for assistance to the government on prosecutorial motions. Statute section 994(n) directed the commission to "assure that the guidelines reflect the general appropriateness [of sentence reductions] to take into account a defendant's substantial assistance in the investigation or prosecution of another person who has committed an offense." The statute says nothing to suggest that the prosecutor should have sole authority to decide when and whether substantial assistance has been provided. The commission, however, in guidelines section 5K1.1 provided: "Upon motion of the government stating that the defendant has provided substantial assistance . . . the court may depart from the guidelines." The appellate courts upheld the commission's decision. Had they not, trial judges would have been able to exercise much greater control.

This has from the outset been a gaping hole in the guidelines and undermines the claim that the commission was primarily motivated to reduce disparities, for two reasons. It is anything goes once the motion is made. Judges have discretion to impose any sentence they believe warranted. The rule inevitably created vast disparities between serious offenders, especially in drug and organized crime settings, who had information prosecutors wanted or needed and as a result benefited, and small fry who had little or nothing to offer and seldom benefitted. Kindhearted prosecutors have long gotten around this by making the motion on the basis of disingenuous claims of assistance. In its 1991 self-evaluation, the commission excluded departures following substantial assistance motions from its analysis: those disparities in its judgment did not count.

F. Sentencing "Relevant Conduct"

The single feature of the federal sentencing guidelines that American state officials, and judges, officials, and academics outside the United States, find most astonishing is the commission's decision to base guideline application on the defendant's "relevant conduct," including conduct alleged in charges that were not filed, that were dismissed, or that resulted in acquittals. More than once when I have described the relevant conduct policy outside the United States, listeners have assumed they misunderstood and asked me to repeat what I said.

There is no statutory basis for relevant conduct sentencing. The commission invented it. Many state sentencing commissions considered, usually briefly and dismissively, whether to adopt a "relevant conduct" or "real offense" policy. Each rejected the proposal out of hand. To most people, the idea that offenders can be sentenced for crimes with which they were not charged or of which they were acquitted is inherently distasteful and obviously unjust (Tonry 1981; Reitz 1993).

The commission offered three major justifications, all demonstrably mistaken or misconceived. The first, that relevant conduct offense sentencing would prevent a shift of power to the prosecutor by breaking the link between charges and punishments, has been discredited since the earliest days (e.g., Federal Courts Study Committee 1990).

The second is that *Williams v. New York*, 337 U.S. 241 (1949), long ago held that judges have authority to look beyond the conviction offense and have always done so. The problem with this argument is that *Williams* was decided in the heyday of indeterminate sentencing when judges were expected to individualize sentences in every case and announced sentence lengths were only nominal because parole boards set release dates. The pre-*Booker* guidelines were premised on the commission's view that judges' discretion should be vastly more narrowly constrained than under indeterminate sentencing. The rationale of *Williams* has little relevance to modern determinate sentencing. *Williams* in any case held that judges in sentencing *may* take account of nonconviction behavior and uncharged or unproven behavior. The guidelines indicate that they *must*.

The third is a claim that the federal criminal law is incomparably more complex than state criminal laws and that many federal offenses in their labels and elements provide no meaningful basis for measuring culpability. Mail and wire fraud and RICO (racketeer-influenced corrupt organizations) offenses are examples. If a majority of federal offenders were convicted of mail fraud, the commission's point might have been arguable. In practice, however, drug and immigration crimes make up a large proportion of the federal criminal docket. In 1993, for example, drug offenders constituted 18,352 of 41,838 convictions reported to the commission (US Sentencing Commission 1994, table 22). In 2013, drug offenders constituted 31.2 percent of sentenced offenders and immigration offenders another 31.2 percent; another 10.1 percent were firearms offenders (US Sentencing Commission 2013, table 3).

Many of the rest were convicted of common law crimes such as theft, robbery, and embezzlement. Most federal crimes are conceptually uncomplicated: drugs, immigration, firearms, and common property offenses. In 2013, only 13 percent of sentenced offenders were arguably white-collar criminals (fraud, embezzlement, bribery, tax, forgery, and antitrust, and many of those, especially embezzlement, were minor offenses). Thus, except for immigration offenses, most modern federal criminal cases look much like state cases.

The commission's argument also understated the complexity of state criminal codes. Many offenders are convicted of inchoate offenses, including conspiracy. Many state codes were based on the Model Penal Code, which defined felonies broadly and classified them into only three classes, on the indeterminate sentencing rationale that sentencing should be based primarily on the offender's personal characteristics. States wrestled with these problems and solved them without adopting relevant conduct sentencing. Knapp (1984) and Parent (1988), the founding executive and research directors of Minnesota's commission, described how that state did it. There was no more need for relevant conduct sentencing in the federal system than in the states.

G. Prohibiting Community Punishments

The only freestanding sentences authorized by the guidelines are imprisonment and, for cases not otherwise subject to 6-month or longer prison terms, probation and fines. They allow no independent role for community punishments such as house arrest, intensively supervised probation, restitution, or community service. They also allow no significant space within which mediation or restorative justice programs can operate.

Fines, in many Western countries the most commonly imposed sanction, are conspicuously underdeveloped. Although the Congress in section 994(a)(1) charged the commission to promulgate "guidelines for use by the court in determining the sentence to be imposed . . . including (A) a determination whether to impose a sentence to probation, a fine, or a term of imprisonment," fines are not authorized as a sole sentence for individuals except for trifling cases. Instead, guidelines section 5E1.2(a) provides: "The court shall impose a fine in all cases, except [when the defendant lacks ability to pay]." Thus fines are effectively available for individuals only as add-ons to prison or probation sentences or in lieu of probation. For cases involving corporate defendants, it is a different matter. Fines are the almost invariable punishment; prison sentences for responsible executives are exceedingly rare.

The guidelines do not permit use of other nonincarcerative sanctions as independent sentences. Guidelines sections 5F1.1–3 authorize use of community confinement, home detention, and community service, but only "as a condition of probation or supervised release." In 1993, only 14.8 percent of convicted offenders received straight probation (i.e., without confinement conditions), and thus in less than one-sixth of federal convictions was it possible for a judge to sentence a defendant to an intermediate sanction (US Sentencing Commission 1994, p. 67). By

2013, that one-sixth had fallen to one-fourteenth; only 7.1 percent of offenders received straight probation.

There is much experience in the United States and Western Europe with use of intermediate sanctions that the commission could have drawn on. Sentencing commissions in North Carolina, Oregon, Pennsylvania, and Washington explicitly incorporated intermediate sanctions into their guidelines as independent sanctions (Morris and Tonry 1990). A commission task force headed by then-commissioner Helen Corrothers offered concrete proposals for building intermediate punishments into the guidelines (US Sentencing Commission 1990*b*). The commission took no action.

H. Integrating Mandatory Minimum Sentence Laws

Mandatory minimum sentence legislation enacted in the 1980s required prison terms that were longer than most prisoners sentenced before that would have served (US Sentencing Commission 1987*b*), and longer than a sentencing commission aiming to proportion sentences to offense severity would prescribe. The commission dealt with this by prescribing sentences even longer than the laws required.

There were two ways the mandatory minimums could have been handled. The first was to develop a comprehensive set of guidelines for all offenses based on knowledge of past practices and conscious policy decisions to make changes. If mandatory minimum sentence laws required longer sentences than those that resulted from that process, policy statements could instruct that the statute took precedence and trumped the guidelines. An asterisked note for affected offenses would have said: "The provisions of an applicable mandatory minimum sentence law setting a lengthier minimum sentence shall take precedence over the guidelines."

The other approach was to integrate the sentences mandated by statutes into the guidelines and scale other penalties around them. This necessarily would increase the severity of guideline sentences generally.

A metaphor makes the options more vivid. Imagine a sentencing guidelines grid as a lattice. Under the mandatories-as-trumps option, long minimum sentences for specific crimes would poke through the lattice and tower above it. Under the commission's integrative approach, the entire lattice was lifted, as if the mandatory minimums were posts, and the sentences for many other crimes were lifted also.

One consequence can be illustrated by an example from typical state mandatory minimum laws. In Arizona in the early 1990s, a majority of felony defendants were charged with offenses subject to mandatory minimums, but many fewer were sentenced under such statutes. That is because the mandatories typically applied only to completed offenses; attempts and conspiracies were not covered. Defendants who agreed to plead guilty to attempted robbery or conspiracy to commit robbery were not subject to the minimum (Knapp 1991). That option was not available under the federal relevant conduct rule.

The commission decided to raise sentences for many drug crimes, including inchoate offenses, even more than was required by the mandatory penalty provisions. In the federal law as it existed in 1987, minimums for many drug crimes were pegged for offenses involving 500 and 5,000 grams. For powder cocaine, 500 grams triggered a minimum 5-year sentence and 5,000 grams a minimum 10 years. The commission could easily have provided that people convicted of offenses involving 500–4,999 grams receive 5 years and those of 5,000 or more grams receive 10. Instead it established intermediate quantity levels with sentences scaled between 5 and 10 years: 2,000 and 3,500 grams, respectively, were made subject to 78- and 97-month minimum guideline sentences, thereby specifying even harsher sentences than were required by the statute (US Sentencing Commission 1997*a*). The same approach was taken under the 100-to-1 rule for crack cocaine sentences, which meant that a minor sale of 5 grams elicited a 5-year sentence and still tiny sales of 7 or 9 grams meant even longer prison terms.

The commission gratuitously raised sentences for drug offenders in three other ways. First, under the relevant conduct policy, sentences increased substantially for defendants who were not convicted under statutory sections subject to the mandatory minimums but whose offenses involved the triggering quantities. Second, the commission decided that sentences for people convicted of drug-related conspiracies and attempts—offenses, as in my Arizona example, not then subject to mandatory minimums—should be calculated by reference to penalties for completed offenses involving the same amount. This raised sentences for inchoate offenses substantially. Third, the commission chose to base drug quantity calculations on the combined weight of the drug and the medium in which it was conveyed—baking soda for crack or blotter paper for LSD—rather than the weight of the pure drug itself. Paul Hofer (2012) observed:

> This has proven a recipe for arbitrary variation, and an invitation to probation officers to increase penalties based on water weight, baking soda, and other inert ingredients. The Parole Commission guidelines were based on *pure* drug amounts, and laboratory analyses included in presentence reports today routinely provide pure amounts. But the Commission followed the Anti-Drug Abuse Act and based punishment on total weight, which caused such outrageous outcomes that the approach was dropped for guideline calculations involving LSD and marijuana plants (but remains in force for determining the applicability of a statutory minimum). For other drugs, the approach perversely increases punishments for offenders *lower* in the distribution chain, where drugs are cut for retail distribution. (2011, pp. 21–22; emphasis in original)

The commission was aware of how controversial its guidelines were, and why. Carrying out a congressional mandate, the commission in its early years completed an ambitious and sophisticated analysis of the effects of mandatory sentencing laws on federal sentencing. It concluded that mandatory penalties are unwise and unsound because they remove incentives to plead guilty and thereby increase trial rates, case processing times, and workloads; they foster prosecutorial manipulation in charging and plea bargaining; they often result in imposition of sentences that are unduly harsh; and they do not permit judges to take into account special circumstances concerning the defendant that might justify some other sentence. These are, of course, the same charges that critics lay against the federal guidelines. Capturing this point precisely, in what may initially have been a Freudian slip, the commission, on the first page of its mandatory sentencing report, refers to its own "mandatory" guidelines (US Sentencing Commission 1991*b*). From that day until *Booker* was decided, implicitly conceding the point, the commission generally described its guidelines as mandatory.

I. The Sentencing Machine

The 43-level sentencing grid was one of the commission's worst blunders.[20] It confirmed skeptics' worst stereotypes of arbitrary sentencing by numbers. There were two major problems, both foreseeable. First, the guidelines were not facially credible. The effectiveness of a guidelines system depends on the willingness of officials to accept and apply it. If the guidelines' logic and plausibility are not immediately apparent, if they look mechanical and arbitrary, judges and others will be alienated. The best evidence of this is the more than 200 federal district court judges who declared the guidelines unconstitutional.

This was commonly referred to at the time as the problem of the "sentencing machine" (Blumstein et al. 1983, p. 159). Judges and lawyers believe their function in sentencing is to impose fair, deserved, and appropriate punishments. Sentencing by use of a process akin to a bank's calculation of a credit risk score is antithetical to that. Judges and others who are alienated by what appears to be a mechanical and arbitrary set of standards are unlikely to invest much effort in preventing efforts by lawyers to circumvent it. That's what has happened since the guidelines' earliest days (e.g., Nagel and Schulhofer 1992).

The problem of the sentencing machine was well known. It is one reason why state guidelines systems have relatively few offense-severity levels. Minnesota's in 1987 had 10 and in 2013 had 11. Pennsylvania's guidelines, which also cover misdemeanors, in 1995 had 13 and in 2013 had 14. Washington State considered adopting a 26-level grid but rejected it in favor of 14. The rhetorical question was asked, "Could we plausibly explain to a judge why a level-16 crime is more serious than a level-15?" When the Washington commission realized that it could

[20] It resulted in part from the federal commission's lack of understanding of state guidelines and even of the logic of guidelines. Judge Breyer and Judge Jon Newman, then chief judge of the Second Circuit Court of Appeals and an active and influential commission advisor, argued that the guidelines must prescribe sentences for the entire range authorized by statutory maximums. The commission decided to fill the range between 0 and 30 years. The state systems by contrast created guideline ranges for particular offenses—for example, 22–30 months—and permitted judges to impose longer sentences ultimately to the statutory maximum as upward departures, subject to appellate sentence review. This accords with the original logic of sentencing (and parole) guidelines. The recommended or presumptive ranges in guidelines were meant for ordinary cases; extraordinary cases should be handled differently (Gottfredson, Wilkins, and Hoffman 1978).

not persuasively answer that question, it realized it had a sentencing-machine problem.

The contemporaneous Canadian Sentencing Commission unequivocally rejected the idea of a sentencing machine setting "mandatory" guidelines: "As a result of their rigidity, any of these options would meet with extreme resistance from judges as well as from most professionals involved in the administration of the criminal law. Their reservations would be justified" (Canadian Sentencing Commission 1987, p. 294).

The second problem with a complicated sentencing machine is that there will foreseeably be high rates of miscalculation. A major evaluation of four parole guideline grid systems showed that even simple grids produce significant levels of inaccurate calculations (Arthur D. Little, Inc. and Goldfarb and Singer, Esqs., 1981). Complicated grids produce higher error rates. That this is true of the federal guidelines was shown long ago by an FJC study. Forty-seven experienced federal probation officers were asked to calculate "base offense levels" for hypothetical defendants described in sample cases used for discussion at a 1992 sentencing institute for federal judges from the Second and Eighth Circuits. There were enormous differences (Lawrence and Hofer 1992). In a 1996 survey, less than 20 percent of federal probation officers indicated that they believed guidelines' calculations were accurate in most cases they had seen; 40 percent indicated they believed calculations were more likely than not to be incorrect (Probation Officers Advisory Group 1996).

IV. The Stories behind the Stories

The guidelines' shortcomings are inseparable from those of the initial US Sentencing Commission. It was badly managed, highly politicized, and riven by factionalism. Two original commissioners, Paul Robinson (in 1987) and Michael Block (in 1989), and one ex officio member, Ronald L. Gainer, the attorney general's initial designee and for a decade the US Department of Justice's sentencing policy specialist, resigned on principle over the commission's failings.[21] In the mid-1990s, two remaining

[21] Robinson (1987a, p. 1), in his dissent to the official publication of the initial guidelines, reported that Gainer informed the commission that "if he were a voting commissioner, as a personal matter, he would not have voted to support the guidelines in their current form."

initial commissioners, Judge William Wilkins and Ilene Nagel, and an early replacement, Michael Gelacek, holding over after their terms expired until successors were appointed, engaged in open media warfare (Bendavid 1993, 1994*a*, 1994*b*).

No one factor can explain why the federal commission and guidelines were so much less successful than those in the states. Some observers argued that the failure was in imagination. Given that there were seven full-time commissioners, 70 staff members, and 2 years to develop guidelines, a better-managed commission would have consulted widely and learned from the state experiences.[22] That did not happen. Kay Knapp, the first staff director, had been research director and then executive director of the Minnesota Sentencing Guidelines Commission; internal politics forced her out within a year. Otherwise, no senior commission staffer was hired during the development period from the Minnesota, Pennsylvania, and Washington commissions that had established guidelines systems. Nor, I know from talking with the senior staff and chairmen of the state commissions at the time, were any of them asked to serve as consultants or advisors.

The federal commission failed to draw on the intellectual capital amassed in the states and to learn from the mistakes, successes, and policy processes of its predecessors. All of the policy and practice issues the US commission faced had already been addressed. Many of its most serious mistakes—including the "relevant conduct" policy, the guidelines' alienating detail and unnecessary complexity, the daunting 43-level grid—could have been avoided by learning from state experience.

The problem may partly have been that the initial commissioners lacked personal knowledge of sentencing. Judge Frankel (1973) envisioned sentencing commissions as specialist agencies that would draw on expert knowledge. None of the initial commissioners, however, had any prior experience or expertise with sentencing guidelines or sentencing policy. Only two, federal district court judge William W. Wilkins, Jr., and retired court of appeals judge George MacKinnon, had ever practiced criminal law, and only Wilkins had sentenced a convicted offender. Judge Wilkins had been a federal trial judge only since 1981.

[22] State commissions typically have part-time members and 5–10 staff.

Judge MacKinnon was appointed directly to the US Court of Appeals for the DC Circuit in 1969, and had never served as a state or federal trial judge. Judge Stephen Breyer was appointed to the First Circuit Court of Appeals in 1980 directly from the staff of the US Senate and had no prior judicial experience. Two of the other original commissioners, Michael Block and Ilene Nagel, were social scientists without legal training. Helen Corrothers had worked with corrections agencies. Paul H. Robinson was a law professor.

Some observers, more conspiracy-minded, note that three initial members were former congressional aides, some with well-known political ambitions: Breyer (Senator Edward Kennedy), Wilkins (Senator Strom Thurmond), and Robinson (Senator John McClellan). All had good reasons to want to maintain good relations with the conservative Republicans who then controlled the Senate. Everyone involved with the commission (I was for a short time a consultant) recognized that Wilkins and Breyer were the most powerful commissioners. Both were widely known to be aspirants for higher office. Both made it. Wilkins was unsuccessful in an effort to be appointed FBI director, but was appointed in 1986 to the US Court of Appeals for the Fourth Circuit. Breyer was appointed to the US Supreme Court and encountered little opposition from Senate Republicans.

Almost all outside observers agree that the initial commission was badly managed. The US General Accounting Office (1990), when asked by the Congress to assess the commission's management and operations in its early years, described an agency in disarray. Much of the critique concerned individual commissioners who created a volatile and unpleasant working environment (1990, pp. 3, 12–15):

> "The extensive involvement of individual commissioners in what would normally be staff activities . . . contributes to the organizational disarray we found" (p. 12);
>
> "Commissioner involvement in research . . . raises another concern . . . the potential for the research to reflect the perspectives and interests of the commissioner conducting the project" (p. 14);
>
> "According to former staff directors, it was difficult to manage in an environment where they could not maintain authority over the staff because of commissioner involvement" (p. 14);

> "Part of the problem has been finding qualified candidates who would be willing to take the [research director's] position, given perceptions that the working environment is complicated by commissioner involvement in research and other matters" (p. 15).

"Out-of-control internal politics" is one way to characterize the problems described in the General Accounting Office report. "Failure of management" is another. Good managers know how to recruit and motivate capable staff, develop and carry out a work plan, create and maintain a congenial working environment, work with and accommodate important constituencies, and control obstreperous appointees.

None of those attributes characterized the commission. In 4 years it had four staff directors. General counsel came and went at the same rate. The commission lacked a research director for several years during the development and implementation phases when empirical analyses were fundamentally important to its work (US General Accounting Office 1990, p. 14). William C. Rhodes (1992), one early research director, wrote a devastating critique of the competence of the commission's congressionally mandated 1991 self-evaluation. Joel Garner, a nationally prominent researcher who long had worked for the National Institute of Justice, joined the commission as research director in 1990–91 in the face of warnings from friends. He explained that he had many years of experience working in a politically contentious government agency, that things had gotten so bad that they were bound to improve, and that he would be starting work as the commission rebounded. He soon quit.[23] Qualified research directors proved elusive, and the position was for a time abolished.

The process by which the guidelines were developed illustrates the commission's management problems. Except for the General Accounting Office study and a few newspaper articles, there is almost no literature on internal commission processes. This account accordingly draws on extensive discussions with former commissioners and commission

[23] "'When I worked there, some of the staff called the commission an information-free environment,' says Joel Garner, the commission's research director in 1990 and 1991. 'It was worse than that. It was an evil place. . . . I've been a bureaucrat for almost two decades, and I've served in lots of different administrations, but this was remarkable'" (Bendavid 1993, p. 18).

staff and my experience as a member of the commission's first research advisory board and for a short time as an occasional paid consultant.

The commission had no overall strategy for developing guidelines. Separate teams under the leadership of professor/commissioners worked on incompatible guideline drafts. One team, led by commissioner Paul Robinson, worked on "just deserts guidelines" that would calibrate sentences to detailed assessments of offenders' culpability. The logic came from criminal law "elements analysis," in which crimes are deconstructed into their mental and physical components. Mental states include purpose, knowledge, recklessness, negligence, and inadvertence. Physical elements include such things as the amount of property loss, the degree of harm, and the circumstances. Both mental and physical elements can be scaled for seriousness. All physical elements being equal, a purposeful crime is more serious than a negligent one. A theft of $500 is more serious than a theft of $50. An armed robbery is more serious than an unarmed one. Because most definitions of crimes include four or more physical elements, separate mental elements can be specified for each.

The insurmountable problem of the proposed just deserts guidelines lay in their complexity. Guidelines for robbery, for example, had to distinguish not only between attempted and completed robberies but also on the basis of whether a weapon was involved and what kind (handgun, other gun, knife, blunt instrument), how the weapon was used (carried, shown, pointed, discharged or otherwise used), whether injuries or death were caused and, if so, how serious, and how much property was involved or lost.

To deal with that complexity, a system of "punishment units" was created, into which any element could be translated. Injuries might be valued at 0 to 1,000 points, the nature of any weapon at 0 to 500, the manner of weapon use at 0 to 500, property loss at 0 to 1,000. The sentence would be determined by summing the points associated with each physical and mental element. Some elements, such as property loss, are hard to accommodate in such a scheme. If a $500 theft equals 50 units and that leads to 90 days in jail, what sentences should corporate fraudsters receive for billion-dollar crimes? To deal with such problems the scheme called on judges to calculate the square and cube roots of property values above thresholds and to plug the answers into the sentencing calculation. Not surprisingly, judges and other outsiders who were shown confidential drafts were bewildered. After many months the proposal was abandoned.

Unfortunately, the other guidelines drafting team had by that time given up its effort. Led by economist Michael Block and sociologist Ilene Nagel, the team sought to devise crime-control guidelines based on research on deterrence and incapacitation. Penalties would be set that had optimal deterrent effects or that would cost-effectively incapacitate those at highest risk for future crimes. The effort soon foundered on the insuperable difficulty that existing crime-control research gave no adequate answers to such questions as "What is the optimal deterrent sentence for a $5,000 theft?" or "Who among 3,000 robbery defendants has a 40 percent likelihood of committing a serious violent crime within the next 5 years?" Research on deterrence and incapacitation then was and now is utterly incapable of answering such questions (Apel and Nagin 2011; Nagin 2013; Travis, Western, and Redburn 2014, chap. 5).

Andrew von Hirsch, on the basis of extensive discussion with commission members and senior staffers, provided a similar but less detailed account:

> Shortly after the commissioners were appointed, however, problems began to be apparent. A first draft of the guidelines was written in the spring of 1986 by one of the commissioners [Robinson], and then jettisoned. The next two drafts emanated from the Chairman's office, were circulated for public comment, and then abandoned after an unfavorable response. It was only in the winter of 1986 that other commissioners were drawn actively into the process. The final draft was written at a late date in some haste to meet the submission deadline. (von Hirsch 1988, p. 2)

Many of the guidelines' most fundamental problems derive from the aborted Robinson "just deserts" draft. Because to that point the only drafting had been the doomed efforts headed by academics, there was nothing else to build on. The Robinson draft's legacies include the guidelines' daunting complexity, the enormous guidelines grid, and "relevant conduct sentencing." Within the logic of the Robinson draft, those features made sense. If every mental and physical element of every crime had to be translated into a punishment unit score, the guidelines had to specify which elements were material and how they were to be scored. Complexity was conceptually essential. If punishment unit totals for a robbery could range from 200 to 3,000, the guidelines had to be complex and to contain many gradations of offense seriousness. Closely scaling punishment severity to offense seriousness was also conceptually essential. Finally, in a system in which plea bargaining is ubiquitous, "real offense sentencing" made sense. Otherwise, plea-bargaining lawyers could manipulate the sentencing system at will by agreeing which offense elements would be admitted by the defendant and thereby precisely determine sentences.

An initial official set of draft guidelines was scheduled for release for public comment early in the fall of 1986. When the commission finally started work on what became its official proposal, there was nothing to do but adapt the Robinson draft. The concept of punishment units disappeared. So did the square and cube roots. However, the enormous guidelines grid, the complexity, and real offense sentencing survived in the first guidelines draft that was publicly released. In later drafts, in response to adverse comment, real offense sentencing became "relevant conduct" sentencing. This meant that calculations began with the offense of which the defendant was convicted. Increments were to be added on a "real offense basis." The guidelines that took effect and that survive to this day reject the premises and logic of the Robinson draft but contain much of its apparatus.

The process by which the federal guidelines were devised thus explains many of their most disliked features. It does not explain, however, why they are so harsh, why the commission so narrowly limited the use of probation and precluded use of other community punishments as stand-alone sentences, or why sentences for many drug offenses were made even longer than statutes mandated.

The explanation for those policy choices lies elsewhere. Part of it was bad management. Part of it was the commissioners' lack of sentencing experience and knowledge of sentencing guidelines. Part was hubris. The largest part was that the crime-control policies of the Reagan administration were oriented more toward toughness than fairness. The commissioners Reagan appointed sought to show that they too were tough on crime and had little sympathy for "lenient" judges. Judge Frankel's sentencing commission proposal to the contrary was predicated on the notion of an expert nonpartisan administrative agency, the ideal that sentencing should be just, and the aspiration that detailed sentencing policy should be insulated from politics. The individuals who dominated the commission's work in its early years did not share those beliefs.

V. What Next?

Federal sentencing was less just and less fair in 2015 than it was in 1985. In the earlier year, more than one-third of convicted offenders received straight probation, and 14 percent received split sentences of probation and a few weeks or months of confinement. For them, unwarranted disparities in prison sentences were not much of an issue. For the half of convicted offenders sentenced to imprisonment, the US Parole Commission's guidelines evened out the worst disparities.

By contrast, the 87.3 percent of convicted federal offenders who received straight prison sentences in 2013 had little recourse against disparately severe punishments. Parole release no longer existed. Appeals of sentences to higher courts were possible, but under the deferential "abuse of discretion" standard of review set by the Supreme Court in *Gall v. United States*, 522 U.S. 38 (2007), few succeed.

The system in 1985 was fairer. Reasonable people can differ on the merits, and justice, of basing release decisions on the Salient Factor Score, with its predictive premises, that the US Parole Commission developed and long used. Surely, though, some defensible, systematic set of criteria is better than no criteria at all, as in many determinate sentencing systems, or the overly detailed criteria of the mechanistic federal guidelines.

Federal sentencing in 2015 is more unjust and unfair for three reasons. First, commission policy decisions made sentencing much more severe. A large part of the increased severity occurred because that is what the commission wanted; it aimed to increase punishments for many crimes. Partly it results from tight limitations on sentences to probation and other community punishments. Partly it resulted from many discretionary decisions made by the commission to make sentencing more severe than the 1984 act required or directed. Partly it resulted from the abolition of parole release and its replacement by the "truth in sentencing" requirement that prisoners serve at least 85 percent of the sentence imposed.

Second, federal legislation enacted between 1984 and 1996 mandated minimum 5-, 10-, and 20-year, and longer, prison sentences for drug and violent offenders; these were much longer than had been served for those offenses under the prior regime. Commission decisions concerning sentences for drug crimes exacerbated the effects of mandatories. Paul Hofer, the leading authority on federal sentencing data, recently observed: "Average prison time served by federal offenders more than doubled after introduction of the guidelines, and this was due in large part to the [commission's] linkage of the guidelines with the mandatory minimum penalties" (Hofer 2012, p. 185).

Third, the combination of detailed, mechanistic guidelines, the relevant conduct policy, and mandatory minimum sentence laws gave federal prosecutors unprecedented power to offer plea bargains that are too good to be turned down. That is not because the sentences offered are mild but because the sentences threatened are enormous. As a practical matter the prosecutor, not the judge, determines which defendants, if any, warrant special consideration and which will serve lengthy prison sentences. Federal Court of Appeals judge Gerald Lynch observed:

> The prosecutor, rather than a judge or jury, is the central adjudicator of facts (as well as replacing the judge as arbiter of most legal issues and of the appropriate sentence to be imposed). Potential defenses are presented by the defendant and his counsel not in a court, but to a prosecutor, who assesses their factual accuracy and likely persuasiveness to a hypothetical judge or jury, and then decides the charge of which the defendant should be adjudged guilty. Mitigating information, similarly, is argued not to the judge, but to the prosecutor, who decides what sentence the defendant should be given in exchange for his plea. (Lynch 2003, pp. 1403–4)

A. Attributing Blame

Not all the problems in federal sentencing can fairly be attributed to the commission and its guidelines, but a large majority can. The commission made many low-visibility but important policy decisions that exacerbated the effects of other punitive changes in federal law.

The Congress enacted the 100-to-1 crack cocaine sentencing law, but the commission made it, and other mandatory minimum sentence laws, even harsher by setting higher guidelines sentences for many crimes than the laws required. The Congress enacted the 85 percent time-to-be-served truth-in-sentencing law, but the commission made the sentences to which the law applies longer or harsher than they need have been in three ways. It made the relevant conduct policy mandatory, which meant that judges were directed to increase sentence lengths to take account of prior alleged crimes of which defendants had not been convicted and other aggravating factors set out in the guidelines. It forbade judges to mitigate sentences on the basis of most commonsensical offender characteristics. By severely limiting imposition of straight probation sentences, it assured that many more people were sentenced to imprisonment and thereby affected by the 85 percent rule.

Some might say that the commission had no choice to do otherwise, given the political climate of Washington, DC, in the 1980s. That cannot be right. Many of the commission's decisions were both radically severe and so low profile that few recognized their import at the time (Tonry 1992*a*). The commission did not have to nullify the presumption that most first offenders should be diverted from prison. It did not have to define probation as "zero months" imprisonment. It did not have to narrowly limit use of fines as freestanding punishments. It did not have to ignore the explicit statutory "capacity constraint" language to tailor the guidelines to fit available prison capacity. It did not have to adopt the relevant conduct standard or give prosecutors exclusive control over sentence reductions for "substantial assistance."

That they need not have done all these things can be seen by comparing the experiences of the federal and North Carolina sentencing commissions. Tough-on-crime attitudes were at their harshest during the early 1990s when the North Carolina Sentencing Commission did its work. This is the period when every state enacted Megan's laws and more than half enacted truth-in-sentencing or three-strikes laws or both (Travis, Western, and Redburn 2014, chap. 3). North Carolina is a conservative southern state, and its commission observed the politics and the rhetoric of the day by creating "mandatory" imprisonment guidelines for serious violent and high-level drug offenses. However, it also provided for diversion of most people convicted of lesser crimes to community penalties and created capacity constraint guidelines that made North Carolina the most successful state in the country at managing the size of its prison population (Wright 2002).

The difference was not in the political climate, but in the quality of members and leaders of the two commissions. North Carolina chairman Judge Thomas Ross made good faith efforts to develop principled, fair guidelines. Federal chairman Judge William Wilkins, despite statutory directives that the federal guidelines do the same, did not. The federal commission adopted a bunker mentality and rejected the experience and technical knowledge accumulated in the states. The North Carolina commission made serious efforts to learn from experiences elsewhere, including the unfortunate federal experiences, and hired and retained Robin Lubitz, deputy director of the Pennsylvania Commission on Sentencing, as its executive director. The federal commission had no plausible management plan for developing guidelines; no reasonable person would have expected competing academics' proposals for "just deserts" and "crime control" guidelines to produce something viable and realistic. They did not. The failure to have a fallback locked the federal guidelines into a structure and an approach from which they never recovered.

In the end, though, the federal guidelines had enormous—albeit negative—influence. As the ABA Standards for Sentencing Procedures and Alternatives and the American Law Institute's Model Penal Code—Sentencing stories demonstrate, the federal experience became a serious impediment to guidelines efforts in the United States. Negatives cannot be proven, but it is likely that the federal experience halted what otherwise might have been a march of progress toward development of effective presumptive sentencing guidelines systems throughout the United States.

B. Reinventing Federal Sentencing

The federal sentencing guidelines need not have failed so dismally. Reviving them as an instrument of justice is not impossible. The best way to do that would be for the Congress to enact new enabling legislation for development of presumptive sentencing guidelines of the sort that Judge Frankel envisioned and that operate successfully in Minnesota,

North Carolina, Kansas, and Washington. The book on the current federal commission could be closed; it could be given residual authority over cases sentenced under its guidelines, as was done with the US Parole Commission when parole release was prospectively abolished under the Sentencing Reform Act of 1984.

A new commission developing presumptive guidelines of the sort Judge Frankel envisioned would, ironically, be working in a more hospitable legal environment than did any of the early guidelines commissions. Under *Blakely v. Washington*, 542 U.S. 296 (2004), judges in a presumptive system may not impose sentences in excess of the upper boundary of applicable guidelines unless the defendant pleads guilty or a judge or jury finds beyond a reasonable doubt that facts have been proven that justify the harsher punishment. This means that the greatest injustices in sentencing, disproportionately severe punishments, cannot happen casually.

When *Blakely* was decided, many people assumed it meant the end of presumptive guidelines, because judges and prosecutors would not tolerate a system that so limited their powers. Ohio for that reason made its previously presumptive guidelines advisory. Commissions in Kansas, Minnesota, North Carolina, and Washington made minor adjustments and retained their existing systems (Frase 2013). As a matter of procedural fairness, those systems were improved. Facts justifying harsher punishments must be charged and proven. That has always been the legal requirement in other common law legal systems. Only behavior that is charged and proven beyond a reasonable doubt, or admitted, may be taken into account at sentencing (e.g., Australia: Freiberg 2001, 2014; England and Wales: Ashworth 2001, 2010).

On the basis of the experiences of state sentencing commissions, and 30 years unhappy federal experience, a new federal commission would be highly unlikely to adopt relevant conduct sentencing, to disregard directives about diversion of first offenders from imprisonment or take account of correctional resources, to forbid judges to take account of offender characteristics that most believe are germane, to discourage use of community punishments, or gratuitously to exacerbate the punitive effects of mandatory minimum sentence and similar laws.

The US Congress is unlikely to enact legislation to create a new sentencing commission. The next best thing would be for the current commission to revive the aborted effort initiated in the mid-1990s by commission chair Richard P. Conaboy to revise and simplify the guidelines. Even Justice Breyer (1999), for many years the guidelines' most outspoken apologist, long ago called for simplification. The agenda should be the same as Judge Conaboy's—to reconsider and substantially address the policy subjects described in the preceding paragraph. The commission undoubtedly has the authority to do so. One faint 1984 echo of Judge Frankel's call for establishment of a politically insulated commission is that the 1984 Sentencing Reform Act provides that changes the commission proposes take effect automatically 6 months later unless the Congress votes to reject them. Leadership and vision are all that is needed.

4

Sentencing Theories

SENTENCING AMERICAN-STYLE IS DIFFERENT from sentencing in other developed Western countries in at least five respects.[1] First, punishments are more severe. The United States has capital punishment, life-without-possibility-of-parole (LWOP) and three-strikes laws, decades-long minimum sentences, and an imprisonment rate exceeding 700 per 100,000 population. Most other Western countries have none of these laws, and the average imprisonment rate is 100 per 100,000.

Second, American officials have vastly more discretionary authority than officials elsewhere. The US Supreme Court declared in *Bordenkircher v. Hayes*, 434 U.S. 357 (1978), and *Castle Rock v. Gonzales*, 545 U.S. 748 (2005), that American prosecutors possess almost unlimited discretion to decide whether to file charges and for what, and whether to dismiss them. American judges choose sentences from within broad ranges authorized in statutes: often from probation to 20, 30, or more years, or life, subject to applicable mandatory minimum sentence laws and in some states to sentencing guidelines. In a few jurisdictions, weak appellate review systems affect the tiny percentages of cases not resolved

[1] None of these five points is controversial among comparative law scholars or would be controverted in substance by many, if any, though of course details vary from country to country. Much fuller discussion and documentation can be found in series of essays by specialists on individual countries in Tonry and Frase (2001), Tonry (2007), Tonry (2012*a*), and Tonry (2016), and concerning mandatory minimum sentences in Tonry (2009*a*). The countries covered in those works include Australia, Belgium, Canada, Denmark, England and Wales, Finland, France, Germany, the Netherlands, Norway, Poland, South Africa, and Sweden.

by guilty pleas. In other developed countries, prosecutors have less discretion about charging and little over dismissals; in many a "legality principle" prescribes precisely what charge should be filed. In many European civil law systems, the judge is not restricted by the charges the prosecutor files and may convict a defendant of a more or less serious offense if that's what the evidence supports. Judges outside the United States operate within much narrower ranges of sentencing authority and are subject to well-established norms about appropriate sentences and to meaningful systems of appellate review.

Third, most American prosecutors and judges are elected. Many of the rest are chosen at least in part on the basis of political and ideological considerations. With very limited exceptions in Switzerland, where some judges and prosecutors are chosen in nonpartisan elections, those in other countries are either career civil servants or are selected at young ages under nonpartisan merit-based systems. Because of those differences, American officials are more susceptible to influence by political considerations, and are more sensitive than officials elsewhere to public opinion and emotions. Judges and prosecutors in other developed Western countries are socialized into professional value systems that emphasize rationality, neutrality, and equal treatment and emphatically reject the proposition that political considerations or public attitudes and emotions are relevant or ethically appropriate for them to take into account in their work.

Fourth, American legislators often precisely prescribe minimum sentences for people convicted of certain offenses, irrespective of extenuating circumstances of the offense or mitigating characteristics of the offender. Mandatory minimum sentence and similar laws exist in every American jurisdiction and sometimes affect large percentages of felony cases. In other developed Western countries, the idea that sentences must be based on considerations of justice in the individual case is paramount everywhere. The laws of some continental European countries include "minimum" sentences, and a few narrowly focused laws in other common law countries prescribe "mandatory minimum" sentences. Notwithstanding that language, however, judges elsewhere have authority to impose lesser sentences "in the interest of justice" or under similar wording. Unless judges in America willfully and disingenuously evade application of a law specifying a mandatory minimum, three-strikes, or LWOP sentence, it must be imposed. In no other developed Western country do judges need to be evasive or disingenuous in order to impose what they believe to be just punishments.

Fifth, prevailing ways of thinking about punishment among American policy makers and practitioners have no equivalents elsewhere. The signature laws of the tough on crime period were motivated almost entirely by political rather than substantive considerations. Judges were often accused of "leniency" and denied authority to take account of special circumstances in individual cases. No credible arguments could be made then or now that such laws were effective crime control measures or were cost-effective.[2] The implications of the enactment of such laws for thinking in principle about punishment of offenders are seldom discussed.

The critical implication is that those laws were not predicated on ideas about just treatment of individual offenders, either in the retributive sense of linking punishments in particular cases to offenders' blameworthiness or in the instrumental sense of relating punishments received by individuals to plausibly likely preventive effects. They were instead primarily "expressive." Traditional ways of justifying punishments of individuals were not part of the calculus. Sentencing in every other developed Western country, by contrast, is primarily animated by

[2] Some readers may find this a surprising statement. I discuss the relevant research in chapter 6. It is supported by the recently reported findings of the National of Sciences Committee on the Causes and Consequences of High Rates of Incarceration (Travis, Western, and Redburn 2014, chaps. 2 and 5). That committee, like all National Academy of Sciences bodies, was organized so as to be multidisciplinary, ideologically and politically diverse, and representative of a mix of scholarly and professional perspectives. Some scholars at some times have made claims that such policies were effective. James Q. Wilson (1975) and others (e.g., Bennett, DiIulio, and Walters 1996) argued that scientific evidence broadly supported many of the severe sentencing policy initiatives of the 1980s and early 1990s. However, they represented a small minority viewpoint. A claim by Bennett et al. (1996), for example, that proposed policies were justified by the existence of youthful "superpredators" was widely repudiated at the time and again recently by a National Academy of Sciences panel on juvenile justice (Bonnie et al. 2012). The weight of the evidence that such policies were neither instrumentally effective nor cost-effective was clear during the 1980s and 1990s, as is shown in the findings of a series of National Academy of Sciences panels (e.g., on deterrence and incapacitation: Blumstein, Cohen, and Nagin [1978]; on sentencing reform initiatives including mandatory penalties: Blumstein et al. [1983]; on criminal careers: Blumstein et al. [1986]; and on control and prevention of violence: Reiss and Roth [1993]; and elsewhere, e.g., on incapacitation: Cohen [1983]). The state of the art of knowledge on the deterrent and incapacitative effects of punishment has changed little since 1985.

concerns to impose just or appropriate sentences on individuals in terms of traditional retributive considerations of culpability, wrongdoing, or offense gravity. Consideration of possible preventive effects is not absent but is almost always subsidiary.

These five characteristics interact. Punishments became unprecedentedly severe in the United States because governors and presidents, legislators, prosecutors, judges, and parole boards responded in various ways to political incentives and changes in public attitudes. Broad discretions allowed practitioners to alter their practices substantially without legislative changes. That was the primary reason the imprisonment rate doubled between 1973 and the mid-1980s (Blumstein and Beck 1999). Laws enacted between 1984 and 1996 attempted to compel judges to impose much more severe punishments. That's why the imprisonment rate doubled again between 1985 and 2000 (Raphael and Stoll 2013).

During the indeterminate sentencing period before 1975, ideas, laws, institutions, and practices also intersected, but in ways that were coherent and meaningfully related to prevailing ideas about treating offenders justly and appropriately. The central institutions were the indeterminate sentence and the parole board. The signal practices were individualized exercises of discretion affecting individual offenders by judges, parole boards, and prison officials. The underlying ideas were that the principal causes of crime are defective or incomplete socialization, inadequate skills and education, and psychological maladjustment; the end of punishment is crime prevention; the means are mostly rehabilitation and incapacitation; and offenders should not be punished or their lives impeded more than is minimally necessary. Consequentialist theories of punishment provided normative justifications for those ways of doing business and criteria for assessing whether the system was working properly.

The components fit together nicely. The institutions provided frameworks for exercise of broad discretions that should be used to maximize offenders' rehabilitative prospects and minimize state intrusions into their lives. Even during its heyday, both critics and supporters recognized the system's limitations—insufficient resources, ineffective programs, and abuses of discretion—but its legitimacy and desirability were widely accepted. When the draftsmen of the Model Penal Code began work in 1949, their aim was not to reconsider or replace indeterminate sentencing but to perfect it. And when the completed code was formally approved by the American Law Institute in 1962, that's what it attempted to do. That is also what the National Commission on Reform of Federal Laws attempted to do in 1971 when it offered a detailed proposal for a comprehensive federal criminal code.

When indeterminate sentencing imploded in the 1970s, all the main components fell into disrepute. The decisions judges, parole boards, and prison officials made were not transparent, and the decision makers were not accountable to law or higher authorities. Individualized decision making was rife with risks of bias, stereotyping, and idiosyncrasy. No institutions or procedures existed to guard against them. And in principle, indeterminate sentencing was unconcerned about different treatment of offenders convicted of comparable crimes. Consequentialist theories, which justified practices and decisions in terms of their effects, allowed little space for ideas about fairness, consistency, and human moral autonomy. When support for indeterminate sentencing collapsed, its core institutions, practices, and ideas were all found wanting.

New American systems of determinate sentencing could have been built that incorporated a new set of interrelated institutions, practices, and ideas. Parole release and indeterminate sentencing might have been abolished, sentencing laws or guidelines might have set standards for sentencing that were closely tied to the seriousness of crimes, and appellate sentence review might have policed judges' compliance with the standards. Retributive theories of punishment could have provided normative justification and criteria for assessing whether the system was working properly. A few states, most notably Minnesota, Oregon, and Washington, tried to do that and for differing periods largely succeeded.

Overall, however, and in time even in the states that tried, that didn't happen. Some of the reasons are well known—resistance by judges to changes that reduce their discretion, resistance by prosecutors to changes that reduce their plea-bargaining leverage, politicization of crime control policy, and widespread adoption of rigid, severe, expressive laws. The result was a motley of states with determinate and indeterminate systems, in each case with and without guidelines, appellate sentence review, and parole release, and overlain by various of the new expressive laws. More recent initiatives that focus on rehabilitation or justify themselves in terms of their putative good consequences, including drug and other problem-solving courts and restorative justice programs, make state-by-state diversity even greater.

That summary focuses on recent political and other adventitious developments that created new laws and institutions that together produced incoherent and unjust sentencing systems. What it neglects is the importance of ideas. The consequentialist ideas that made sense of indeterminate sentencing could have been succeeded by retributive ideas that would have made sense of determinate sentencing. That didn't happen, except for short periods in a few places. American sentencing systems are incoherent because American ideas about sentencing and punishment are incoherent. There are no widely shared criteria to be used to assess whether systems are working properly and justly. Until that changes, American sentencing will remain inconsistent, arbitrary, severe, unjust, and often hypocritical.

What will happen in coming years cannot be predicted. Optimists, influenced by a seeming convergence in views by Right on Crime conservatives and decarceration-promoting liberals, would expect widespread recent criticism of current levels of imprisonment and current policies to portend major changes. Pessimists would expect that those elements of American culture, politics, and history that produced and accepted mass incarceration and current policies will endure, pressures for change will abate, and inertia will leave things largely as they are. Future historians will explain what happens and why.

In hopes that the optimistic forecasts prove right, in this chapter I trace the development of thinking about punishment over the past century and suggest how it must change if punishment patterns and policies are to change. Successive patterns of thought made sense of indeterminate and—for a time—determinate sentencing. Punishment theories and theorists, however, have not kept up with policy developments. To be useful, they need to do that. The final section of this chapter explains some of the ways that might be done.

I. The Theoretical Vacuum

For a time, in the 1970s and 1980s, it appeared that retributivism might replace the consequentialist framework that long shaped American policies and practices. Instead, by the mid-1990s, incapacitative policies such as "dangerous offender" and "sexual predator" laws, deterrent policies such as mandatory minimum sentence and three-strikes laws, and rehabilitative policies such as drug courts and correctional treatment programs had proliferated. Restorative and community justice programs that celebrated case-by-case problem-solving were established in many places. None of these initiatives was predicated on, or can be reconciled with, the retributive premise that punishments for crime, if they are to be just, must take account of concerns about horizontal (treating like cases alike) and vertical (treating different cases differently) equity.

Proponents of retributive theories have made little effort to address proportionality-busting policies, nor have they expressed much interest in trying to do so. Here is an illustration: "In principle, retributivism can lay out the outer limits for punishment. . . . But beyond this, a retributive conception of proportionality need not have much in the way of precision to say about the particular details of punishment's implementation" (Markel 2010, p. 950).

Nor have proponents of consequentialist theories made much effort except concerning restorative justice (e.g., Braithwaite and Pettit 1990, 2001). In any case, consequentialist theories necessarily encompass what Jeremy Bentham called frugality—in modern terminology, parsimony—the proposition that no punishment is justifiable if it is more severe than is necessary to achieve the sought-after consequence. Parsimony for Bentham encompassed two conceptions of proportionality (Frase 2009*a*). Both are predicated on the belief that causing suffering, including to offenders in the name of punishment, is in Bentham's terms "wicked," an "evil" to be avoided. The alternative-means test requires that there be no less costly way to achieve the sought-after goal. No punishment may properly be imposed if some approach other than punishment would do as well. The ends-benefits test requires that the pains to victims to be avoided by punishment must be greater than the pains the offender would suffer if punished. If not, punishment cannot be justified. Few modern American sentencing initiatives pass either test.

Philosophers and other theorists mostly talk retributivism. Consequentialists mostly don't talk punishment. In any case, policy makers and practitioners are not listening. That's a pity. In theory, theory ought to matter. What can be done?

Two strategies are available. The first is to measure new policies with traditional normative calipers and, if they don't measure up, declare them unprincipled and morally unjustifiable. Having called spades spades, let them be. The harshest laws commonly prescribe prison sentences measured in decades and lifetimes. Drug laws often mandate sentences far longer than those imposed on many violent and sexual offenders. Some three-strikes laws call for 25-year-to-life sentences for property and minor drug crimes. None of that can be squared with concerns for proportionality or parsimony. The belief is widespread within the theory class that these laws are per se unconscionable and unprincipled, the product not of normative considerations or ethical analysis but of emotion, cynicism, and political posturing. That may explain why they are seldom the subjects of sustained analysis.

Restorative justice and some treatment programs, notably drug courts, have been discussed by retributive theorists. Typically they are criticized for failing to comport with proportionality requirements, and the proposed way forward is to approve of them (only) to the extent that dispositions in individual cases are consistent with conventional ideas about retributive proportionality (e.g., Robinson 2003 [restorative justice]; Husak 2008, 2011 [drug courts]). That will be a difficult challenge to meet. Restorative justice and treatment programs presuppose that outcomes and dispositions must be individualized to be effective. Such programs will continue whether or not theorists approve of them.

The other way forward is to engage new policies and practices on the merits, identifying their express or implicit normative rationales, assessing them in their own terms, and considering when and whether they can be reconciled with traditional retributive and consequentialist ideas.. This is worth doing in its own right. Antony Duff (2001, 2011) has for many years been trying to do that in relation to restorative justice.

That kind of engagement is not easy. Most of the available theorizing has been around for a long time. Little of it attempts systematically to explore normative arguments for initiatives that appear to be facially incompatible with traditional theories. Arguments, in any case, are easier to carry out when they have at least two sides. Shadowboxing is the alternative. Shadows are not challenging opponents. They don't hit back.

Nineteenth-century theorists had an easier time. Jeremy Bentham, the developer of the first comprehensive proposals for a utilitarian punishment system, made his disdain for Immanuel Kant's retributive analyses clear.[3] Kant, and later Georg Wilhelm Friedrich Hegel, usually viewed as the initiators of modern retributive theories, returned the favor.[4] They could disagree so publicly because each set out his views in detail. There were two sides to the argument. In our time, it is not easy to find theoretical writing that offers well-developed, principled justifications for new initiatives.

No one offers sustained, normative justifications for three-strikes laws, mandatory minimums, LWOPs, drug courts, or "dangerous offender" laws. People offer political arguments, such as that the public wants or is reassured by harsh sentencing laws, or is sympathetic toward drug-dependent offenders, or supports electoral candidates who are tough on crime, and programs should be adopted for those reasons. People offer policy arguments, such as that crime will be prevented through deterrent or incapacitative effects of harsh punishments, or that successful treatment will diminish drug abuse and related criminality. Some analysts observe that criminal justice policies are often adopted primarily for expressive reasons—as much or more to demonstrate that *something* is being done than because policy makers believe they will have any effects on crime (e.g., Garland 2001; Freiberg 2007).

Presumably principled arguments can be made. Such arguments would explain why the aims pursued are legitimate for governments to pursue and when, why, and to what extent individual offenders' interests

[3] Unlike Kant and Hegel, Bentham insisted that punishment theory had nothing to do with ideas about individual rights or respect for the moral autonomy of individuals. Commenting on the French Revolution and the Declaration of the Rights of Man to which it gave rise, he acerbically observed that the idea of "natural rights is simple nonsense: natural and imprescriptible rights, rhetorical nonsense, nonsense upon stilts" (quoted in Harrison 1995, p. 87).

[4] Kant stressed the difference between his ideas and Bentham's: "The law concerning punishment is a categorical imperative, and woe to him who rummages around in the winding paths of a theory of happiness looking for some advantage to be gained by releasing the criminal from punishment or by reducing the amount of it" (Kant 1965 [1798], p. 100).

Hegel was as adamant: "This superficial [characterization of crime] as an *evil* is the primary assumption in the various theories of punishment as prevention, as a deterrent, a corrective, etc., and conversely what is supposed to result from it is just as superficially defined as a good. . . . As a result of these superficial points of view, however, the objective consideration of *justice*, which is the primary and substantial point of view in relation to crime, is set aside" (Hegel 1991 [1821], p. 125).

and autonomy may appropriately be limited or disregarded in order to achieve them. There may be plausible principled arguments for why some shoplifters are imprisoned for decades under three-strikes laws, or why many drug dealers are punished more severely than rapists, but so far they have not been offered. The United States Supreme Court has upheld the constitutionality of applying three-strikes laws to property offenders and the continued confinement of "dangerous offenders" after their prison sentences have expired.[5] The explanations, however, have at base been nothing more than assertions that legislatures possess constitutional authority to enact such laws. That is a legal not a normative conclusion, and demonstrates the truism that being legally allowable is not the same thing as being morally justifiable.

Normative analyses of less punitive new initiatives are little richer. Drug and other problem-solving courts, new rehabilitation programs, and reentry programs raise issues that were well ventilated a generation or two ago, but have largely disappeared from public and scholarly discussion. C. S. Lewis (2011 [1949]) and Antony Burgess (1962) challenged the morality of efforts to coerce offenders to change in the interest of crime prevention or public protection. Frank Allen (1959, 1964), Kenneth Culp Davis (1969), and Norval Morris (1974) cautioned about dangers that administrators would misuse their broad powers to individualize treatment. Others warned of the dangers of idiosyncratic and racially biased decision making (e.g., American Friends Service Committee 1971).

Few such arguments are made in our time. The principal issues discussed are instrumental: How good is the evidence about the effectiveness of treatment programs; how well-tailored are they to offenders' risks and needs; how well are they implemented? Concerns about the morality of their use, risks of abuse, and coercing people to participate in them are seldom expressed. Nor is Norval Morris's (1974) objection that participation in treatment programs as a result of threats of imprisonment or parole release denial is inherently coerced and by definition

[5] *Kansas v. Hendricks*, 521 U.S. 346 (1997), upheld the constitutionality of indeterminate confinement of "sexual predators" following expiration of prison sentences imposed for specific offenses. *Ewing v. California*, 538 U.S. 11 (2003), upheld the constitutionality of a 25-years-to-life sentence for the theft of three golf clubs. *Lockyer v. Andrade*, 538 U.S. 63 (2003), upheld the constitutionality of a 25-years-to-life sentence for a $153 theft from a K-Mart.

involuntary. Consents in other settings are seldom recognized as voluntary when elicited by threats.

It has to be a Good Thing to explore whether and how recent innovations in punishment policies and practices can be justified in principle, in general and in their application to individual cases. Legislators, judges, and prosecutors have not done that, but that is not the business they are in.

Even if policy makers and practitioners pay little or no attention in the here and now to what theorists argue or conclude, it is better that legal institutions and practices be deconstructed and dissected, and the results displayed. Prevailing attitudes change. Policies and practices change. Arguments and analyses that are not influential in one time often become so in another.[6] When indeterminate sentencing fell from favor in the 1970s, for example, theorists rediscovered the languishing ideas of Kant and Hegel and elaborated new retributive theories that built on them.

Changing attitudes concerning racial discrimination and homosexuality provide familiar examples. Patterns of discriminatory and differential treatment that were commonplace a half century ago, and were widely justified, are almost unthinkable now. After attitudes changed, policies that were formerly unthinkable, such as enactment of gay marriage laws, were widely adopted. The propositions that black people can be forbidden to eat in restaurants, sleep in hotels, ride at the front of a bus, swim in a public swimming pool, or sit on the main floor of a movie theater are unimaginable to Americans under 50. So are anti-miscegenation laws forbidding marriages between people of different

[6] This is equally true of empirical research on punishment practices. For nearly two decades research findings accumulated, and went unacknowledged in policy circles, that correctional boot camps for young offenders were ineffective at reducing later offending or achieving lasting improvements to offenders' self-esteem or social functioning (Wilson, MacKenzie, and Mitchell 2008). Times have changed. Notorious deaths of young people pushed too hard were publicized. Support for boot camps crumbled. The negative research findings were often, but only then, invoked as reason to end the programs. The same pattern underlies contemporary belief in the effectiveness of drug abuse treatment. The research findings—drug abuse is a chronic relapsing condition, most treated drug users relapse, the best predictor of treatment success is time in treatment, even if coerced—did not change (e.g., Anglin and Hser 1990). What changed, and led to the drug court movement, was policy makers' decision to shift focus away from "most relapse" and toward "relapsing condition . . . time in treatment" (President's Commission on Model State Drug Laws 1993).

races. Those propositions, and laws enforcing them, were commonplace and widely accepted in the world into which 60-year-old Americans were born.

Examination of policies and practices that unnecessarily damage individuals' lives can demonstrate that they are not worth having. In the longer term, that demonstration may prove influential even if in the short term blind eyes cannot see and deaf ears cannot hear. In the long term, mandatory minimum sentence laws requiring sentences measured in decades, three-strikes and LWOP laws, and capital punishment will be as unthinkable in the United States as antimiscegenation laws are now. They are unthinkable now in most of the rest of the developed Western world.

II. Normative Analyses

Changing ideas about justice were an important part of the developments associated with the decline in support for indeterminate sentencing in the 1970s and with the initiatives adopted during the sentencing reform period from 1975 through the mid-1980s. In legal, philosophical, and policy worlds, utilitarian ideas were predominant in the English-speaking countries from the middle of the nineteenth century through the 1960s. For a time, in the 1970s and early 1980s, it appeared that retributivism might replace the utilitarian framework that long shaped policies and practices and the thinking of philosophers and other theorists. That did not happen.

The major tough-on-crime initiatives of the 1980s and 1990s neither implicitly nor explicitly took into account the interests of the offenders whose lives they affected. None of them is predicated on the retributive premise that responses to crime—if they are to be just—must take account of concerns about horizontal and vertical equity in the distribution of punishment. They do not honor the two utilitarian parsimony principles that punishments should not be more painful or intrusive than is necessary to achieve their preventive aims and that punishments are not justifiable if their aims can be achieved as well or better through other less-punitive means. Nor do they honor the utilitarian "least restrictive alternative" idea that the draftsmen of the Model Penal Code (1962) and the Model Sentencing Act (1972) regarded as fundamental.

The harshest contemporary laws prescribe prison sentences measured in decades and lifetimes. Drug laws often mandate sentences for minor trafficking offenses far longer than many imposed on violent and sexual offenders. Three-strikes laws typically require minimum 25-year sentences for a wide range of violent offenses but also for some property and drug offenses (Zimring, Hawkins, and Kamin 2001). LWOPs are often imposed for offenses other than murder (Ogletree and Sarat 2012, chap. 1). None of that can be squared with either the retributive proportionality principle or the utilitarian parsimony principle.

Failure to satisfy requirements of traditional frameworks for thinking about just punishments is not necessarily a fundamental defect if there is some other plausible set of normative justifications. It is conceivable—though unlikely, inasmuch as from Aristotle and Plato on no one has developed a third framework—that the severe and disproportionate burdens recent laws impose on offenders can be justified in other ways. No one, however, has offered any such justifications. Below I discuss what I call anormative theories of punishment, but as the term indicates these are not normative ideas about just punishments for individual offenders. They are political ideas about punishment that give no weight to offenders' interests.

Some people justify tough-on-crime policies on the basis that the public supports harsh sentencing laws or is morally affronted by drug use and trafficking. Others observe that criminal justice policies are often adopted primarily for expressive reasons (e.g., Garland 2001; Simon 2007). None of these assertions, however, address the question: How can we justify doing *that* to *this particular* offender? Both the traditional frameworks viewed that as the critical question.

From early in the nineteenth century until the 1970s, punishment theories, institutions, policies, and practices in the English-speaking countries were based largely on consequentialist ideas. The academic and real worlds lined up nicely. Practitioners and policy makers may not have read Cesare Beccaria (2007 [1764]), Jeremy Bentham (2008 [1830]), or Enrico Ferri (1921), or known who they were. Nonetheless, they were in broad agreement with them that the primary purpose of punishment is to minimize harms associated with crime and state responses to it. Most of the institutions that comprise contemporary criminal justice systems—penitentiaries, training schools, reformatories, probation, and parole—were invented in the nineteenth century and premised on the pursuit of that purpose (Allen 1981; Mennel 1983). So were individualized and indeterminate sentencing systems for dealing with adult offenders and the parens patrie rationale that long underlay the juvenile court (Platt 1969; Rothman 1971).

Near the end of that 150-year period, the Model Penal Code (1962) laid out a blueprint for the mother of all consequentialist punishment systems. Offenses were defined broadly and were categorized only into misdemeanors and three levels of felonies. Precise delineation of the seriousness of crimes was considered unimportant and unnecessary. The critical question was whether the defendant was guilty. Once that was determined, the judge was given broad discretion to decide what sentence to impose. Probation was available for any offense, including murder. If the judge believed that the maximum prison term authorized for a crime was too severe, he or she could sentence the offender as if he had been convicted of something less serious. If a prison sentence was ordered, the parole board decided when the prisoner would be released. The prison authorities could award and withdraw time off for good behavior. Consistent with the utilitarian principle of parsimony, presumptions were created to ensure that offenders were not punished more severely than was necessary: judges were directed not to send people to prison, and parole boards were directed to release inmates when they first became eligible, unless specified conditions existed to justify some other decision. Allusions to retributive ideas appear only three times, and faintly at that. Nonincarcerative penalties should not be imposed or inmates released on parole if doing so would "unduly depreciate the seriousness of the offense." One of the overall purposes of the code was to ensure that disproportionately severe punishments were *not* imposed (Tonry 2004).

Stop for a minute and think about that: retributive ideas were almost absent from the most influential American criminal law document of the twentieth century. The code was developed under the aegis of the American Law Institute, then and now the most prestigious law reform organization in the United States. Lawyers then could not (and still cannot) simply join. They had to be nominated by current members and approved by a membership committee; membership is widely considered a great honor, the capstone of a successful career, and ostensibly limited to people of great accomplishment. The code was developed over a 13-year period by a group of influential practitioners, including judges, prison commissioners, prosecutors, parole board heads, defense lawyers, and academics. Work was directed by Herbert Wechsler, America's leading academic criminal lawyer. Draft versions of sections were successively considered—and approved provisionally and then finally—at annual meetings of the American Law Institute. The voters were not primarily criminal lawyers or academics but mostly commercial and business lawyers and federal and state judges. The code was drafted and approved by people who were neither radicals nor woolly-headed intellectuals. They were midcentury America's most establishmentarian lawyers, together with a group of leading criminal justice practitioners, and they did not believe that retributivism and proportionality should be central considerations in sentencing.

If retributive ideas and instincts are so common, how can it be that they had so little influence on the Model Penal Code? The answer is that right-thinking people in the 1950s and 1960s believed that retributivism was atavistic. Harvard law professor Sheldon Glueck, a leading intellectual of indeterminate sentencing, observed decades earlier:

> The old argument was that punishment was necessary as a "just retribution" or requital of wickedness. No thoughtful person today seriously holds this theory of sublimated social vengeance, nor that "expiative theory" which is the reverse of the shield of retribution. (1928, p. 456)

Even if it was true that the appropriateness of retribution for crime was "the unstudied belief of most men," as Jerome Michael and Herbert Wechsler observed, that intuition was not enough (1940, p. 7). Conventional wisdom and commonly held intuitions can be wrong, as widely held beliefs in earlier times about racial inferiority, homosexuality, and gender roles demonstrate. That is what the drafters of the Model Penal Code believed. Retributive instincts were ignoble, and wrong. The conventional ways of thinking during the era of indeterminate sentencing, the zeitgeist, the prevailing sensibilities, rejected retribution and favored rehabilitation and to a lesser extent its consequentialist siblings deterrence and incapacitation.

In our time, by contrast, retributive ideas seem an inherent part of thinking about crime, even if they have had little recent influence on policy except in the vindictive sense that policy makers have generally preferred harsher punishments to milder ones. Social and experimental psychologists instruct that human beings are hardwired to react punitively to crime (Darley 2010). Evolutionary psychologists explain that natural selection favored human beings with that wiring; individuals with clear senses of right and wrong and willingness to act on them would, it is said, have been better community members and thereby fostered cohesion, increased the odds of community survival, and perpetuated the gene pool that predisposed people to be retributive (Robinson, Kurzban, and Jones 2007). Some influential modern philosophers of the criminal law argue that those punitive intuitions justify retributive punishment theories (Moore 1993).

Sensibilities, however, were changing when the American Law Institute released the completed Model Penal Code in 1962. The timing could not have been worse. Harbingers of discontent had already begun to appear (e.g., Lewis 2011 [1949]) and would reappear with increasing frequency (e.g., Burgess 1962; Allen 1964; Davis 1969). By the mid-1970s, dissatisfaction was widespread. Policy makers rejected many features of indeterminate sentencing and favored new approaches based on retributive ideas. Individualized, indeterminate sentencing was out. Retributive, determinate sentencing was in.

Whatever it was that changed policy makers' and practitioners' minds also influenced theorists. Consequentialism lost ground and influence. Retributivism came into vogue. In the 1950s, Norval Morris (1953), John Rawls (1955), and H. L. A. Hart (1959) attempted to reconcile general utilitarian rationales for punishment as an institution with retributive approaches in making decisions in individual cases. Herbert Morris (1966) and Jeffrey Murphy (1973) offered benefits-and-burdens theories which, a bit obscurely, argued that the gravamen of crime is obtaining unfair benefit from others' law-abidingness and that punishment should balance things out. John Kleinig (1973), in the first book about punishment with "desert" in its title, assessed the relevance of retributive considerations to the justificatory questions surrounding punishment. Joel Feinberg (1970) and Jean Hampton (1984) argued in different ways for expressive theories, and Herbert Morris (1981) and

Antony Duff (1986) for communicative ones. Michael Moore (1993) offered an intuitionist account. Among the criminal lawyers, Norval Morris (1974) elaborated his theory of "limiting retributivism," Alan Dershowitz (1976) his of "fair and certain punishment," and Andrew von Hirsch (1976) his of "just deserts." By the early 1980s, it was not unreasonable to believe that a corner had been turned and that policy makers, practitioners, and theorists would long march to the beat of distant retributive drums.

That did not happen except for a few years. In the late 1970s and the early 1980s, some legislatures enacted statutes meant to encourage proportionate sentences, and abolished parole release in order to assure that offenders served them. Sentencing commissions adopted guidelines based on retributive premises. The rhetoric of "just deserts" entered the political and policy lexicons in the United States and shortly thereafter in Australia, Canada, and England and Wales.[7]

The retributive moment in policy circles, however, quickly passed. Except in lip service, the aim to apportion punishments according to offenders' relative blameworthiness largely disappeared. Many of the sentencing laws enacted in the United States in the 1980s and 1990s, including mandatory minimum, three-strikes, truth-in-sentencing, and LWOPs, paid no heed to proportionality. Drug laws mandated sentences for street-level dealers far longer than those typically received by people convicted of serious assaults, robberies, rapes, and many homicides. Three-strikes laws mandated lengthy and life sentences for repeat property and drug offenders. LWOP laws allowed lifetime sentences for a wide range of crimes, including for first degree murder but also, in many states, for lesser offenses.

No plausible retributive theory would regard people who committed murders, manslaughters, rapes, and robberies as equally blameworthy, but that is how the many punitive laws treated them. All retributive theories regard disproportionately severe punishments for particular

[7] Minnesota's sentencing guidelines commission, for example, explicitly debated the choice between "just deserts" and "modified just deserts" as the rationale for the guidelines it promulgated in 1980 (this example and others are discussed in von Hirsch, Knapp, and Tonry [1987]). The Australian Law Reform Commission (1980), the Canadian Sentencing Commission (1987), and the Home Office of England and Wales (1990) each endorsed "just deserts" as a guide to policy making.

crimes to be unjust by definition, but legislators blithely enacted three-strikes laws that subjected murderers, robbers, rapists, burglars, shoplifters, auto thieves, and low-level drug sellers alike to mandatory minimum 25-year sentences.

If principled rationales were implied by developments such as these, the principles might have been said to be consequentialist—deterrence by means of threats of harsh punishment, incapacitation by means of lengthy periods of confinement, and moral education by means of the messages severe punishments ostensibly convey about right and wrong.[8] That claim, however cannot be made with a straight face. Both in former times and in ours, all mainstream normative theories of punishment include some version of Bentham's parsimony principle or Kant's absolute prohibition of disproportionately severe punishments (e.g., N. Morris 1974; Braithwaite 2001*b*).

New, less overtly punitive initiatives also pay little heed to those ideas. They focus on results, not on proportionality or parsimony. Drug courts, and other problem-solving courts targeting mentally ill offenders, domestic violence, and gun crimes, began in the early 1990s and by 2010 numbered in the thousands (Mitchell 2011). Drug courts are predicated on the beliefs that drug treatment can work, that drug dependence is causally related to offending, and that coerced treatment backed up by firm judicial monitoring can reduce drug dependence and use. Other problem-solving courts are based on parallel logics. Proponents of problem-solving courts regularly announce that they are influenced by ideas about therapeutic jurisprudence, a school of thought that urges incorporation of therapeutic ideas into legal doctrines and processes (Wexler 2008*a*, 2008*b*; Wexler and Winick 2003; Winick 1997, 2005). David Wexler (1995), its most influential proponent, however, insists that therapeutic jurisprudence is not a punishment theory at all but a series of policy prescriptions.

A vast recent literature on correctional treatment asserts that many kinds of treatment programs—for sex offenders; for drug-dependent

[8] Scandinavian punishment theorists point out that moral educative messages must respect proportionality concerns; otherwise the moral messages about what is more serious than what get muddled, which undermines rather than reinforces basic norms about right and wrong (e.g., Lappi-Seppälä 2011).

offenders; on anger management, cognitive skills training, vocational training—can reduce offending (MacKenzie 2006). Correctional managers in many countries including the United States are paying attention and incorporating treatment ideas and programs into probationary sentences, prison regimes, and prisoner reentry programs. A National Academy of Sciences committee recently summarized much of the evidence:

> Contrary to the commonly quoted conclusion that "nothing works," the evidence shows that some approaches work for some offenders and that other approaches show promise. Post release interventions that have shown measurable effects include treatment for substance abuse, especially when combined with frequent testing for drug abuse, and cognitive behavioral therapy. Comprehensive, multiservice employment and training programs and mentoring programs hold promise but require rigorous evaluation. (Petersilia and Rosenfeld 2007, p. 2)

In most developed countries, restorative justice programs are proliferating, sometimes as alternatives to the criminal justice system, sometimes as complements, sometimes as integral components. The governing logic is not treatment effectiveness or proportionality but reconceptualization of crime and responses to it (e.g., Braithwaite 2001*a*; Braithwaite and Pettit 2001). If crime is seen not only as wrongful behavior by an offender and harm to a victim but also as a problem to be solved, or a rupture in relations among offender, victim, and community, or a sign of social or community breakdown, the best solution cannot simply be to punish and stigmatize the offender. It should instead be to solve the problem, restore good relations, or rebuild civic institutions and community solidarity while acknowledging the offender's wrongdoing and the victim's needs.

The rationales of drug courts, correctional treatment programs, and restorative justice are not the same, and they are not the same as the rationales for mandatory minimum sentences, three-strikes laws, and LWOPs. What all these programs and policies share, however, is that they do not give much weight to proportionality in deciding what should be done in individual cases, to calibrating punishments to the gravity of the offender's wrongdoing.

III. Underexamined Policies

Except concerning restorative justice (e.g., Braithwaite and Pettit 1990, 2001), few efforts have been made to justify proportionality-defying punishments on the normative merits. Braithwaite and Pettit, like most writers on punishment theory, accept that concerns for proportionality should set upper bounds on responses to crime. Subject to that constraint, treating like cases alike is not a major objective. The overriding goals are a process that respects the interests of the victim, the offender, and the community, and achievement by unanimous agreement of a forward-looking plan for acknowledging wrongdoing, restoring or building relationships, and enhancing the offender's life chances. Restorative justice programs with those aims pose entirely different issues than do sentencing policies meant to require condign punishment.

Philosophers and other theorists have mostly denounced proportionality-defying punishments (e.g., von Hirsch and Ashworth 2005). Half-hearted attempts have been made to explain why concerns to protect offenders from disproportionately severe punishments have not influenced such policies. Typically they focus on repeat offenders. The English scholar Nigel Walker (1991) offered an outlaw argument: recidivists, through their obliviousness to community behavioral norms, forfeit any claim to have their liberty interests taken into account when punishment decisions are made. This is not unlike the logic of the medieval punishment of banishment, which deprived the banished of all claims on others, including the claim not to be killed. People who have been law-abiding enjoy an immunity from disproportionate punishment because of a presumption of harmlessness, but

> someone who has harmed or tried to harm another person can hardly claim a right to the presumption of harmlessness: he has forfeited that right, and given society the right to interfere in his life. . . . The justification [of the right to interfere] is not a duty based on retribution but the offender's forfeiture of an immunity. (Walker 1996, p. 7)[9]

[9] Walker throughout his career offered a consequentialist account of punishment, so it is fair enough that he did not worry greatly about proportionality. The forfeiture/immunity argument, however, on its face assumes that normative justification relating to severe treatment of the individual recidivist offender is required. That implicitly acknowledges that such punishments would otherwise be unjust.

Australian law professor Arie Freiberg offered as devil's advocate a social contract argument: "massive loss of liberty" following a third or subsequent offense "no longer has to be justified on the basis of the gravity of the precipitating offense . . . but can be justified simply on the basis that the implicit social contract has been fundamentally breached by the offender, thus bringing the contract to an end" (2001, p. 41; cf. Freiberg 2007).

Walker's and Freiberg's forfeiture arguments, however, are declamations, not theories. They do not explain whether proportionality is or is not an important consideration in punishing first offenders, whether loss of immunity or contractor status makes proportionality concerns completely irrelevant, or whether any limits exist. Most likely everyone agrees that there must be limits, and that capital punishment or LWOPs for tax evasion, shoplifting, prostitution, and possession of marijuana are excessive, even for recidivists. Most people would find many contemporary punishments for serious crimes to be disproportionately severe or unjustifiably intrusive if they or a loved one were subjected to them. It is always easier to endure suffering by strangers, but that reality provides no moral justification for disproportionately severe punishments.

Not much more attention has been paid to the general questions of whether and to what extent offenders should be punished more severely because they have offended before. To Americans, the answer is obvious that they should be, and a lot. Three-strikes laws offer an extreme example. Sentencing guidelines offer less extreme but less widely recognized examples. Under many sentencing guidelines systems, prior convictions can result in prison sentences two, three, or four times longer than would be imposed for a first offense (Reitz 2010). To Scandinavians, it is obvious that prior offenses ordinarily are irrelevant to punishments for new crimes and when they are relevant should not count for much (Asp 2010; Lappi-Seppälä 2011). To Brits and Australians, it is obvious that they should count some, but subject to tight limits (Lovegrove 1988, 1997; Baker and Ashworth 2010).

The widely divergent self-evident significance of prior convictions in the United States, the Scandinavian countries, England and Wales, and Australia shows that the subject is not self-evident. In the English-speaking countries, at least, almost everyone—judges, probation officers, ordinary citizens, offenders—shares an intuition that previous convictions justify imposition of a harsher punishment for the new crime (Roberts 2008), but no one has offered a good explanation why that intuition should be acted upon.

There have been a few wobbly attempts to justify the recidivist premium in retributivist terms (Bennett 2010; Lee 2010), but in the end they collapse into arguments that the additional punishment is justifiably predicated on either the offender's bad character or his or her defiance or disrespect of the court. Neither is easily reconciled with traditional liberal ideas. Bad character and rude behavior are not bases for convictions, much less punishments, of nonoffenders; it is hard to see why offenders should suffer for them. Andrew von Hirsch (2010) and others have argued that the increased punishment is not an increase at all but a "progressive loss of mitigation" of the deserved punishment that is granted to first or sometimes second or third offenders because their wrongdoing may have been primarily situational or out of character. All three arguments collapse into little more than rationalizations for an intuition that cannot otherwise be justified.

Consequentialists have a seemingly easier incapacitative or deterrent case to make, but it quickly runs into parsimony problems. The current state of the art of the evidence as assessed by the National Academy of Sciences Panel on the Causes and Consequences of High Rates of Incarceration does not demonstrate that contemporary crime control strategies have significant preventive effects:

> CONCLUSION: The increase in incarceration may have caused a decrease in crime, but the magnitude is highly uncertain and the results of most studies suggest it was unlikely to have been large.
>
> CONCLUSION: The incremental deterrent effect of increases in lengthy prison sentences is modest at best. Because recidivism rates decline markedly with age, lengthy prison sentences, unless they specifically target very high-rate or extremely dangerous offenders, are an inefficient approach to preventing crime by incapacitation. (Travis, Western, and Redburn 2014, p. 337)

The recidivist premium thus cannot be justified on consequentialist grounds either.

More fundamentally, the outlaw and recidivist premium theories implicitly make consideration of all the interests of offenders contingent. If prior convictions or serious crimes justify disregarding the interests of repeat offenders, presumably other circumstances could allow disregarding them for first offenders. Many mandatory minimum sentence laws for drug crimes do exactly that: they require much longer minimum sentences for first offenders than are imposed on other, including repeat, offenders convicted of more serious crimes. A series of examples follows of issues raised by recent policy initiatives that need exploring.

A. Three-Strikes, Mandatory Minimums, and LWOPs

Laws of these types nearly always defy conventional ideas about proportionality and parsimony. Theorists tend simply to denounce them. Even assuming that cases for such laws could sometimes be made on consequentialist grounds, analysis need not stop there. Distinctions need to be made. Washington State's pioneering three-strikes and sexual predator laws, for example, were drafted narrowly by people who worried about dangers of overbreadth (e.g., Boerner 1992). California's were not. As a result, Washington's laws potentially apply only to a handful of offenders each year, California's to many thousands.

Normative analyses of three-strikes, minimum sentence, and similar laws accordingly should consider first whether they can ever be justified and, if so, for what kinds of offenses and under what circumstances, and what lengths of sentences they may under different circumstances justly specify. Analyses should, however, also address whether there are some categories of offenders who should be contingently or always exempt from their coverage. Examples include the mentally handicapped, minors, people without prior convictions, people whose convictions are based on accessorial guilt or limited involvement, and defendants who raised excusing or mitigating defenses such as diminished capacity, self-defense, necessity, or duress for which there was some credible basis but that were or would have been unsuccessful at trial.

A developing literature on "empirical desert," which argues that criminal law doctrine and punishment policies should take account of widely held intuitions and beliefs, is germane (e.g., Robinson 2008). The fundamental claim is that citizens' perceptions of the legitimacy of state institutions and processes are influenced by the extent to which they reflect prevailing ideas about justice. Substantial evidence in the United States and elsewhere shows that ordinary citizens would support punishments much less severe than most judges impose or than severe modern laws require (e.g., Roberts et al. 2003; Gwin 2010). Public opinion studies show that representative samples of the public opposed the federal 100-to-1 law for crack and powder cocaine offenses when they learned that crack and powder cocaine are pharmacologically indistinguishable, that most crack dealers are black, and that black dealers typically received much longer prison sentences than white dealers (Bobo and Thompson 2006, 2010). Similar widely held beliefs disapprove of punishing drug dealers and property offenders more severely than rapists, robbers, assaulters, and burglars.

The problems of horizontal and vertical equity are especially acute for LWOPs. Many such laws were enacted with support from death penalty opponents on the supposition that they would serve as alternative punishments for people who might otherwise be sentenced to death. As enacted, however, many are applicable to other offenses. In 2012, nearly 50,000 people were serving LWOPs, many following convictions for offenses other than murder. In 8 states, more than a third of prisoners serving LWOPs had not been convicted of homicide. In Washington state, the figure was 54 percent (Nellis 2013). Even offenses committed by young offenders who cannot constitutionally be sentenced to death have resulted in LWOPs, including for nonhomicidal crimes, although the Supreme Court eventually declared that unconstitutional.

Three-strikes, LWOP, and mandatory minimum laws can be narrowly or broadly drawn and present greater or lesser problems of vertical equity when compared with laws governing sentences for other offenses. Unless they are subjected to searching normative analyses, all of these differences will continue to pass unnoticed and unjustified.

B. "Sexual Predator" and "Dangerous Offender" Laws

Every legal system has mechanisms for incapacitating people who are believed to be unacceptably dangerous to others. The most intellectually honest is to employ civil commitment procedures that authorize confinement of people who are determined on the basis of convincing clinical evidence to be unacceptably dangerous to themselves or others. Such a commitment must carry with it the possibility that committed individuals may later petition for release on the basis of clinical evidence that they are no longer dangerous. Under those circumstances they should, of course, be released.

Policy makers often are not willing to allow many violent and sexual offenders to be dealt with by mental health authorities. Approaches vary. The Netherlands and other European legal systems distinguish between "sanctions," which are deemed punishments and whose imposition should be guided by considerations of proportionality, and "measures," which can serve other including incapacitative purposes. People confined under measures receive indeterminate placements and are released when no longer deemed to need confinement (de Keijser 2011; cf. von Hirsch 2011). These laws are, however, seldom used to require lengthy confinement. The United States and England use "dangerous offender" and "sexual predator" laws that authorize extended confinement even after a prison sentence has expired (Frase 2011; Baker and Ashworth 2010).

Both approaches raise numerous normative issues. Why criminal law approaches rather than civil commitments? May any offense serve as the basis for such a disposition? In the Netherlands, drug-dependent repeat property offenders sometimes are confined on an indeterminate basis as measures for purposes of drug treatment, though seldom for more than 2 years. Under England's habitual offender law in the first half of the twentieth century, most of those indeterminately confined were chronic property offenders (N. Morris 1951). If the basis of confinement or continued confinement is a prediction that the offender will commit future crimes, not a conviction for past ones, must individuals affected be held in more congenial conditions than offenders serving sentences?

Like people quarantined because they have infectious diseases, people quarantined because they are believed to be unacceptably dangerous should be held in normal, comfortable living conditions subject only to controls on their movement. That is the German policy. The small number of offenders held in preventive detention because they are believed to be unacceptably dangerous have spacious, well-furnished private rooms; attractive and well-outfitted sports, crafts, and entertainment facilities; paid jobs; and opportunity to buy and cook their own meals.

Dangerous offender laws can operate like scalpels or like bludgeons. Scalpels are better. California's three-strikes law is a bludgeon, potentially applying to thousands of offenders each year. England's dangerous offender law is comparably broad (Jacobsen and Hough 2010). Washington State's sexual predator law, by contrast, is a scalpel, carefully drafted, in light of civil liberties concerns and dangers of overuse, to apply only to a small category of offenders (Boerner 1992). Finland's and Germany's dangerous offender laws also are scalpels, affecting only small numbers of cases (Lappi-Seppälä 2001, 2016; Weigend 2016).

A generation or two ago there was a robust literature on ethical issues posed by deterrent and incapacitative sentencing policies (e.g., N. Morris 1974; von Hirsch 1985; Tonry 1987). The issues, seldom discussed in recent decades, have not disappeared; they have been ignored. Only one of them—concerning whether previous convictions justify increased sentences for later offenses (the "recidivist premium")—has received recent attention (e.g., Roberts and von Hirsch 2010). One issue that needs revisiting is the problem of false positives; most prediction instruments for serious crimes have at least 2-in-3 false positive rates, meaning that most people held for incapacitative reasons would not have reoffended if they had been released (Morris 1974). A second is the use of ethically suspect prediction factors such as race, gender, age, marital status, class- and race-linked social variables such as education, employment record, and residential stability (Starr 2014).[10] A third is whether increased punishment on the basis of past crimes (a major factor in most prediction instruments) violates the ethical principles underlying the double jeopardy doctrine (Tonry 1987). A fourth is whether incapacitative punishments effectively constitute anticipatory punishments for crimes that would not have been committed if the offender was released (von Hirsch 1985).

[10] This is not a merely theoretical question. Virginia's sentencing guidelines direct judges to consider gender, age, and marital status in deciding whom to sentence to imprisonment (Virginia Criminal Sentencing Commission 2010). Gender, age, and marital status are strongly correlated with race, which means that they result in systematically more severe punishments of minority offenders (Starr 2014). In the 1970s and 1980s this was commonly seen as a prima facie reason not to include them in sentencing or parole release criteria or more generally as factors in prediction instruments (Gottfredson, Wilkins, and Hoffman 1978; Hoffman 1991).

C. Drug Courts and Other Rehabilitative Programs

Many rehabilitative programs fail both retributive and consequentialist tests. Offenders receive neither proportionate nor parsimonious handling. The issues requiring ventilation were familiar a generation ago (e.g., Allen 1959, 1981; N. Morris 1974). Can efforts to alter the personalities of offenders ever be justified? Can they be justified for some kinds of offenders but not others? Or in relation to some kinds of problems, needs, or deficits, but not others? C. S. Lewis was especially worried about interventions that attempt to change offenders' personalities: "To undergo all those assaults on my personality which modern psychotherapy knows how to deliver; to be re-made after some pattern of 'normality' hatched in a Viennese laboratory . . . —who cares whether this is called Punishment or not?" (Lewis 2011 [1949], p. 93). Lewis was worried about preoccupations of his time; in our time possibilities of chemical and electronic behavioral controls are even more worrying. The same worries apply to many kinds of changes contemplated by treatment programs. May participation be coerced overtly or by means of offers that are too good to be turned down ("Otherwise, it's off to prison for you")? In most settings, agreements made under threats are regarded as involuntary. How can we protect against overzealous, bigoted, or idiosyncratic exercises of the treaters' powers over the treated? How should concerns about misuse of power be balanced with treatment or crime-preventive aims? Must the burdens imposed by treatment programs satisfy proportionality or parsimony concerns (Husak 2011; O'Hear 2011)?

D. Restorative Justice

Restorative justice has received much more attention from punishment theorists than have rehabilitative programs or punitive sanctions for at least three reasons. First, it is largely a bottom-up development promoted by grassroots activists and largely operates outside or parallel to the criminal justice system. A large, multinational, and introspective community of activists and scholars promotes restorative justice, writes about it, and argues about it. Second, it springs from socially positive human instincts concerned, as the standard rhetoric proclaims, with rebuilding relationships among offenders, victims, and communities. One of its formative texts, John Braithwaite's *Crime, Shame, and*

Reintegration (1989), argues that the criminal justice system is ineffective and that its destructive shaming should be replaced by an emphasis on reintegration of offenders into communities, on solving problems that give rise to offending, and on empowering victims. This stands in stark contrast to policy and political arguments for punitive sanctions which turn offenders into nameless, faceless stereotypes. Third, its proponents have generated a body of theoretical writing to which others can respond (e.g., Braithwaite and Pettit 1990, 2001; Walgrave 2008).

Not surprisingly, a sizable literature explores normative dimensions of restorative justice programs, as well as differences between retributive and restorative approaches (e.g., Robinson 2003; von Hirsch et al. 2003). Much of it has consisted of attempts to reconcile restorative processes with proportionality concerns. Other recurring issues concern whether restorative processes should be independent of the justice system or incorporated within it, whether programs should be available for all offenses or only for some, and how to assure that offenders do not suffer unduly from the absence of procedural and evidentiary protections afforded by the justice system (Walgrave 2008).

III. Imagining the Future

No one knows what American attitudes toward punishment will be like in 2025. In 2015, sentencing laws and practices are extraordinarily severe compared with those in other countries. Whether retributivism, or punishment theories more generally, will have a role to play in 2025 outside classrooms and academics' offices remains to be seen. Philosophers and other theorists of punishment have remarkably little to say that is useful or illuminating about contemporary American sentencing laws and practices, the proliferation of restorative and community justice programs, or the widespread revival of coercive correctional treatment programs. They should. If the time comes, as no doubt it will, when policy makers seriously reconsider contemporary approaches and attempt to devise new ones, some at least will look for theoretical critiques of the recent past and normative justifications for possible futures. It will be a pity if the work has not been done to help them.

The following chapter sets out a normative framework for reinventing American sentencing systems so that they less often do harm and more often do justice. Doing that will require broadly shared understandings of what justice requires. It is difficult to find much justice in the laws enacted during the tough on crime period, but there are things to learn from the indeterminate sentencing and sentencing reform periods that preceded it. Indeterminate sentencing's aspiration to tailor sentences to offenders' circumstances and needs warrants emulation. So does the parsimonious principle of trying to avoid unnecessarily severe or intrusive punishments. The sentencing reform aims of the 1970s and early 1980s—official accountability, procedural fairness, transparency, and rationality—are inherent parts of any system that makes decisions about important interests of individuals.

5

Sentencing Principles

MOST OF THIS BOOK CONCERNS empirical evidence, practical experience, and analysis of policy choices concerning the punishment of convicted criminals. The subjects covered are deeply rooted in American history, culture, and institutions, so much so that it can be difficult to distinguish between fundamentals and serendipity. American prison sentences, for example, are exceedingly long by international standards, often measured in decades and lifetimes. Sentences of 2 or 5 or 7 years are commonplace. Many Americans assume that current practices are in the nature of things: "Serious crimes deserve serious punishments."

Most people in all countries no doubt believe that, but in most other Western countries notions of what counts as a serious punishment are very different, as table 1.3 showed. Prison sentences as long as a year are unusual, longer than 5 years are exceedingly rare, and longer than 20 years are almost unheard of. In many countries, they are not legally possible. In much of continental Europe, the longest nominal lawful sentence for any single crime is 12, 15, or 20 years, sometimes but not always with an exception for murder. Time spent in prison is usually at least a third less.

In Finland, during a recent period of heightened emphasis on crimes against women, the normal sentence for rape was raised from 18 to 24 months (12 to 16 months after automatic reduction for remission). There was considerable controversy about politicization of sentencing policy. Many believed the new norm to be disproportionately severe compared with punishments for other comparably serious crimes (Lappi-Seppälä and Tonry 2011, p. 28). Most Americans probably think 2 years or 16 months surprisingly slight.

I mention this example not to discuss optimal lengths of prison sentences but to demonstrate that what we are accustomed to powerfully shapes what we believe to be normal or right or possible. Human beings are inherently ethnocentric. We know our own lives and environments and measure new things in light of that experience. It is almost inevitable. Spend time in another country with someone who has traveled little and listen to how often things are criticized or commented on because they seem strange—which often simply means different from home. That mentality usually changes in people who have traveled often and to many places. What at first seems strange often turns out, on reflection, to be just another way of doing something.

We can't ever completely escape the influence of our background and experience. We can't somehow see things from a neutral, independent perspective. The American philosopher Thomas Nagel (1986) observed that there is no "view from nowhere." We are somewhere, and where we stand affects what we can see.

Even so, like a traveler who has been in many countries, we can try to look at things in broader perspectives than usual and in light of a diversity of experiences and examples. In this section, I provide a general sketch of what a just system for punishing criminals would look like if informed by widely shared post-Enlightenment ideas and developed from scratch. It has four main, remarkably simple but often not observed, elements:

- *Justice as Fairness*: Processes for responding to crimes should be publicly known, implemented in good faith, and applied evenhandedly.
- *Justice as Equality*: Defendants and offenders should be treated as equals; their interests should be treated with respect and concern when decisions affecting them are made.
- *Justice as Proportionality*: Offenders should not be punished more severely than can be justified by their blameworthiness or the gravity of their offenses relative to the severity of punishments justly imposed on others for the same and other offenses.
- *Justice as Parsimony*: Offenders should not be punished more severely than can be justified by valid, normatively based purposes for which they are being punished.

The sketch is not of any country's current system. Each evolved in its own way, which affects what people see as desirable, natural, or essential. Among Western countries American sentencing least fully complies with these four principles.

Political philosophers since John Locke in seventeenth-century Scotland have agreed that one main function of the state is to maintain order and provide conditions of security and stability that enable citizens to plan and live the lives they choose. The criminal law and its institutions are not the only, or the most important, sources of order. Basic social institutions like the family, the church, the school, the community, and the workplace do the heavy lifting of inculcating and reinforcing social norms and values. Many European judges, public officials, and scholars believe that the criminal law's functions are inherently residual, backing up the primary sources of order. Many Americans believe that the criminal law's instrumental functions are more important than that, and that criminal sanctions significantly shape people's choices and behavior.

For my purposes here, there is no need to choose between those views. Criminal events occur in every country. Responding to them in ways that enhance order and reinforce important norms is a core state responsibility. Every country has created institutions to do that.

My interest is in how the criminal law and its institutions can be designed and used to reinforce basic social norms and influence behavior while respecting the interests and human rights of individuals caught in the arms of the criminal law. The four principles provide a framework. Ordinarily discussions of punishment theory center on ideas about proportionality and parsimony. I begin instead with other principles that should underlie any criminal justice system that respects core Western values. Two recently deceased American philosophers, John Rawls and Ronald Dworkin, showed the way.

I. Fairness

John Rawls in his 1971 *A Theory of Justice*, the most influential book on political philosophy of the past half century, provided a metaphor for thinking about the conditions of justice in a free society. He imagined a deliberative device, which he called the original position, in which representative people would design the characteristics and institutions of a just society. They would deliberate behind a veil of ignorance, by which he meant that they would have general knowledge of human nature and institutions but would not know what kinds of people they themselves were or would be. If the deliberators knew that, they would consciously and unconsciously be tempted to support arrangements to the advantage of people like themselves. Rawls's deliberators thus would not know whether they would be of any particular race, ethnicity, nationality, or religion; of any particular sexuality or gender; rich or poor; smart or stupid; healthy or unhealthy; materialistic, artistic, or spiritual. The object was to create conditions in which deliberations, arguments, and conclusions about justice would not be self-interested.

Rawls's book addressed many subjects and catalyzed an enormous critical literature. I draw from it only one theme, "justice as fairness," which was also the title of one of his most influential articles (1958). It is a simple though powerful idea, known to all American lawyers who have pondered the meaning of the constitutional guarantee of "due process of law." It is simply that rules or laws should be known and knowable, that procedures should be consistently and evenhandedly applied, that processes should be transparent, and that the identity of the person affected should not matter. Turned into an aphorism, the claim might be that "without fairness there can be no justice."

II. Equality

Ronald Dworkin (1986) observed that the legal concept of equality requires that all people be accorded "equal respect and concern." Commitment to a legal concept of equality cannot possibly literally require equal treatment, he said, that all people be treated in the same way in all circumstances, or even that all people of particular relevant characteristics be treated in the same way. Objectives, salient characteristics, resource limitations, policy considerations, and imperfect knowledge necessarily justify differentiation between cases. Equality, Dworkin said, should be conceptualized not as a right to equal treatment but to "treatment as an equal." This requires that individuals and their interests be treated with equal respect and concern. Individuals are not entitled to particular outcomes, but are entitled to fair consideration of their claims under criteria that are known and substantively defensible.

He was writing about challenges to affirmative action programs in higher education that aimed to increase the admission of black and other minority applicants. Rejected white applicants with the same or stronger academic records and Law School Admission Test scores than some admitted minority applicants filed lawsuits alleging denial of equal treatment. Dworkin insisted that their applications deserved fair consideration. The critical question, however, concerned not their qualifications but the criteria under which they were evaluated. He considered the substantive reasons why universities wanted to increase the participation of members of minority groups. He concluded that they were sufficiently convincing in that place and that time to justify use of criteria meant to increase the numbers of minority students. Since the additional criteria were valid, white applicants had no basis for complaint when their applications were rejected. Their applications had been considered with equal respect and concern under all the relevant criteria, and been rejected on the merits.

What is important is the proposition that fundamental ideas about equality require that people be treated as equals, which in turn requires that their interests be treated with equal respect and concern. In the criminal justice system at its best, this takes the form of individualizing decisions about individuals to take account of ethically and morally salient differences between cases, One may agree or disagree with Dworkin's conclusions about the substantive case for affirmative action in higher education and yet agree that the kind of process and the kind of analysis he describes are important if individuals are to be treated fairly. The key questions should always be whether the criteria for decisions are justifiable and, if so, whether they have been fairly applied.

Values of justice as fairness and justice as equality should be respected in the handling of all criminal cases at all times. An unfair process or procedure or a failure to accord respect and concern to a person's interests are objectionable whenever and at whatever stage they occur. In a sense these values can be thought of as horizontal, affecting every case at any stage.

Sentencing and punishment, by contrast, raise issues that might be thought of as vertical. They concern the ways and the extent to which appropriately convicted offenders should or may be treated differently in relation to a vertical scale of increasingly severe punishments.

Two core ideas recur—that punishment should be proportionate to the seriousness of the crime, the offender's blameworthiness, or valid objectives sought to be achieved, and that punishments should be no more severe than can be justified in relation to the system's underlying normative rationales. These are the principles of proportionality and parsimony that were discussed in chapter 4. Although it is customary to associate proportionality with retributive theories and parsimony with consequentialist ones, conceptions of both principles are part of every mainstream punishment theory.

III. Proportionality

The term "proportionality" is commonly associated with retributive views deriving from the writings of Immanuel Kant and Georg Wilhelm Friedrich Hegel. Retributivists differ on details but agree on the core propositions that offenders should be punished because for moral reasons that is the right thing to do and that punishments must or at most may be proportioned to the seriousness of the offender's crime. "Positive" retributivists believe that offenders must be punished as much as they deserve, and neither more nor less (e.g., Robinson 1987*b*; M. S. Moore 1993). "Negative" retributivists believe that offenders may be punished as much as they deserve, but never more, but need not be punished that severely (e.g., Mackie 1982; Duff 1986).

Failing to respect proportionality concerns undermines the moral bases of the criminal law. If, for example, shoplifting were punished more severely than robbery or rape, the law on its face would send the perverse message that shoplifting is the most serious of the three offenses and that people who commit it deserve greater blame and harsher punishment. That is morally incoherent and incompatible with nearly all people's views of the relative seriousness of those harmful behaviors.

Proportionality, however, is not only a retributive value, but also appears in two forms in consequentialist theories. Modern consequentialist theories differ in details but agree on the core propositions that punishments must be justified by their beneficial effects and should not be more severe than is required to achieve those effects.

Classical utilitarians like Jeremy Bentham believed that punishment can be justified only to the extent that the suffering experienced by offenders is offset by greater suffering by others that will be prevented. This in substance is a consequentialist parallel to negative retributivism: the not-to-be-exceeded limit is set not by blameworthiness or offense seriousness but by preventive effects. Punishments not justified by prevention of greater sufferings by others are "wicked" because they impose suffering for no good purpose.

Supporters of restorative justice, a contemporary consequentialist view, explicitly adopt a form of negative retributivism. For them, the important objectives of organized responses to crime are to repair broken or damaged relations among the victim, the offender, and the community while treating offenders and victims with respect and concern. If restorative processes culminate in unanimous agreements among participants for substantially different consequences in comparable cases, so be it. Proportionality is not fundamentally important to them, relative either to offense severity or to case resolutions in other similar cases. But there is a human-rights limit: the upper bound of proportionate sentences the justice system might appropriately impose on retributive grounds (Braithwaite and Pettit 1990; Braithwaite and Pettit 2001).

Bentham, the archetypal consequentialist, proposed substantive proportionality limits on punishments imposed for utilitarian reasons. For Bentham the primary means of crime prevention was deterrence. The primary aim is to avoid human suffering by preventing crime. If that cannot be done, the secondary aim is to minimize suffering. Utilitarian theory is premised on a model of rational calculation that Bentham called the "felicific calculus." Penalties should provide incentives to commit less rather than more serious crimes. Punishment should be greater for a completed crime than for an attempted one to provide an incentive to discontinue, and conversely an increment of additional punishment for carrying through. Punishment should be greater for robbery than for theft or shoplifting, in order to provide incentive to commit the less serious offenses, and for murder than for robbery to provide a disincentive to kill the robbery victim. Punishing shoplifters more severely than robbers or rapists would create perverse disincentives.

Some people, probably most, subscribe to mixed theories in which punishments may be justified by their crime-preventive effects, but only so long as they do not exceed what would be justified by considering only the seriousness of the crime. This is a form of negative retributivism.

Retributive considerations provide outer limits, but anticipated crime-preventive effects may be taken into account in deciding what to do within them (e.g., N. Morris 1974; Frase 2013).

Proponents of the severe sentencing laws of the 1980s and 1990s probably did not think at all about issues of proportionality, in either the retributive moral responsibility sense or the consequentialist rational incentives sense. Alternatively, they may have been motivated by some implicit notion that proportionality does not matter in punishing drug, violent, and repeat offenders. That's tantamount to saying that notions of justice are irrelevant to the criminal law.

IV. Parsimony

Consequentialist theories necessarily encompass what Bentham called frugality—the proposition that no punishment is justifiable if more severe than necessary to achieve the sought-after preventive effect. Parsimony for Bentham encompassed two separate ideas, each providing a reason to limit punishment. Each is predicated on the proposition that causing suffering to anyone, including offenders in the name of punishment, is an evil to be avoided (Frase 2009*a*).

The alternative-means test requires that there be no less costly way to achieve the sought-after preventive goal. No punishment may properly be imposed if some other method would do as well or better. If, for example, automobile theft can more effectively be prevented by requiring installation of ignition locks than through the deterrent effects of criminal sanctions, the case for reliance primarily on sanctions cannot be made. A similar analysis would forbid imprisonment of most drug-dependent offenders, since there has long been convincing evidence that drug treatment costs less than imprisonment and is more effective in reducing both drug use and offending (Anglin and Hser 1990; Chandler, Fletcher, and Volkow 2009; National Institute on Drug Abuse 2014).

The ends-benefits test requires that the victim suffering sought to be avoided by punishment be greater than the pains the offender would experience by its imposition. If not, punishment cannot be justified. Extreme examples of sentences that violate the ends-benefits test are unfortunately common in the United States. They include, for example, every property offender sentenced to a minimum 25-year sentence under California's three-strikes law. They also include the vast majority of people sent to prison under lengthy sentences for drug possession or sales, including by definition those who were drug-dependent.

Bentham's is a conceptual framework. The calculations required present insuperable challenges. Measuring and then weighing the suffering avoided for would-have-been victims of prevented crimes and that of punished offenders is impossible in relation to individual cases. Suffering is intangible, and it is impossible to know whether any crimes would be prevented, and if so how many. The challenges at an aggregate level are no fewer. The framework is nonetheless important because it focuses attention on the moral need to avoid needless suffering.

Economists have attempted to make such calculations, but the end product is seldom useful. The American literature on costs and benefits of imprisonment, for example, has mostly been ideologically motivated to justify the use of imprisonment (e.g., M. A. Cohen 1988, 2005). As a result, the estimated costs of crime to victims are typically enormous, because they include inflated estimates of the intangible costs of "pain and suffering."[1] Estimates of costs of imprisonment by contrast are typically understated because they include no estimates of the intangible costs of offenders' experience of imprisonment or of its collateral effects on social service budgets, prisoners' families and children, or ex-prisoners' reduced employment prospects, lifetime earnings, and life expectancies. If the full costs of imprisonment were estimated and taken into account and uninflated estimates of intangible suffering were used, imprisonment for most public order, prostitution, drug, and property crimes, and many violent crimes, would seldom pass the ends-benefits test.

Parsimony is generally associated with Bentham (1970 [1789]), or in modern America with Norval Morris (1974), and with consequentialist

[1] "Pain and suffering" estimates were originally based on jury damage awards in contested personal injury lawsuits (M. A. Cohen 1988). Such cases—typically involving all or some of horrific crimes, sympathetic victims, and deep-pocketed defendants—are inherently unrepresentative of the mine-run of cases and generate exaggerated estimates of the costs of crime. A more recent "contingent valuation" method asks research subjects how much they would be willing to pay in higher taxes or insurance premiums to reduce the incidence of crime Y by a designated amount, often 10 percent. Simple calculations are then made to determine the costs of crimes. No one has offered a convincing explanation for why or how the numbers generated relate to anything in the real world.

and hybrid theories generally. The same idea, however, is fundamental in all mainstream retributivist theories, whether positive or negative. Parsimony for retributivists relates not to things that are empirically measurable but to moral notions of desert. No punishment is justifiable if it exceeds the deserved proportionate punishment, or the upper bound of morally justifiable deserved punishments. Anything more is gratuitous and unjustifiable.

V. Commonality

The preceding four principles are not controversial. Both retributive and consequentialist theories of punishment support them, albeit sometimes for different reasons. Retributivists and most consequentialists endorse the *principle of proportionality*, insisting that just punishments be proportioned to offenders' blameworthiness. Retributivists regard this as a categorical imperative, a fundamental requirement of justice. Utilitarians believe punishments must be scaled to the seriousness of crimes because only in this way would rational would-be offenders be given incentives to commit less rather than more serious crimes (e.g., theft rather than robbery or rape). Restorative justice advocates believe that proportionality concerns set upper limits on punishments. Many people believe that proportionate sentences are intuitively more credible in the eyes of citizens. People who regard the legal system as legitimate because it reflects prevailing notions of right and wrong are more likely to comply with its demands (Robinson 2008).

Both retributivists and consequentialists support the *principle of parsimony*. They use different words for it and mean different things by it, deriving from their respective notions of justice in punishment, but they agree that punishments that exceed what their version of that notion justifies are inherently unjust. Retributivists believe that any punishment more severe than can be justified by the seriousness of the crime is by definition unjust. Consequentialists believe that infliction of suffering on offenders can be justified only by equal or greater reduction of suffering by others. Any punishment that cannot be justified in that way, or that is more severe than is necessary to achieve valid goals, is by definition unjust.

Both retributivists and consequentialists believe in the *principle of fairness*. Procedural regularity is for both an essential precondition to any just process that can result in state intrusion into individuals' lives. Retributivists believe that respect for human beings' moral autonomy is a first principle. The capacity for moral choice is what makes us human; punishment attaches consequences to actions for which individuals are morally responsible. Since the nature of the act and the extent of the actor's blameworthiness determine the amount of punishment that is deserved, getting the facts right necessarily requires fair processes and procedures.

Consequentialists also believe there must be good reasons for the state to interfere in individuals' lives. Even though Bentham denounced the idea of human rights as an empty concept, he repeatedly indicated in specific contexts that the state in the name of crime prevention cannot intervene in peoples' lives except when they have brought it upon themselves. Otherwise, people should be left alone. For example, he did not believe the insane should be punished because they lacked normal capacities to regulate their behavior. He would forbid punishment of people who were ignorant of the law they violated and of people who, because of drunkenness, lacked capacity to control their behavior. Getting the facts right is critical to determining who should and should not be punished. That requires fair processes and procedures.

Both retributivists and consequentialists believe in the *principle of equality*, that punishments should reflect consideration of the circumstances of individual offenders. Both call for individualization of punishments, retributivists to assure proportionality, consequentialists to assure effectiveness. Many retributivists believe that all the circumstances of the crime and all the characteristics of the offender must be taken into account if a valid assessment is to be made of his or her blameworthiness or culpability; Nigel Walker (1991) called this the "Recording Angel's" perspective. Even Kant discussed ways that punishments could be individualized to reflect the offender's individual circumstances. He wrote, for example, that a wealthy person who committed a crime for which a poor man might be fined might be imprisoned in harsh conditions so that the burdens of punishment would be comparable. Consequentialists believe in individualization because the optimal preventive sanction or package of sanctions cannot be determined without taking into account the risks and needs presented by each offender.

Proponents of retributive and consequentialist views seldom look for commonalities but instead focus on abstract differences. When, however, commonalities are sought, as I have done here, they emerge. That does not mean, of course, that proponents of the two ways of thinking do not differ in important respects. They do, most fundamentally in their starting points. Retributivists see punishment as morally deserved and a Good Thing. Consequentialists see punishment as a Bad Thing, justifiable only when it achieves net reductions in human suffering. That difference in the end may imply important differences in how individual cases are dealt with. Nonetheless, when the implications in real life of the two ways of thinking about punishment are considered, the four common principles, the four common characteristics of a process of penal justice, emerge. Processes must be fair, offenders must be treated as equals, and punishments must be parsimonious and proportioned to the seriousness of crimes.

The four principles together embody the best features of indeterminate and determinate sentencing. Individualization and parsimony were fundamental themes of indeterminate sentencing: punishment should optimally address the individual offender's circumstances and never be more severe than is necessary to achieve its aims. Indeterminate sentencing was weakest on fairness and proportionality. Decisions were seldom governed by established, published rules, and appeals from them were seldom available. In principle, even offenders convicted of trifling crimes could be held indefinitely.

Many initiatives during the sentencing reform period sought to address those weaknesses. Proportionality and fairness were fundamental themes. Official accountability, transparency, and consistency were key objectives. Parsimony and pursuit of equal treatment through individualization received less emphasis. Arie Freiberg (2001) observed that the new systems, because often too rigid and mechanical, risked replacing the old problem of unwarranted, unjust disparities with a new problem of unwarranted, unjust parities.

During the tough on crime period, all four principles were eclipsed by policy makers' emphases on pursuit of personal, political, and expressive goals. Three-strikes laws, LWOPs, mandatory minimums, and many truth-in-sentencing laws paid no heed to any of them. In the next chapter, I set out proposals for twenty-first-century sentencing systems that acknowledge them all.

American sentencing systems must be reconstituted so that they less often do harm and more often do justice. It is difficult to find much justice in many of the laws enacted during the tough on crime period, but there are things to learn from the indeterminate sentencing and sentencing reform periods that preceded it. Indeterminate sentencing's aspiration to treat offenders as equals by tailoring sentences to their personal circumstances and characteristics warrants emulation. So does the parsimonious principle of trying to avoid unnecessarily severe or intrusive punishments. The sentencing reform aims of the 1970s and 1980s, with their emphases on fairness and proportionality, are inherent parts of any sentencing system which aspires to be just. All four of the principles of punitive justice matter.

6

Sentencing Futures

MASS INCARCERATION NEEDS TO BE unwound and prevented from recurring. This can happen only if fundamental changes are made in sentencing laws, institutions, policies, and practices. At rhetorical levels at least, there appears to be broad agreement that mass incarceration was a huge mistake. It has been much less effective at preventing crime than many people envisioned; it does huge damage to offenders, their families, and their communities; it wastes vast amounts of money. And, not unimportantly, it gives and has long given America bad press throughout the world.

In the 1950s and 1960s, the American criminal justice system was a model for the countries of Europe as they rebuilt their legal systems after World War II and to the leaders of newly independent countries emerging from colonialism in Africa, Asia, and Latin America. American advisors and ideals played major roles in the development of the UN's Universal Declaration of Human Rights (1948), the European Convention on Human Rights (1950), and aspirational documents around the globe. The same impulses were manifested within the United States in the Model Penal Code (1962), the Model Sentencing Act (1963), and the reports of the national crime commissions of the 1960s and early 1970s.

In recent decades, the United States has served as an object lesson of all the things that can go wrong when criminal justice systems become deeply enmeshed in partisan politics, ideological conflict, and public emotion. They should be reconstructed in ways that make them once again sources of pride, beacons for all the world to admire and emulate.

Institutions and processes need to be rebuilt so that they reflect and live up to fundamental Western ideas about justice and fairness. The moral responsibility, human dignity, interests, and needs of defendants and offenders should be restored to their place at the center of the criminal justice system. People's freedom, property, reputations, and lives are at stake. Everything the criminal justice system does should acknowledge that. That does not mean, of course, that victims' interests or state interests in security and crime prevention should be ignored. They are important, but there is no zero-sum game. Treating offenders unjustly does not honor victims, affirm moral values, or make a safer society.

Sentencing systems must be redesigned to allow individualized consideration not only of offenses but also of offenders' personal characteristics and circumstances. Policy initiatives of the 1980s and 1990s made that impossible. They need to be repealed and replaced with new laws and institutions that allow judges and corrections officials to respond, justly and appropriately, to wrongdoing, as most have always wanted to do.

There are good reasons, including the widespread belief that current policies are cruel, wasteful, and counterproductive, to hope that American criminal justice policies will return to the mainstream of those in Western countries as they were before the 1980s. If that happens, crime will once again be seen as a regrettable but inevitable feature of human life to which the state must respond, in ways that are proportionate and humane, acknowledge wrongdoing, reinforce moral values, and help offenders reestablish good lives for themselves and their loved ones. Responses to crime should once again reflect the Judeo-Christian credo, and I assume those of most faiths, that sins should be hated but sinners loved.

American sentencing and corrections systems too often treat individuals unfairly. They too often result in severe punishments that bear no relation to the seriousness of the crimes for which they are imposed. They too often do unnecessary damage to offenders and their children and their prospects for living satisfying, law-abiding lives. They do not express respect and concern for the people whose lives are at stake.

American sentencing and corrections systems are wasteful and ineffective. Those are reasons to redesign them, but not the most important reasons. A new correctional subindustry flying the flag of "justice reinvestment" promotes laws aimed simultaneously at saving money and reducing recidivism. Both are worthy goals, but the changes made in their name have so far only nibbled at the edges of the problems and left in place the laws and institutions that produced mass incarceration and its unhappy effects. Until they are changed, none of the fundamental wrongs will be righted.

Numerous, but mostly meager, changes have been made. Prosecutors and other practitioners have moderated some practices. The scope of some sentencing laws has been slightly narrowed; standards for parole release eligibility have been slightly broadened; criteria for parole and probation revocation have become less rigid; prisoner reentry programs have been created; treatment programs have been expanded. None of the major tough-on-crime legislation of the 1980s and 1990s, however, has been repealed.

Even the few ballyhooed changes have been modest. The conversion of the federal 100-to-1 crack cocaine sentencing law to a still unjust 18 to 1 is one example. Limited amendments to New York's Rockefeller Drug Law are another. Former US Attorney General Holder's announcement that low-level, nonviolent federal prisoners who had already served 10 years in prison and had no significant criminal history would be considered for commutations is a third.

No legislature, however, has repealed a three-strikes, life-without-parole (LWOP), or truth-in-sentencing law or created a broad-based mechanism for assessing the need for continued confinement of people serving long prison terms. Except in Michigan in 2002, no legislature has repealed all or most of its mandatory minimum sentence laws. Until these things happen, nothing substantial will change. Mass incarceration will continue. The United States will remain an outlier among Western nations.

Few politicians are yet willing to acknowledge publicly that many of the laws enacted in 1984–96 were unjust and unwise. The cases to be made for major changes are moral ones, not politically risk-averse claims about minor and first-time offenders, cost-savings, and recidivism reduction. Citizens voted for referenda to legalize marijuana, authorize its medical use, and narrow California's three-strikes laws because they were right things to do. Judges weakened the federal sentencing guidelines and California's three-strikes law because the guidelines and the law were unjust. Initiatives to roll back mass incarceration and rebuild American sentencing systems must be justified in those terms.

This chapter explains what must be done. It has four main sections. The first explains why the case for change must in large part be made on normative grounds. The laws and policies that produced mass incarceration were adopted because policy makers believed or said they believed that to be the right thing to do and not simply because they were cost-effective or crime-reductive. The argument that must be made is that the status quo is unjust, cruel, and needlessly destructive.

The second section discusses the formidable body of evidence that shows that the policies that led to mass incarceration could not be justified in crime prevention terms when they were enacted and cannot be justified now. To the extent that they were predicated on the beliefs that lengthy prison sentences and mandatory minimum sentence, LWOP, three-strikes, and truth-in-sentencing laws are effective or cost-effective preventers of crime, they were misconceived.

The third lays out concrete steps that need to be taken. Judges impose sentences, but that is the last step in a process that begins with legislatures' criminalization of behavior and includes the discretionary decisions of police and prosecutors. The proposals thus include changes in criminal codes and police and prosecution practice. They include repeal of most or all the severe sentencing laws enacted in the 1980s and 1990s, creation of sentencing commissions and presumptive guidelines systems, enactment of new statutory constraints on judges' sentencing authority, and reestablishment or revivification of parole boards and parole release.

The fourth section concerns measures needed to roll back mass incarceration. That will not happen for many decades unless systems are created that allow for reconsideration of the need for continued confinement, and major reductions in sentence lengths, of people locked up in prisons. Marc Mauer and Nazgol Ghandnoosh (2013) observed that if the American prison population declines by 1.8 percent per year, as it did in 2012, it will take 89 years to reach even the 1980 level, and that was nearly double the rate in 1973 when the increase began. The changes in sentencing laws and policies proposed in section III will reduce the flow of people into prisons and shorten the time they spend there, but will not substantially reduce the number of people already in prison in 2020. Imprisonment rates rose for 16 years after American crime rates began their historic decline in 1991, and in 2015 there were only a few thousand fewer people in prison than the all-time high. Sentence lengths in the United States became so great that inmates simply accumulated. Many people were admitted to prison to serve 25 year, life, and LWOP sentences under laws enacted in the 1980s and 1990s. Few of them have yet been released because their sentences have expired.

Taken together, the proposals illustrate in some detail what just systems of American sentencing would look like. They incorporate the best features of the indeterminate systems that existed in all 50 states and the federal system from the 1930s to the mid-1970s and of the short-lived sentencing reform period that immediately followed it. A just system would be based on the four principles of punitive justice discussed in chapter 5:

- *Justice as Fairness*: Processes for responding to crimes should be publicly known, implemented in good faith, and applied evenhandedly.
- *Justice as Equality*: Defendants and offenders should be treated as equals; their interests should be treated with respect and concern when decisions affecting them are made.
- *Justice as Proportionality*: Offenders should not be punished more severely than can be justified by their blameworthiness or the gravity of their offenses relative to the severity of punishments justly imposed on others for the same and other offenses.
- *Justice as Parsimony*: Offenders should not be punished more severely than can be justified by valid, normatively based purposes for which they are being punished.

Those are not airy-fairy propositions. They describe what any person would want for themselves or their loved ones if accused or convicted of crime. They are minimal requirements of justice.

I. Moral Values

Fundamental change will occur only when it becomes widely accepted that the policies that led to mass incarceration are morally wrong. A handful of liberal reform advocates have long said this. Many of the spokesmen for Right on Crime now also say it. In 2014, former House majority leader Newt Gingrich and Van Jones wrote: "It would be hard to overstate the scale of this tragedy. For a nation that loves freedom and cherishes our rights to life, liberty and the pursuit of happiness, the situation should be intolerable. It is destroying lives and communities." Other prominent conservatives whom I quoted in chapter 1, along with many liberals, say similar things.

Some conservative critics of the status quo, however, make no such admission. Instead they propose new policies for nonviolent offenders, say that current policies cost too much, and promote policies aimed primarily at saving money and reducing recidivism. Former Texas governor Rick Perry observed, "There are thousands of non-violent offenders in the system whose future we cannot ignore." Former drug czar William Bennett declared: "Conservatives are known for being tough on crime, but we must also be tough on criminal justice spending. That means demanding more cost-effective approaches." The Right on Crime Statement of Principles, endorsed by, among many others, Gingrich, Perry, Bennett, former attorney general Edwin Meese, and former Florida governor Jeb Bush, lists five objectives of the criminal justice system: "Protecting the public, lowering crime rates, reducing re-offending, collecting victim restitution, and conserving taxpayers' money." Fairness and justice are conspicuously absent.

Many liberal reformers express similar views (e.g., Alexander 2012). They say that too many non-violent property and drug offenders are in prison and that something needs to be done about it. They duck the challenges presented by violent and repeat offenders. Mass incarceration will not be unwound and prevented from recurring until Americans acknowledge that sentencing policies are too rigid and too severe. The essential changes—fewer people sent to prison, more community punishments, shorter sentences, greater flexibility for judges and parole boards —are needed for all offenders.

There is no free lunch. Anodyne calls to unwind mass incarceration by changing policies for nonviolent first offenders will not make a big difference. Those are not the people whose confinement produced the world's highest imprisonment rate. Meaningful changes will require greatly reduced use of prison sentences, and much shorter ones, for nearly all offenders, whether or not they are first-timers, and whatever their offenses. That includes repeat and violent offenders. That's the reality.

For the past 30 years, most liberal advocates of change made the fundamental mistake of arguing disingenuously. Instead of saying that current policies are cruel and unjust, and should be changed for those reasons, they usually argued that current policies—which they often believed to be unjust—should be changed because they were ineffective or too costly. Supporters of correctional alternatives, exemplified by most reentry initiatives, usually claim that their use will reduce costs and lower recidivism rates. This is no doubt true for some programs, but as a broad generalization it is a mistake. Thirty years of evaluations have shown that most "alternatives" cannot keep their promises and at best reduce reoffending rates by no more than a few percentage points. However, at worst they result in recidivism rates no higher than if the same people had been sent to prison. Correctional alternatives also can save a lot of money *if* they are used in lieu of imprisonment. In recent decades they were instead often used not as prison alternatives but as supplements to probation, were rigidly enforced, experienced high failure and revocation rates, and resulted in increased total costs and more people in prison (Morris and Tonry 1990).

Some well-managed, well-funded, well-targeted programs with especially effective or charismatic leaders have been persuasively shown to be able to divert offenders from prison, save money, and significantly reduce reoffending. Few real-life programs are like that. A 2001 report of the US Surgeon General showed that violence prevention pilot programs shown by rigorous evaluations to be effective seldom achieve the same results when widely implemented. Taking programs "up to scale" state-wide is remarkably difficult. Economist Mark Kleiman, a strong advocate of some probation programs, predicts of efforts to establish programs on a large scale: "The most likely result would be failure; few programs successful at the pilot level turn out to scale up effectively" (2009, p. 125).

The problems of going to scale are well-known. Bureaucratic inertia sets in, key staff especially program entrepreneurs leave, and budgets get cut, making program integrity difficult to sustain. Among treatment programs that are evaluated, "implementation failure" is the most common finding. Literature reviews and meta-analyses regularly conclude that programs reduce reoffending, but they suffer from "publication bias." Evaluations that find no effect are seldom published; the published literature represents mostly the unknown percentage of evaluations that find positive effects. Some correctional programs no doubt produce significantly better than average results, but it is unreasonable to assume that most do or will.

The strategy of disingenuous argument has failed because it does not acknowledge that adoption of current sentencing policies was not motivated primarily by concerns about cost savings or effectiveness. Mandatory minimum, three-strikes, truth-in-sentencing, "dangerous offender," "sexual psychopath," and LWOP laws were enacted not on the basis of research findings, cost-benefit studies, impact projections, or meta-analyses, but because policy makers believed them to be intuitively plausible, morally appropriate, or politically expedient. They were enacted because their supporters believed that "we" deserve protection from "them," and that "they" have forfeited any claim to have their interests or human rights taken into account. Instrumental arguments about costs and effectiveness, especially weak ones, seldom win over people motivated by moral beliefs. Few supporters of capital punishment change their views when they learn there is no convincing evidence that the death penalty deters killings. The ultimately moral arguments about disproportionate punishments, ruined lives, and social injustice need to be made explicitly if minds are to be changed.

It is an oversimplification to characterize views about crime control and punishment policies in terms of conservative and liberal, but those categories are commonly used and capture at least central tendencies among people who fit into them. For 40 years, conservative policy advocates made normative claims: offenders deserve to be severely punished, procedures that let guilty people off are wrong, "lenient" sentences depreciate the seriousness of crimes, victims' needs and interests are more important than those of offenders, and severe policies do and should denounce wrongful conduct.

Liberals typically ducked the normative claims and responded with instrumental ones, arguing that particular policies and practices are ineffective, cost too much, and divert funds from more important public needs. Or, accepting conservative assumptions and values, liberal advocates argued that their policy proposals do what conservatives want done, but better. The programs they propose, they say, cost less and reduce recidivism rates more.

Normative arguments concerning criminal justice policy have generally defeated instrumental ones since the mid-1970s. During the recessions of the late 1970s and early 1990s that made Jimmy Carter and George H. Bush one-term presidents, liberal law reformers in countless legislative hearing rooms argued that severe sentencing and corrections policies were unwise. They were unaffordable and would force unwanted budgetary trade-offs between prisons and schools, higher education, and highways. The arguments fell on deaf ears. In the political climates of both recessions, the movement toward harsher sentencing policies accelerated.

During the latest recession, policy makers in some states have made modest changes to severe sentencing and corrections policies. That's good. That is more than happened during the Reagan, Bush I, Clinton, and Bush II administrations, and may portend a change in the political climate. When the good times once again roll, however, as they are in 2015 as I write these words, changes that are adopted primarily to save money or improve efficiency, rather than because they are the right thing to do, are not likely to last.

No one should be surprised that normative arguments trump instrumental ones. The proposition that punishments should be harsher because that will better acknowledge victims' suffering is a normative claim about what is due victims. The proposition that violent or repeat offenders have forfeited any right to have their interests considered is a normative claim about appropriate consequences for wrongful behavior. The proposition that laws that punish minor offenses disproportionately severely are unjustifiable is a normative claim about unjust punishment. The proposition that laws that punish minority offenders disproportionately severely are unjust is a normative claim about social justice. The proposition that no punishment should be so severe that it ignores possibilities of redemption is a normative claim about human dignity.

The five propositions in the preceding paragraph are in the abstract irreconcilable. Different people subscribe to various of them in different degrees. I described the claims as normative. Others would describe them as moral. However they are described, they express deeply held beliefs about how offenders should be treated and about the weight that should be given to their interests in deciding how to respond to crimes they have committed.

Given a choice between doing what seems morally right and doing something else, most people prefer the morally satisfying choice, even if it costs more. If the morally preferable choice is rejected because it seems unaffordable, it is with a feeling of regret, an uncomfortable sense of doing the wrong thing for the wrong reason. Given the chance later on to do the right thing, most people jump at it.

To the extent that contemporary crime control policies are based on normative beliefs, their proponents and supporters are unlikely to repudiate them for instrumental reasons. Those policies will be repudiated, or support for them weakened, only if enough people can be persuaded that they are unjust and cannot be morally justified. That will not happen unless normative disagreements are brought into the open and engaged directly. Sometimes, at least, when that happens, minds change. Lawrence Bobo and Victor Thompson (2006, 2010) found, for example, that whites' support for the federal 100-to-1 law that punished crack cocaine offenses much more severely than powder cocaine offenses plummeted when they learned about its disproportionate effects on black offenders. The successful 2012 and 2014 referenda narrowing California's three-strikes laws were built on claims that punishments for many offenders were unjustly severe and ruined lives to no good purpose. The proposals that follow are premised on the view that many contemporary policies must be changed because they are morally wrong. Before setting out those proposals, I briefly summarize the evidence on the deterrent and incapacitative effects of punishment to show that it does not support a straight-faced claim that current policies are justifiable because they are effective crime prevention measures.

II. The Effects of Sanctions

In 2015 it is not controversial to assert that the crime prevention effects of mass incarceration have been much less than many people supposed or hoped, that there is little reason to believe that harsher punishments have greater deterrent effects than milder ones, that incapacitating people by locking them up for lengthy periods is an ineffective crime prevention strategy, or that the experience of imprisonment makes many offenders more, not less, likely to commit crimes later in their lives. The National Academy of Sciences Committee on the Causes and

Consequences of High Rates of Incarceration reached all those conclusions and explored and explained the evidence justifying them in detail (Travis, Western, and Redburn 2014, chaps. 3 and 5).

Those conclusions are not novel, though they are based on much more, and scientifically more rigorous, evidence than was available in earlier times. A series of National Academy of Sciences (NAS) panels in the 1970s and 1980s that surveyed the evidence then available on deterrence, incapacitation, sentencing, and criminal careers offered much the same conclusions.[1]

There is one subject, however, on which knowledge about the effects of criminal justice programs has changed substantially. Two early NAS panels reviewed the evidence on the effectiveness of correctional rehabilitation programs. They concluded, consistent with the "nothing works" conventional wisdom of the time, that little credible scientific evidence showed them to be effective at reducing reoffending (Sechrest, White, and Brown 1979; Martin, Sechrest, and Redner 1981). Since then masses of experimentation and research have combined to show that many well-designed, well-targeted, and well-run correctional programs can reduce reoffending. A recent NAS report examined the evidence and reached that conclusion (Petersilia and Rosenfeld 2007). So have many recent surveys of the relevant evidence (e.g., MacKenzie 2006; Cullen 2013). Many things can "work."

Under the right conditions, better programs can reduce reoffending more effectively than mass incarceration, and at substantially lower cost. Operating new programs successfully on a large scale, meeting Kleiman's challenge, will require substantially greater public investment and better correctional management than have in recent decades been common. Finding the necessary public funds will not be easy.

Elected officials in many states have recently been attracted to Justice Reinvestment proposals to save money by lowering prison populations and to reduce recidivism rates by running better community programs (Lavigne et al. 2014). In principle, cost savings from less prison use should be

---

[1] The conclusions on the effects of sanctions in the 2014 report are consistent with the findings of National Academy of Sciences panels on deterrence and incapacitation (Blumstein, Cohen, and Nagin 1978), sentencing (Blumstein, Cohen, Martin, and Tonry 1983), criminal careers (Blumstein, Cohen, Roth, and Visher 1986), and violence prevention (Reiss and Roth 1993).

recycled to support better community and treatment programs. In practice, officials generally prefer to divert most or all of any savings to meet other state budgetary needs (Austin et al. 2013).

New research showing the effectiveness of some correctional programs has thus far had little influence on sentencing policy. Social science evidence has in general been conspicuously absent from legislative policy making about sentencing since the early 1980s. Legislatures enacted many hundreds of state and federal laws in the 1980s and 1990s that mandated long prison sentences that were ostensibly aimed at preventing crime through deterrence and incapacitation. These included mandatory minimum sentence and LWOP laws in every state and the federal system, three-strikes and truth-in-sentencing laws in more than half the states and the federal system, and the US Sentencing Commission's "mandatory" guidelines. Although there is no basis for believing these laws significantly reduced crime rates, the evidence is compelling that they are a major reason why American imprisonment rates are four to five times higher than they had been from the 1930s to the early 1970s (Raphael and Stoll 2013; Travis, Western, and Redburn 2014, chaps. 2 and 3).

For much of the twentieth century before 1975, faith in goodwill and good effects, not research findings, underlay indeterminate sentencing. If major developments since 1975 had been predicated on widely accepted research findings, imprisonment rates and patterns, and criminal justice policies, things would have evolved very differently.

Research has interacted with policy in several ways in the past 40 years. The developments during the sentencing reform period from 1975 to the mid-1980s provided a classic example of evidence-based policy making. Pilot studies suggested federal parole guidelines might work. Federal parole guidelines were developed, implemented, and evaluated. They were successful at reducing disparities and increasing consistency. Drawing on that experience, voluntary sentencing guidelines were developed (Gottfredson, Wilkins, and Hoffman 1978). They proved unsuccessful, but were succeeded by presumptive sentencing guidelines which achieved their primary goals of rationalizing sentencing, reducing unwarranted disparities, making processes fairer and more transparent, and making judges accountable for their decisions (Tonry 1996, chap. 2).

That period of admirably evidence-based policy making proved short-lived. By the mid-1980s, credible evaluations showed that voluntary sentencing guidelines had little effect on sentencing patterns and did not reduce disparities (e.g., Rich et al. 1982). By contrast, presumptive sentencing guidelines developed by a sentencing commission reduced racial and other unwarranted disparities, brought greater consistency to plea bargaining, and enabled states to improve resource planning (e.g., Knapp 1984). From an evidence-based policy perspective, the implications were straightforward: parole and presumptive sentencing guidelines work; voluntary guidelines do not. Nonetheless, parole guidelines, despite their successes, withered away, the movement toward adoption of presumptive sentencing guidelines stalled, and voluntary sentencing guidelines became the industry standard.

Mandatory minimum sentence, three-strikes, truth-in-sentencing, and LWOP laws offer a diametrically opposed example of the limited influence of research findings. Little solid research evidence justified their enactment or survival. During the 1980s and early 1990s, however, they were the most commonly adopted sentencing policy changes.

A. Deterrence

Many of the harshest laws were ostensibly premised on beliefs or assumptions about the deterrent effects of mandatory and severe punishments. From a crime control perspective, such beliefs and assumptions were misguided.

Daniel Nagin and Steven Durlauf in an influential article examined evidence on the deterrent effects of sanctions and the effects on crime of imprisonment and policing. About deterrence, they concluded: "In summary, the literature on whether increases in prison sentence length serve as a deterrent is not large, but several persuasive studies do exist. These studies suggest that increases in the severity of punishment have at best only a modest deterrent effect" (Durlauf and Nagin 2011, p. 31). They also concluded that the effects of imprisonment on prisoners were on average criminogenic rather than crime-preventative (e.g., Nagin, Cullen, and Lero-Jonson 2009) but that a sizable literature indicates that police actions have preventive effects (e.g., Evans and Owens 2007). As a result they proposed that prison use be greatly reduced and savings be transferred to more effective and less costly police crime-prevention efforts.

The National Academy of Sciences has repeatedly constituted panels to examine scientific evidence on the preventive effects of sanctions. Each cautioned skepticism. Academy reports are especially authoritative. The panels typically include the leading subject matter specialists. Members are chosen so as to be representative of diverse disciplines, to reflect a wide array of political and theoretical perspectives, and to include people from government, the private sector, and universities. I've described the findings of the 2014 report of the Committee on the Causes and Consequence of High Rates of Incarceration. Two years earlier, the National Academy of Sciences Panel on Deterrence and the Death Penalty concluded that there is no credible evidence that the death penalty is a more effective deterrent to homicide than other sanctions that might be imposed (Nagin and Pepper 2012).

These conclusions, however, are not novel. After the most exhaustive examination of the subject ever undertaken, the 1978 National Academy of Sciences Panel on Research on Deterrent and Incapacitative Effects concluded, "In summary . . . we cannot assert that the evidence warrants an affirmative conclusion regarding deterrence" (Blumstein, Cohen, and Nagin 1978, p. 7). Daniel Nagin, a principal draftsman, was less qualified: "The evidence is woefully inadequate for providing a good estimate of the magnitude of whatever effect may exist. . . . Policymakers in the criminal justice system are done a disservice if they are left with the impression that the empirical evidence . . . strongly supports the deterrence hypothesis" (Nagin 1978, p. 4).

The National Academy of Sciences Panel on Understanding and Controlling Violence reached a similar conclusion in 1993. After documenting that the average prison sentence per violent crime tripled between 1975 and 1989, the panel asked, "What effect has increasing the prison population had on violent crime?" and answered, "Apparently very little" (Reiss and Roth 1993, p. 10). That answer took account of both deterrent and incapacitative effects.

Every major comprehensive review of the deterrence literature over the years has reached similar conclusions. Philip J. Cook, in a classic, much-cited survey, long ago concluded that existing studies showed that "there exist feasible actions on the part of the criminal justice system that may be effective in deterring [certain] crimes. . . . [but the studies] do *not* demonstrate that all types of crimes are potentially deterrable, and certainly they provide little help in predicting the effects of any specific governmental action" (Cook 1980, p. 215).

A meta-analysis by Travis Pratt and colleagues (2006) produced a main finding on deterrence, one "noted by previous narrative reviews of the deterrence literature," that "the effects of severity estimates and deterrence/sanctions composites, even when statistically significant, are too weak to be of substantive significance (consistently below -.1)" (Pratt et al. 2006, p. 379). The most recent, and an especially exhaustive, survey of the evidence by America's foremost authority on the subject, Daniel Nagin (2013), reached the same conclusion.

Surveys of the evidence on deterrence by bodies created by governments of other countries have reached the same conclusion (e.g., Canadian Sentencing Commission 1987; Home Office 1990 [England and Wales]; Törnudd 1993 [Finland]; von Hirsch, Bottoms, Burney, and Wikström 1999 [England and Wales]; Germany 2006; Australia 2013).[2] The Committee on Justice of the Canadian Parliament observed: "If locking up those who violate the law contributed to safer societies, then the United States should be the safest country in the world. In fact, the United States affords a glaring example of the limited impact that criminal justice responses have on crime. . . . [The] evidence from the US is that costly repressive measures alone fail to deter crime. The Committee unanimously agrees that crime prevention is the best policy choice" (Canada 1993, p. 2). Consistent with this, the Canadian Supreme Court in 2015, declaring mandatory minimum sentence laws unconstitutional, wrote "The empirical evidence is clear: mandatory minimum sentences do not deter more than less harsh, proportionate, sentences" (*R v. Nur*, 2013 SCC 15 [2015]).

---

[2] The Legal and Constitutional Affairs Committee of the Australian Senate concluded: "Jurisdictions across Australia have relied, and continue to rely, on incarceration as a deterrent to criminal offending at great cost to the taxpayer and society generally. While governments continue to support the expensive corrections system, it has not been successful in addressing offending behaviour—prison is not a deterrent" (Australia 2013, para. 8.6). The Second [Federal Government] Report on the State of Interior/Domestic Security in Germany, issued by a commission appointed by the federal justice and home affairs ministries, concluded that "harsher and/or longer penalties did not produce less recidivism than lenient penalties did, and that in many instances an informal solution (dismissal, diversion etc.) came out to have been the most effective answer to delinquent acts or criminal behavior" (Germany 2006, paras. 6.4.3.2, 6.4.3.3).

B. Incapacitation

Research on incapacitative effects provides no firmer underpinnings for the proliferation of laws mandating lengthy prison sentences. Some were honestly or ostensibly premised on beliefs or assumptions about incapacitation. Three major strands of evidence are particularly relevant: on "replacement effects" and, from work on criminal careers, on "age crime curves" and "residual career lengths." All three offer strong evidence that locking up large numbers of people to incapacitate them is not an effective crime prevention strategy (Piquero, Farrington, and Blumstein 2003, 2007).

1. *Replacement Effects.* For some categories of offenders, an incapacitation strategy necessarily failed because most or all of those sent to prison were rapidly replaced in the criminal networks of which they were a part. Locking them up did not diminish future offending. Drug trafficking is the paradigm case. Drug dealing is part of a large complex illegal market with low barriers to entry. The net earnings of street-level dealers are low, and the probabilities of eventual arrest and imprisonment are high (Levitt and Venkatesh 2000; Cook et al. 2007). Even so, arrested dealers are quickly replaced by new recruits (Smith and Dickey 1999; Dills, Miron, and Summers 2008; MacCoun and Martin 2009).

It would make little sense for most people who have reasonably good prospects of living a satisfying life to accept the risks of street-level drug dealing. The chances of ruining your life are high, and well-known. For young disadvantaged people with little social capital and limited life chances, with substandard educations and few marketable skills, however, drug dealing too often appears to present opportunities that are not otherwise available. Such young people tend to overestimate the benefits and underestimate the risks (Reuter, MacCoun, and Murphy 1990; Kleiman 1997). This is compounded by peer influences, social pressures, and deviant role models provided by successful dealers who live conspicuously affluent lives and manage to avoid arrest.

The impression that drug dealing will enable a disadvantaged young man or woman to live the good life can be strong. That impression is fundamentally misleading. The likelihood of arrest for any individual sale of crack, cocaine, heroin, or methamphetamine is low—estimates range between one in 500 transactions and one in 1,000—but the likelihood of eventual arrest and imprisonment is very high (Caulkins and MacCoun 2003). The arrests and imprisonments of street-level dealers create illicit opportunities for others. At least in recent decades plenty of other young people have been prepared to seize that "opportunity."

Similar analyses apply to many members of deviant youth groups and gangs. Social pressures encourage participation. It offers opportunities for peer approval, recognition, and self-esteem that are not otherwise readily available in socially disorganized neighborhoods. The teenage years are for many people a time for risk-taking. Teenagers drive recklessly, underestimate pregnancy risks, experiment with drugs, and commit crimes at peak rates. In some inner-city areas of large cities, so many young men have been arrested and gone to prison that those things bear little stigma. In some socially disorganized neighborhoods, those experiences are almost part of the normal life cycle. As gang members and leaders are arrested and taken out of circulation, successors are ready, willing, and available to step into their shoes.

2. *Criminal Careers: Age-Crime Curves.* Research on criminal careers provides other reasons to be skeptical that imprisoning offenders for long periods is a cost-effective crime prevention strategy. Many of those confined would have ceased offending long before their prison terms expire. Criminal careers were a major focus of federally funded crime research in the 1980s and the subject of a National Academy of Sciences panel report (Blumstein et al. 1986). One strand of that literature documented "age-crime curves" (Farrington 1986).

That work shows that very large percentages of young people commit offenses; rates peak in the mid-teenage years for property offenses and the late teenage years for violent offenses, followed by rapid declines (e.g., Sweeten, Piquero, and Steinberg 2013). For most offenders, a process of natural desistance results in cessation of criminal activity in the late teens and early twenties. Desistance is associated with natural developmental processes of maturation. As people enter their twenties, they increasingly have interests and stakes—intimate relationships, marriage, children, jobs, career prospects, hopes for a better life—that are too important to risk. Getting a job, entering into an important continuing personal relationship, and finding God or experiencing other spiritual awakenings are important causes of desistance. Confining people after they would have desisted is inefficient and wastefully expensive. It is also unnecessarily destructive. And since spending time in prison increases the likelihood of later offending, the experience will extend criminal careers of people who would otherwise have settled into conventional lives.

3. *Criminal Careers: Residual Career Lengths.* Another strand of criminal careers research investigated and documented the phenomenon of "residual career length," the period during which an active offender will continue to commit offenses (Blumstein, Cohen, and Hsieh 1982). Most desist in their teenage years or early twenties. Even the most persistent offenders desist relatively young—typically in their thirties (Farrington 2003). This means most—even active—criminal careers are short. In the federal system and most states, first offenders are punished less severely—usually much less severely—than repeat offenders. Under three-strikes laws, dangerous offender statutes, and all sentencing guidelines, criminal history considerations substantially increase sentence lengths, often doubling or tripling sentence lengths imposed on first offenders (e.g., Reitz 2010; Frase 2013). Under three-strikes and "career criminal" or "dangerous offender" laws the multiplier is vastly greater. The short residual career lengths of most offenders mean that there is little incapacitative gain to be realized from imprisoning most offenders for lengthy periods, and especially for sentencing repeat offenders to increasingly long terms.

The implications are straightforward: fewer convicted offenders should be sent to prison, and for shorter times. There are no evidence-based grounds for believing the use of prison sentences generally and lengthy ones in particular have significant crime-preventive effects. There is good evidence that imprisonment fails to reduce later offending and may increase it. There is good evidence that well-designed, well-targeted, well-resourced, and well-run treatment programs can modestly reduce later offending. Treatment programs cost much less to operate than prisons, and are less likely themselves seriously to damage offenders' likelihood of living better lives later on. The conclusion to be drawn: as is current practice in most other Western countries, American criminal justice systems should use prisons much more sparingly than they now do and instead, for purposes of both norm reinforcement and social justice, divert many suspected offenders from the criminal justice system and sentence many others who now wind up in prison to community penalties and programs.

Evidence had little influence in recent decades on American sentencing laws and policies. Other things have driven sentencing policy in the United States since the mid-1980s. The winds of change, however, may be blowing, and evidence may begin to count for something. If so, the American criminal justice system could be very different in coming years.

III. Building Just and Effective Sentencing Systems

The short-term goal should be to reduce the national imprisonment rate by half by 2020, essentially to turn the clock back to where America was in the mid-1980s. The longer-term goal should be to regain by 2030 an imprisonment rate of 160 per 100,000. That was the American norm for half a century before 1973, when the 35-year period of continuous increase began. Reaching the 1973 level would not make the United States "lenient" by international standards. The imprisonment rate would remain double that of the Scandinavians and 50 percent more than the modern average of 100 per 100,000 in Western countries. It would match the least punitive former communist nations.

> *Proposal 1. Numerical Goals: The national imprisonment rate should be reduced by 2020 to the mid-1980s level of 350 per 100,000 and by 2030 to the 1973 rate of 160 per 100,000.*

A. Criminal Codes, Cops, and Prosecutors

The starting point in creating a system of punishment that embodies the four principles of punitive justice is a criminal code that proscribes only behaviors that violate sufficiently important social norms to justify a punitive state response and reinforcement by state institutions. Criminal laws need to be clearly expressed and widely known, and to define as criminal only behaviors that are widely recognized as seriously wrongful.[3] Any adequate criminal law will forbid serious violent

[3] There is a large, growing, and sophisticated literature on criminalization and overcriminalization (e.g., Husak 2008; Simester and von Hirsch 2011). Reducing overcriminalization is a paramount goal of the Right on Crime movement and the American Enterprise Institute.

acts and takings of property; where the boundaries should be drawn beyond that necessarily will vary with time, place, and culture. Socially contested behaviors are almost always better dealt with by other social institutions. Criminalizing behaviors such as drug use, prostitution, and public order offenses that are morally ambiguous and whose wrongfulness is disputed inevitably leads to unequal and inconsistent enforcement of the law.

Proposal 2. Overbreadth of the Criminal Law: Legislatures should revise criminal codes to narrow their scope and define as crimes only behaviors that violate fundamental, widely supported social norms.

A criminal law of appropriate content and scope is not by itself an adequate foundation for a just system of sentencing and punishment. There must also be just and effective systems of policing and prosecution. Police and prosecutors inevitably exercise discretion in responding to incidents, and are ethically bound to enforce law consistently and evenhandedly. There can be no perfect resolution between the need to respond to particular cases appropriately and wisely and the need to treat cases evenhandedly. Unwarranted parities in treatment can be as wrong as unwarranted disparities. For less serious behaviors, informal dispositions of some kinds of cases are inevitable. Police must decide whether to take a young suspect home to his or her parents or to the police station. They must decide whether to give an intoxicated driver a warning, and take or follow him home in their car, or to arrest him. Similar decisions inevitably get made about drug sales, drunken fights, domestic incidents, and a wide range of everyday breaches of public order. Tax authorities and regulatory agencies must decide which few among many thousands of comparable prima facie cases of tax evasion and regulatory violations to refer to prosecution and which to handle civilly.

For very serious harms such as homicides, rapes, armed robberies, public corruption, and major white collar crimes, there will seldom be much doubt about prosecution. In many less serious cases, special circumstances may support a decision not to prosecute. In legal systems governed by the "expediency principle," such as in the English-speaking countries and the Netherlands, prosecutors are allowed discretion to decide what should be done (Tonry 2012*a*).

Some legal systems attempt to regulate police and prosecution decisions. Many continental European systems are guided by a "principle of legality," which on its face forbids exercises of discretion in individual cases and directs police and prosecutors simply to enforce and apply the law evenhandedly. The principle is derived from the underlying normative equality premise of the *Rechtsstaat*, the state that treats every citizen equally under applicable laws (Pifferi 2012).

Prosecutors in legality principle countries such as Germany or Sweden are expected to deal with cases only on their merits and under established rules. Cases may be dismissed because of doubt about a suspect's guilt or the adequacy of the evidence or under diversion policies applicable to all qualifying cases, but not simply because the individual prosecutor decides that prosecution is inappropriate for a particular case or suspect. Sweden's rules and policies for the control of prosecutorial decision making are among the most developed in any country. Defendants or victims who believe a prosecutor is handling their case inappropriately may file an administrative appeal within the prosecution system. There are no negotiated charge dismissals, and the judge is not bound by the prosecutor's charging decision. The defendant may be convicted of a less or more serious offense than the formal charge. The aim is to assure that every citizen under particular circumstances is dealt with by the state in the same way (Asp 2012).

In many European systems, whether or not prosecutors are subject to the legality principle, prosecutors oversee police investigations. European prosecutors are often members of the judiciary with the same obligations of neutrality, objectivity, and impartiality as any other judge (Jehle, Smit, and Zila 2008; in Italy: Nelken 2013), or they are separately organized but bound by the same ethical principles as judges (e.g., in the Netherlands: van de Bunt and van Gelder 2012). In the Netherlands, police are authorized to dispose of some kinds of cases informally, but under rules developed by the prosecution service.

Equivalent legal and conventional constraints on the powers of police and prosecutors do not exist in the United States. Police are almost always organized at municipal levels with chiefs appointed by the mayor or city council. Except for abuses of authority, excessive use of force, corruption, and actions motivated by invidious bias, police decisions are effectively unreviewable. Most American chief prosecutors are locally elected at county level. The US Supreme Court, in *Bordenkircher v. Hayes*, 434 U.S. 357 (1978) and *Castle Rock v. Gonzales*, 545 U.S. 748 (2005), held that their discretionary decisions are largely immune from judicial review. Whatever the extent to which strong equal treatment and fairness norms motivate police and prosecutorial decision making in the United States, it is only because local officials have chosen to establish and enforce them and individual practitioners have chosen to observe them.

The American prosecution system is characterized by a powerful ideology of local autonomy. Prosecutors typically pride themselves on reflecting attitudes, preferences, and beliefs in their local communities (Boerner 2012; Miller and Caplinger 2012). They resist efforts from outside to create general rules or policies guiding their decisions and practices (Wright 2013).

Criminal courts resolve the cases prosecutors bring before them. However, differences in how prosecutors operate have important implications for thinking about how judges ought to sentence convicted offenders. In principle, and probably also in practice in some legality principle countries, it is reasonable to suppose that all mentally competent people who have been identified and apprehended by the police for a moderate or high severity crime will be diverted from prosecution under established policies or prosecuted and, if probative evidence is available, convicted. In such places, the proposition that treatment as an equal requires imposition of comparable punishments for comparable crimes makes sense.

By contrast, in the United States, where most chief prosecutors are locally elected, that proposition is much harder to justify. Among closely comparable cases for which mentally competent people have been identified and apprehended, some may not have been charged at all; some with a lesser or greater offense; some with the same offense, which was later downgraded as part of a negotiated guilty plea; and some with the same offense. The argument that treatment of people as equals requires that people convicted of the same or comparable crimes should receive comparable punishments is considerably less compelling when the relationship between the offender's blameworthy act and the offense of which he or she is convicted is so contingent and attenuated.

The organization of American police and prosecutors, and the constitutional independence of prosecutors, makes European-style controls on their behavior unimaginable in any foreseeable American future. Even so, police and prosecutors can change their procedures and adopt rules to make their decisions fairer and reduce the use of imprisonment. In chapter 1, I described German conditional dismissals, Dutch and Belgian transactions, and penal orders in Scandinavia that are used in large percentages of criminal cases, sometimes with, but more often without, criminal convictions. Defendants are provided opportunities to resolve criminal charges by agreeing to pay fines, make restitution, and perform community service. The proposed disposition is not bargained but offered on a take-it-or-leave-it basis. These policies save time and money, reinforce social norms by attaching consequences to criminal acts, and enable many suspects to avoid the stigma and collateral effects of criminal convictions.

American police, under prosecutorial supervision, and prosecutors should adopt such systems. For less serious offenses, including most misdemeanors and minor drug, property, and public order felonies, defendants should ordinarily not be required to plead guilty. Further actions could be taken against defendants who unreasonably failed to do what they agreed to do. "Unreasonably" appears in that sentence as an important qualification against agreed actions, such as payment of large fines or restitution by indigent offenders, that simply set up offenders for failure.

For more serious offenses, guilty pleas could be required, but this should be a last resort for reasons related to the specific character of American legal systems. In most continental European countries, records of criminal convictions are not publicly accessible and are not routinely available to prospective employers (Jacobs 2015). There are no "ban the box" campaigns, because employment applications almost never have a criminal record box to check. Even convictions do not have the stigmatizing effects they do in the United States, where the information is readily available and substantially lessens offenders' employment prospects. They also trigger major collateral consequences in the United

States such as disenfranchisement, disqualification from occupations, and ineligibility for a wide range of social welfare programs.

> *Proposal 3. Prosecutorial Dispositions: Laws should be enacted directing prosecutors to establish, and police and prosecutors to implement, structured programs for disposition of criminal cases, usually without formal guilty pleas, by means of defendants' agreements to pay financial penalties, make restitution, and perform community service.*

B. Sentencing Systems

Sentencing systems can be devised that incorporate the four principles of punitive justice. The principles can also be used as a frame of reference for assessing existing systems. Assuming an adequate body of substantive criminal law and a fair system of adjudication, specifying the contours of just sentencing systems should be straightforward. Details necessarily will vary depending on prevailing normative ideas about the justification and distribution of punishment. Knowledge of how institutions such as plea bargaining operate in practice, however, needs to be taken into account.

C. Repealing Rigid and Unjust Laws

Anyone familiar with American sentencing can repeat the litany of tough-on-crime sentencing laws enacted in the 1980s and the first half of the 1990s: mandatory minimum sentence laws (all 50 states), three-strikes laws (26 states), LWOPs (49 states), and truth-in-sentencing laws (28 states), in some places augmented by equally severe "career criminal," "dangerous offender," and "sexual predator" laws. These laws required sentences of historically unprecedented lengths for broad categories of offenses and offenders.

Some of these laws were unprecedented not in their nature but in their severity. Mandatory minimum sentence laws have long existed. Many states enacted "habitual offender" laws in the 1920s and 1930s, usually targeting chronic property offenders, but by the 1970s prosecutors seldom sought to apply them (Tappan 1949; Brown Commission 1971). "Sexual psychopath" laws were enacted in several waves before the

1980s, but they were typically narrowly defined, infrequently applied, and seldom mandated decades-long or life sentences (Sutherland 1950*a*, 1950*b*; Jenkins 1998). LWOPs, three-strikes, and truth-in-sentencing laws by contrast, are largely inventions of the 1980s and 1990s.

Three things make the modern laws unprecedented. The first is their severity. When the 1980s began, mandatory minimum sentence laws seldom required more than 1 or 2 years in prison (Shane-DuBow, Brown, and Olsen 1985). LWOPs require lifetime imprisonment. Three-strikes laws require a 25-year minimum sentence, and often life. Many mandatory minimum sentence laws for drug and violent offenses require 10, 20, or more years' imprisonment, and few require fewer than 5 years.

The second distinctive characteristic of modern laws is their breadth. California's three-strikes law applied to any third felony, and some gross misdemeanors, if the defendant had two previous felony convictions for any of a long list of drug and violent felonies. Many states' LWOP laws apply to offenses other than homicide, and most until recently applied to offenses committed by minors (Ogletree and Sarat 2012; Nellis 2013).[4] Many mandatory minimum sentence laws apply to relatively low-level offenses: the numerically most important examples are the lengthy minimum sentences often mandated for low-level, often addicted, drug dealers. Truth-in-sentencing laws apply to wide swathes of drug and violent offenses and usually forbid parole release before 85 percent of the sentence has been served.

The third distinctive characteristic is that modern laws flatly defy conventional notions of proportionality. California's three-strikes law required minimum 25-year sentences for property felonies and gross misdemeanors. Drug laws often require longer sentences for trafficking in minor amounts than are required for offenses almost anyone would consider much more serious. Consider table 6.1, which shows guidelines sentences prescribed in the 2013 edition of the US Sentencing Commission's Guidelines Manual.

[4] Until the US Supreme Court in *Graham v. Florida*, 560 U.S. 48 (2010), and *Miller v. Alabama*, 132 S. Ct. 2455 (2012), declared mandatory sentences of life without the possibility of parole unconstitutional for juveniles as cruel and unusual punishments under the Eighth Amendment to the US Constitution.

TABLE 6.1. US Sentencing Commission, recommended guidelines sentences, 2013

Offense	Severity level	Recommended sentences
Assault, intent to kill	27	70–87 months
Sale of crack, 28 grams	**26**	**63–78 months**
Robbery, firearm used	26	63–78 months
Theft, more than $1,000,000	22	41–51 months
Robbery	20	33–41 months
Aggravated assault, firearm discharged	19	30–37 months
Stalking, domestic violence	18	27–33 months
Theft, more than $200,000	18	27–33 months
Sexual abuse of a ward	14	15–21 months

Sale of 28 grams of crack cocaine was a level 26 offense subject to a 63–78 month sentence. Until 2010, sale of five grams, a trivial amount, a sixth of an ounce, triggered that sentence. Most such sellers are young, disadvantaged, minority people, who are often themselves drug-dependent. The recommended sentence is slightly less than for assault with intent to kill, and the same as for robbery involving use of firearms. It is greater than for theft of $1,000,000, robbery, aggravated assault in which a firearm was discharged, stalking or domestic violence, or sexual abuse of a dependent minor. The crack cocaine sentence, unlike the others shown in table 6.1, is mandatory. Although the *Booker* case made the federal guidelines "advisory," which means judges can impose other sentences, federal statutes mandate a minimum 60-month sentence for the crack seller. For all the other offenses shown in table 6.1, judges have discretion to impose lesser sentences.

Go figure. Very few people consider a small, unadorned street-level drug sale to be a more serious crime than a robbery or a serious assault with a firearm. It is hard to argue with a straight face that selling a small quantity of drugs for $20 or $30 is more serious than stealing $1,000,000. Gross disproportionality like that is not reconcilable with any mainstream theory or principle of punishment.

All such laws should be repealed. They often result in unjustly and disproportionately severe punishments, to no significant crime-preventive effect. Their existence empowers prosecutors to make *in terrorem* threats to defendants that effectively coerce many to plead guilty, including some who are innocent or have valid defenses but don't want to risk receiving decades-long or life sentences. The late Harvard Law School professor William Stuntz observed that "outside the plea bargaining process, such threats would be deemed extortionate" (2011, p. 260). These laws result in widespread circumvention by judges and prosecutors who want to avoid imposing unjustly severe sentences. And, because circumvention is neither certain nor in some places common, they result in massive differences in the sentences received by otherwise comparable defendants who do and don't come before sympathetic judges and prosecutors.

Insofar as life sentences remain lawful, judges will have authority to impose them on people who commit the most heinous homicides. In many other Western countries, the maximum sentence for any one crime, including murder, is 20 years or less. In the United States, Canada, and other English-speaking countries, however, life sentences have traditionally been possible for aggravated homicides. That being so, it is likely that many American jurisdictions will retain life sentences. In almost all Western countries, however, including the United States before 1980, people sentenced to life imprisonment are eligible for parole release. That should be true in the United States in the twenty-first century. All LWOP laws should be repealed.

Some people believe LWOPs are a necessary evil—to provide an alternative sentence for people who otherwise might be sentenced to death. That argument lacks facial plausibility in a country that executes 50 people a year but holds nearly 50,000 in prison serving LWOPs (Nellis 2013). Very few of them were at serious risk of a death sentence. Even if a capital punishment alternative is believed to be strategically necessary to minimize executions, there can be no basis for making LWOPs applicable to defendants other than death-eligible ones. Such laws, if they are kept at all, should be amended to apply only to defendants charged with capital felonies for whom there is a realistic possibility of a death sentence, which as a constitutional matter means only first-degree murder cases.

Proposal 4. Repeal Mandatory Minimums: All three-strikes, mandatory minimum sentence, life-without-possibility-of-parole, and comparable laws should be repealed, or else radically narrowed in scope and severity.

Repeal of all mandatory minimum sentence laws does not mean that judges would lack authority to impose appropriately severe proportionate punishments for serious crimes. Proposals below for creation of more detailed systems of offense classification, lengthened maximum sentences for especially serious offenses or offenders, and appellate sentence appeals provide mechanisms for regulating sentences in such cases.

Mandatory minimum and similar laws are ham-fisted and inevitably sometimes apply to defendants to whom they should not. In most other Western countries with which Americans would ordinarily want their country compared, there are no mandatory minimum sentence laws. The criminal codes of many continental European countries specify minimum sentences for specific offenses, but judges always have authority to impose a lesser sentence if they believe justice so requires. They are not mandatory. Judges may impose less severe punishments when mitigating circumstances exist. Most English-speaking countries' criminal laws contain some, usually a handful, of "mandatory minimum sentence" laws, but, with some exceptions for homicide, only in the United States do the words mean what they say. Nowhere else do such laws prescribe minimum sentences of 10 or 20 years or life. In Australia, England and Wales, and South Africa they contain clauses allowing judges to impose some other sentence in—the typical phrase—"the interest of justice" (Tonry 2009*a*; Ashworth 2010; Freiberg 2014).

There is relatively little discordance among the legal systems of Western countries other than the United States about this. Statutory provisions on minimum sentences elsewhere nearly always create presumptions that can be overcome. This is what presumptive sentencing guidelines systems do. The purposes of mandatory minimum sentence laws can be more justly achieved by establishment of presumptive sentencing guidelines systems that set appropriate punishments for serious crimes but allow judges, for reasons stated, to impose lesser punishments. Prosecutors can appeal decisions with which they disagree.

There is nothing radical about a proposal for repeal of mandatory minimum sentences. Every major criminal law reform proposal of the last 50 years, including the Model Penal Code (1962), the first and second editions of the Model Sentencing Act (1963, 1972; Flood 1963), the American Bar Association Standards on Sentencing Alternatives and Procedures (1994), and the Model Penal Code—Sentencing (2007, 2011), has opposed their adoption and favored their repeal. So have innumerable organizations including the American Bar Association, the American Law Institute, the Commission on Reform of Federal Criminal Laws (1971), and the Commissioners on Uniform State Laws (Uniform Law Commissioners 1979; Perlman and Potuto 1979). Supreme Court associate justice Anthony M. Kennedy headed the ABA Justice Kennedy Commission, which urged repeal of mandatory minimum sentence laws.

> *Proposal 5. Escape Clauses: Any three-strikes, mandatory minimum sentence, life-without-possibility-of-parole, or comparable laws that are not repealed should be amended to include provisions authorizing judges to impose some other sentence "in the interest of justice."*

Mandatory minimum sentence and similar laws were enacted at times when policy makers sought to be highly punitive and when being "tough on crime" was politically expedient. Fear of being labeled "soft on crime" is a major reason why almost no severe sentencing laws have been repealed and why most recent sentencing law changes have focused on first offenders and minor changes to parole and probation revocation procedures and parole eligibility. If prevailing attitudes are changing, the time may come when repeals of the severest laws become more likely. That will be much easier for risk-averse politicians to do if it happens automatically. This can be done by means of "sunset laws" which automatically lapse unless reenacted. The federal Patriot Act, which was enacted shortly after the 9/11 attacks on the World Trade Center and the Pentagon, contained a sunset clause. It should be done with all severe sentencing laws.

> *Proposal 6. Sunset Provisions: Any three-strikes, mandatory minimum sentence, life-without-possibility-of-parole, or comparable laws that are not repealed should be amended to include sunset provisions specifying that they will automatically lapse 5 years after enactment unless reenacted.*

D. Building Just Sentencing Systems.

Just systems have two fundamental characteristics. They operate under published criteria for imposition of punishments in individual cases, and, since human institutions predictably sometimes work badly, they contain fail-safes designed to minimize risks of injustice. Sentencing criteria can be expressed in a number of ways, including statutory provisions, guidelines, case law, and combinations of all three. Fail-safes can be built into the architecture of the sentencing standards and can be provided by various kinds of review systems.

1. *Classification of Felonies.* Just sentencing systems authorize maximum punishments that are meaningfully scaled to the seriousness of crimes. Offenders should not be punished more severely than they can reasonably be said maximally to deserve. Statutes that limit maximum lawful sentences are one protection against that happening. The punishment tariff should be published and generally available in order to make the system transparent, give fair notice to citizens, and provide criteria according to which judges can be held accountable for the sentences they impose.

One straightforward protection against imposition of unjustly severe punishments is if offenses are divided into a sufficiently large number of categories, scaled in relation to the comparative seriousness of crimes. Maximum authorized sentences should be relatively short, at least for ordinary cases.

Most American sentencing systems do not satisfy this requirement. Criminal codes have typically developed by accretion over scores of years or centuries rather than through a succession of comprehensive overhauls. New criminal offenses have been added, old ones redefined, and sentencing provisions enacted and changed piecemeal in response to the emergence of particular issues, notorious cases, and moral panics (Schwartz 1983). Not surprisingly, provisions on maximum sentences are inconsistent and sometimes irreconcilable with proportionality values. This was a major focus of criminal code revision efforts in the 1950s and 1960s, including in the work of the National Commission on Reform of Federal Criminal Laws (1971). The draftsmen of the Model Penal Code sought to address it by dividing all offenses into three classes of felonies.

Many states revised their criminal codes during the 1960s and 1980s, some importantly influenced by the 1962 Model Penal Code, but most did not adopt the code's provision that all felonies be divided into three classes. The code proposed this because it was developed during the indeterminate sentencing era and assumed its continuation (Tonry 1982,

1988). Under indeterminate sentencing, sentence lengths were mostly nominal and parole boards set release dates. In Washington and California, every prison sentence was for "one year to the statutory maximum." In some states, judges could set a maximum sentence lower than the statutory maximum but no minimum. In other states, the judge could set a maximum and a minimum, but usually subject to a limit that the minimum be one-third or not more than one-third of the maximum. Both the maximum and the minimum were usually reduced by a third or more as a time-off credit for good behavior (Rothman 1971).

The Model Penal Code was meant to rationalize and systematize minimum and maximum sentences. It assumed that the identity of the conviction offense was not critically important, since judges and parole boards were expected to individualize sentences in every case. Table 6.2 summarizes the proposals. It sets out three schemes. The "basic" scheme in section 6.06 would allow judges to set minimum sentences but not maximums. The "alternative" scheme in section 6.06A lets judges set minimums and maximums subject to a limit that the minimum not be more than half the maximum. The "extended" scheme applied to defined categories of people involved in organized crime, professional criminals, and especially dangerous offenders.

By modern American standards, the maximums for most cases are short, though they resemble modern limits in most other Western countries. For Class 1 felonies, the most serious, including murder, rape, and aggravated robbery, the minimum was 1–10 years and the maximum life. For Class 2, which included most other serious felonies, minimums were 1–3 years and maximums 10. For Class 3, minimums were 1–2 years, and maximums 5. All of those are gross numbers; section 305.1 of the code contemplated that prisoners would ordinarily receive up to 12 days per month time-off credit for good behavior against both the maximum sentence and the minimum. Section 305.9 created a presumption that inmates would ordinarily be released when they first became eligible. All prison sentences were to be indeterminate, with minimums not to exceed one-half the maximum.[5]

[5] Judges would be given significant discretion over minimum sentences, but in the alternative version of section 6.06 maximums were fixed by law. In the basic version judges would have significant discretion over maximums. Neither proposal commanded decisive support; that is why they were provided in the alternative.

TABLE 6.2. Model Penal Code (1962), Minimum and maximum authorized sentences

Offense class (section)	Minimum*	Maximum*
Felony 1 basic (§6.06 [1])	1–10 years	life
Felony 1 alternative (§A6.06 [1])	1–10 years	up to 20 years, or life
Felony 1 extended (§6.07 [1])	5–10 years	life
Felony 2 basic (§6.06 [2])	1–3 years	10 years
Felony 2 alternative (§A6.06 [2])	1–3 years	up to 10 years
Felony 2 extended (§6.07 [3])	1–5 years	10–20 years
Felony 3 basic (§6.06 [3])	1–2 years	5 years
Felony 3 alternative (§A6.06 [3])	1–2 years	up to 5 years
Felony 3 extended (§6.07 [3])	1–3 years	5–10 years

Sources: Model Penal Code (American Law Institute 1962), sections 6.06, 6.06A, and 6.07.

*Under section 305.1, time-off credits for good behavior could reduce minima and maxima by up to 12 days per month.

Few states adopted the code's sentence classification and parole eligibility provisions. If they had, the provisions would now be obsolete. The drafters assumed that indeterminate sentencing and the values associated with it would continue and that parole release would remain a component of American criminal justice systems.[6] That did not happen; 16 states and the federal system in 2015 did not have parole release systems. Many states that retain parole release enacted some or all of truth-in-sentencing, mandatory minimum, and LWOP laws that eliminate whole categories of prisoners from eligibility for release. Finally, the

[6] In order to individualize sentences, judges could impose probation in any case, including homicide. Courts had other powers. Although 1 year was meant to be the minimum term for a state prison sentence, section 7.08(2) provided that every prison sentence was tentative for 1 year, thus permitting petitions to be filed seeking reductions. Section 6.12 authorized the court to reduce the felony class of the conviction offense if the court concluded that it would be unduly harsh to sentence the offender in accordance with authorized sentencing options including minimum and maximum terms normally available.

code's drafters assumed that policy makers, judges, and parole boards would continue to believe that rehabilitation was the primary aim of sentencing, that imprisonment should be imposed only as a last resort, and that prisoners should be released at the earliest opportunity. Given those provisions and those assumptions, maximum sentences were not very important.

Almost all of those assumptions proved to be wrong. Few people today believe that rehabilitation should be punishment's primary aim. Some people today believe imprisonment should be used only as a last resort no matter what the offense and that prisoners should be released as soon as possible, but many people believe otherwise. In any case, the Model Penal Code's offense classification is an anachronism: it contains too few categories to differentiate offense severities adequately, and thus risks unwarranted parity: treating materially different cases as if they are the same.

The solution is straightforward. Offenses should be divided into many more categories than three, differentiated by their seriousness, with maximum lawful sanctions authorized for each. Reasonable people will differ on how many categories are appropriate, on whether increments of additional authorized punishment for each step of the scale should be the same or different, and on the maximum authorized sanctions for the most serious offenses. If there were 10 felony classes, the maxima might be 2, 4, 6, 8, 10, 12, 14, 16, 18, and 20 years, plus life with eligibility for parole release for first-degree murder. In contemporary Europe, the top is 12–20 years.

Maximum authorized sanctions by definition should apply only to the most aggravated instances of any particular offense. The fallibility of human institutions requires that there be mechanisms to assure that only those most serious crimes are punished especially severely. One first step toward doing this, as the Advisory Committee on the Penal System in England and Wales (1978) proposed, is to specify intermediate maximums for ordinary cases well short of the authorized statutory maximums and to establish criteria that must be satisfied before the intermediate maximum can be exceeded. The Model Penal Code did this by establishing separate maximum penalties for ordinary and exceptional kinds of cases. These proposals are discussed below.

Every state and the federal system should revise their criminal codes to classify all felonies on the basis of their seriousness into a set of categories specifying maximum authorized sentences. Many states have already created classification systems, but not in their criminal codes. More than half of the states in the last 40 years established systems of voluntary or presumptive sentencing guidelines which classified all felonies by seriousness, usually into 10–15 categories. Those are plausible numbers and are validated by their widespread adoption. Because guidelines are not statutes and do not specify lawful maximums, however, they do not set absolute limits. As a result, except in presumptive guidelines states subject to *Blakely*, judges who depart from guidelines can potentially impose sentences up to the statutory maximum. Since in many states these are 20, 25, or more years for many offenses, individual offenders can receive widely disparate sentences that bear no relationship to the seriousness of the crimes of which they were convicted.

> *Proposal 7. Classification of Felonies: Legislatures should revise criminal codes to classify all offenses into 10–15 categories to distinguish meaningfully between the seriousness of crimes, thereby assuring proportionality in maximum sentences and that offenders not receive unjustly severe punishments.*

2. *Authorized Sanctions, Ordinary Cases.* A fair, accountable, transparent sentencing system requires rules that specify what kinds of sentences should typically be imposed in ordinary cases. Assuring that individuals' interests be treated with respect and concern requires that the rules be sufficiently flexible to allow ethically important differences between cases to be taken into account. Unless there are rules, judges will not be able to test their own intuitions against general standards. Unless individual defendants and their counsel know what the rules are, they will not know how to promote the defendant's interests. Unless onlookers know what the rules are, they will not be able to know whether processes are operating in appropriate ways or to form their own views of whether justice is being done. Unless onlookers believe that courts operate as they should, public perceptions of their legitimacy will suffer.

Showing respect and concern to all defendants requires that opportunities exist to argue at sentencing and on appeal that their cases are not typical. Otherwise they will be unable to explain distinctive features of their cases that warrant special treatment, and to receive it if their arguments are persuasive.

Evidence is not available to support confident generalizations about how well existing systems do this. Standards for sentences in ordinary cases are commonplace, but empirical research on compliance with them, or on unwarranted sentencing disparities, is not. Court systems in many countries operate under statutes or guidelines that establish standards for ordinary cases. In continental European countries, statutes often indicate minimum sentences, which judges may disregard for good reasons (e.g., Lappi-Seppälä 2011). In the Netherlands, guidelines for prosecutors' sentencing recommendations are detailed and are commonly said to have substantial influence on judges' decisions (van de Bunt and van Gelder 2012). In England and Wales, the American federal system, and some American states, voluntary sentencing guidelines set standards for sentencing (e.g., Roberts 2012). In Minnesota, Washington, Oregon, North Carolina, and Kansas, presumptive sentencing guidelines set standards (Frase 2013).

Only for some of the last five jurisdictions is there convincing empirical evidence that judges generally comply with standards. It is likely that they do so in most continental European countries, where prosecutors and judges are career civil servants, prison sentences are usually short, and commitment to the legality principle requiring equal treatment of comparable cases is strong. Empirical evidence demonstrating this is not abundant. The best evidence in England and Wales, somewhat dated, is that unwarranted disparities are common and extreme (Hough, Jacobson, and Millie 2003).

In other jurisdictions, including Canada, parts of Australia, and most American states, there is little reason to believe either that there are jurisdiction-wide standards or, if they exist, that they are generally complied with. In American jurisdictions before 1975 when indeterminate sentencing systems were ubiquitous, the prevailing system of individualized, case-by-case, decision making did not imply or operate under general standards. No American state still generally honors the rehabilitative premises of indeterminate sentencing, but many have retained its traditions—broad unregulated judicial discretion, minimum and maximum sentences, parole release—under an overlay of mandatory minimum, truth-in-sentencing, and LWOP laws.

Every jurisdiction, however, should have some system of reasonably detailed standards for sentencing. Judges, like everyone else, are idiosyncratic and have personal intuitions about offense seriousness. Some are especially sympathetic toward offenders who are drug-dependent or come from deeply disadvantaged backgrounds. Some are not. Some believe that imprisonment is seldom or never an appropriate punishment for shoplifting, most auto theft, and other minor property offenses. Some have strong negative visceral reactions to sex offenses and offenders, and consider these cases especially heinous. Some abhor violence in any form, and react especially punitively to it. General standards for ordinary cases, whether expressed in statutes or guidelines, provide at least starting points which, if taken seriously, can moderate the influence of idiosyncratic views.

The evidence in the United States is overwhelming that presumptive sentencing guidelines promulgated by a sentencing commission are the most effective means available to establish enforceable standards for sentences in ordinary cases. I discussed that evidence in detail in chapter 2. Presumptive guidelines systems have been shown to make sentencing more consistent and predictable and to reduce racial and other unwarranted disparities.

Presumptive guidelines classify all felonies (and in some states all misdemeanors) into 10–15 categories scaled to seriousness. Ranges of proportionate, authorized sentences are provided for each category. Judges are expected to impose sentences in ordinary cases in the authorized range, but may impose less severe sentences if they provide written reasons. Prosecutors may appeal the adequacy of the reasons provided.

Presumptive sentencing guidelines have one great advantage that is usually not stressed. Under the Supreme Court's decision in *Blakely v. Washington*, 542 U.S. 296 (2004), they establish meaningful upper limits on the severity of sentences even if statutes do not. Guidelines usually specify ranges within which sentences should normally be selected. The Supreme Court held that the upper bound is equivalent to a statutory sentence maximum. A sentence exceeding a statutory maximum is inherently unlawful; if the prosecution wants a defendant to be punished more severely, it must charge him or her with a more serious offense and prove it or persuade the defendant to admit it. Accordingly, no sentence severer than the top of the applicable presumptive guidelines range can be imposed unless either a judge or jury on a beyond-reasonable-doubt basis finds facts that might justify the harsher sentence, or the defendant admits them. Prosecutors and judges initially feared that *Blakely* would unduly complicate their work, but experience has shown that it did not do so.

Presumptive sentencing guidelines should be established in every state because:

- Sentencing commissions are much better suited than legislatures to develop, monitor, and over time revise sentencing standards.
- Well-designed, well-implemented presumptive guidelines improve consistency and predictability and reduce racial and other unwarranted disparities.
- Well-designed, well-implemented presumptive guidelines improve transparency by making sentencing standards public, making sentencing processes fairer, and making sentencing decisions more consistent.
- Well-designed, well-implemented presumptive guidelines improve accountability by requiring judges to explain why they impose sentences other than those specified in applicable guidelines and thereby providing bases for appellate review of the persuasiveness of their explanations.
- Well-designed, well-implemented presumptive guidelines that incorporate a "capacity constraint policy" make sentencing patterns predictable and improve corrections planning and management by making corrections spending and facilities needs also predictable.
- Well-designed, well-implemented presumptive guidelines establish meaningful upper limits on sentences that may be imposed and thereby prevent the imposition of grossly disproportionate sentences in individual cases.

Proposal 8. Presumptive Sentencing Guidelines: Every state which does not already have one should establish a sentencing commission charged to develop a system of presumptive sentencing guidelines.

3. *Authorized Sanctions, Extraordinary Cases.* Extraordinary cases present high risks of unjustly severe punishments because they magnify the likely effects of judges' idiosyncratic views. This was recognized even in the era of indeterminate sentencing in the United States and in England and Wales. The issues are general ones, though in especially acute forms in the United States since especially severe sanctions are available. Both retributive and consequentialist approaches to punishment require strict upper limits of sanctions scaled to offense severity. This is one setting in which having a sizable number of offense classes is important in order to bound offenders' maximum exposure.

Both the Model Penal Code and the report of the British Advisory Council on the Penal System (1978) proposed that maximum sanctions for ordinary offenses be set, well below the maximums authorized by law, and proposed findings of fact relating to special dangers to the public that must be established before the normal limits may be exceeded.

Section 6.07 of the Model Penal Code authorized longer minimums and maximums for professional criminals, dangerous, mentally abnormal persons "whose commitment for an extended term is necessary for protection of the public," and "multiple offender[s] whose criminality was so extensive that a sentence of imprisonment for an extended term is warranted." These terms were defined closely and narrowly.

The Advisory Council proposed that maximum penalties for ordinary crimes be set at levels encompassing 90 percent of sentences imposed for that crime in a reference period, and that sentences for exceptional cases be indeterminate (though with parole release eligibility not later than expiration of the normal maximum, and with credits for good behavior). The key recommendation: "Consequently we recommend that no court should pass a sentence of imprisonment exceeding the new [intermediate] maximum term unless, by reason of the nature of the offence and the character, conduct, and antecedents of the offender, the court is of the opinion that a custodial sentence of exceptional length is necessary for the protection of the public against serious harm" (1978, p. 92).

Proposal 9. Extraordinary Sentences: Legislatures should revise criminal codes to provide standards for imposition of sentences more severe than authorized for ordinary cases that (a) provide explicit criteria for imposition of such sentences, (b) forbid imposition of punishments more severe than the maximum proportionate sentence for the offense or offenses of conviction, and (c) following Blakely *require that the statutory criteria for exceptional sentences be shown to have been met on the basis of a beyond-reasonable-doubt evidentiary standard.*

4. *Criminal History.* Criminal history counts for much too much in American sentencing. That needs to change. In extreme cases, as for example concerning shoplifting under California's three-strikes law before 2012, prior convictions can increase sentences by 10, 20, or more times. Under many sentencing guidelines systems, prior convictions increase sentence lengths by three to five times (Reitz 2010). Those huge differences are hard to justify in principle, as I explained in chapter 2, and are primary reasons both for the extreme lengths of American sentences and for mass incarceration.

These things happen because Americans have not traditionally thought much about the relevance of criminal history to sentencing or developed nuanced policies concerning it. Other Western countries have explicit policies. In Scandinavian countries, with minor exceptions, prior convictions are considered irrelevant when imposing a sentence for a new crime. In England and Wales, they are to be taken into account only when, in statutory language, they are "recent" and also are "relevant" to the new offense. In other English-speaking countries and most Western European countries, prior convictions are taken into account but subject to limits, usually modest, on how much a sentence can be increased because of them. No American jurisdiction during the indeterminate sentencing period, and only those with sentencing guidelines in 2015, had statutory rules or judicial standards concerning the weight to be given to prior convictions.

Most people who write about punishment theories and policies, including philosophers and lawyers, pay attention almost exclusively to first offenders. That makes analyses easier, but it means that theorizing overlooks a large majority of sentencing decisions. In principle, at least, most people intuitively believe that punishments should be proportionate to the seriousness of crimes. That calculation is easy to make concerning first offenders. All else being equal, armed robberies warrant severer sentences than robberies, robberies than major thefts, and major thefts than shoplifting. That analytical tidiness disappears in relation to the vast majority of offenders for whom the current conviction is not their first conviction. In 2006, for which data from the 75 most populous counties are available, 77 percent of felony defendants had at least one prior arrest, 61 percent had at least one prior conviction, and 49 percent had multiple prior convictions. The typical defendant is thus not a first offender but someone with a prior criminal record, half of the time a substantial one (Cohen and Kyckelhahn 2010, table 4).

That reality makes comparison of sentences, and theorizing about principled approaches to sentencing recidivists, difficult. It is not obvious how to assess the appropriateness of a sentence for a shoplifter with two convictions for shoplifting and one for drug selling compared with those of a burglar who has one prior conviction for prostitution and an unarmed robber with no prior convictions at all. Except in some guidelines states or under three-strikes and similar laws, decisions about the weight, if any, to be given to prior convictions is entirely within the discretion of individual, inevitably idiosyncratic judges. Researchers, of course, have tried to model sentencing to explain differences. Almost always they conclude that prior record and the seriousness of the current offenses are the most heavily weighted factors (e.g., Spohn 2008; Johnson 2012). However, those are averages and provide no insight into the appropriateness or consistency of sentences in individual cases.

Reasonable people differ over the relevance of prior criminality to imposition of just punishments. Some believe prior criminality is irrelevant. If the offender was convicted of a prior offense and has completed the prescribed punishment, that book should be closed. The debt to society has been paid. Like any other citizen convicted of a crime, a recidivist should be punished only as much as he or she deserves for the new crime. Any additional increment of punishment means either that the offender is being punished more severely for the current crime than he or she deserves or is being subjected to an additional, and therefore unjust, punishment for the previous crime in violation of the ideas underlying the double jeopardy doctrine (Tonry 1987).

Other people believe, for reasons that are seldom adequately explained, that prior crimes justify additional increments of deserved punishments. Ambitious, but tortured and unsuccessful, efforts have been made to develop retributive explanations based on recidivists' special duty to behave, disrespect for the state, or failure to learn a punitive lesson (Bennett 2010; Lee 2010). The answer to them is that all citizens have a general duty of law-abidingness and that the criminal law punishes defined proscribed behaviors committed with defined mental states of intention, knowledge, recklessness, or negligence. Being of "bad character" is not a criminal offense. Citizens in a free society are allowed to be eccentric, unconventional, or disrespectful.

The preceding arguments are based on retributivist ideas about deserved punishments. Claims are sometimes made that past offending is the best predictor of future offending and that increasing penalties because of prior convictions will control crime through incapacitation. That is only true if we want to confine large numbers of people for lengthy periods in order to prevent minor drug and property crimes. In 2006 and 2009, only a quarter of state felony defendants were charged with violent crimes (Cohen and Kyckelhahn 2010; Reaves 2013). More than 70 percent were charged with drug, property, motor vehicle, and public order offenses. Only 29 percent of people admitted to state prisons in 2011 had been convicted of violent crimes (Carson and Golinelli 2013, table 4). Imprisonment is an expensive and unjust way to prevent shoplifting, theft, prostitution, and drug dealing. For reasons discussed in the second section of this chapter—age/crime curves, natural desistance, replacement effects, residual criminal career lengths—there is little reason to believe incapacitative crime control policies are generally effective.

Nor is there a stronger case to be made about violence. Even individualized predictions of dangerousness are notoriously unreliable. Increasing all offenders' sentences because of prior convictions is an indiscriminate and wasteful blunderbuss strategy. That is why both "collective" and "selective" incapacitation crime control strategies lost credibility after testing in the 1970s and 1980s (Chaiken and Chaiken 1982; J. Cohen 1983; Blumstein et al. 1986).

The evidence on violence prediction, however, provides little basis for individualization. The evidence has changed little since the 1970s (e.g., N. Morris 1974). For all but tiny categories of offenders, principally members of organized crime and some pathologically disturbed people, predictions of serious violence are wrong at least two-thirds of the time. Most people predicted to be violent in the future are not.

The preceding assertions are not inconsistent with the conventional claim that as many as two-thirds of released prisoners reoffend. The two-thirds claim is misleading, because it entangles people sent to and released from prison (Tonry 2004, chap. 7). Of those *sent* to prison for the first time, one third or fewer commit new offenses. Of those *released* from prison in a particular year, disproportionately chronic property and drug offenders, as many as two-thirds reoffend. The difference in reoffending between first-time and all released prisoners exists because most of those released in a year are chronic offenders serving short sentences. The vast bulk of crimes are property and drug offenses, which are typically committed at high rates by troubled and often mentally ill or drug-dependent people living disorganized lives. These unfortunates cycle in and out of courts, jails, and prisons.

It is difficult to imagine that increasing punishments on the basis of criminal history can meaningfully address the social problems chronic minor offenders represent. Some supporters of indeterminate sentencing believed that concern for public safety justified holding people convicted of minor crimes for extended periods including lifetimes if they were believed to be dangerous (Rothman 1971; Pifferi 2012). This was one reason why the Model Penal Code classified felonies into only three classes and authorized longer sentences in extraordinary cases. Parole boards could delay a prisoner's release until the last minute of the maximum sentence for incapacitative reasons, irrespective of the offense of which he or she was convicted. In our time, most people believe that punishments must be deserved in a retributive sense and that lengthy confinement of people convicted of minor crimes is unjust.

At least in English-speaking countries, however, most people including offenders and judges believe that recidivist offenders deserve progressively harsher punishments (Roberts 2008, 2010). It is a prerational belief that is seldom challenged and never justified except on characterological grounds that ought not to count. It is a prerational belief that should be resisted and cabined by rules. Intuition unguided by rational reasoning, for example in earlier times about the inferiority of black people, the emotionalism of women, and the sexual preferences of gays and lesbians, is never an adequate justification for causing harm to someone.

There is an additional reason why the effects of criminal history on sentences should be tightly constrained. As Richard Frase (2009*b*) has shown in Minnesota, enhancement of sentences on the basis of prior convictions is a principle cause—in Minnesota the principal cause—of racial disparities in imprisonment. Likewise three-strikes laws. They target violent and drug offenders, disproportionate numbers of whom are black and Hispanic. Enacting and enforcing them increased racial disparities in imprisonment. Their repeal would reduce disparities.

Substantially reducing the weight given to criminal history will save money, reduce prison populations, and alleviate racial disparities. This should be done directly by repealing three-strikes, career criminal, and similar laws and enacting statutes limiting the weight of criminal history in sentencing.

Sentence increases based on prior convictions could be handled in various ways. The English approach is to authorize increases on account of prior convictions only if recent and "relevant" to the current offense (Baker and Ashworth 2010). Other English-speaking countries set formulae, such as that the total sentence cannot exceed the most severe punishment that might appropriately have been imposed for the current offense by itself (Freiberg 2014). For American jurisdictions, something more concrete like a percentage limit would be better. It is difficult to imagine any plausible normative justification for increasing a sentence by more than 50 percent of the term that would otherwise be imposed, especially in a country in sentences have traditionally been long.

Sentencing commissions should revise guidelines to reduce the importance of criminal history and ensure punishments are primarily based, as they always should have been, on the offense or offenses of which the offender was convicted. This would to a significant extent occur indirectly if my early proposal to divide felonies into a much larger number of categories with proportionate maximum sentences is adopted. The existence of maximums measured in decades made possible the inordinate weight given to prior convictions in sentencing. Much shorter maximums tailored to offense seriousness will limit it.

Proposal 10. Criminal History: Standards should be established limiting the weight given in sentencing to prior convictions, including (a) statutory provisions limiting the extent to which a sentence may be increased on account of prior convictions, and (b) provisions directing sentencing commissions to limit the weight given to criminal history in determination of authorized sentences. Criminal history enhancements should never result in a sentence more than 1.5 times that which would otherwise have been imposed solely on the basis of the offense or offenses of conviction.

5. *Appeals.* Any system recognizing the four principles of fairness, equality, proportionality, and parsimony must provide mechanisms and opportunities for individuals to contest decisions that affect their interests. Human institutions malfunction. Human beings make idiosyncratic, mistaken, and unreasonable decisions. In a just system, individuals would be able to challenge adverse decisions at every stage of the process, as Swedish defendants and victims may in relation to prosecutorial and sentencing decisions. *Blakely* sets proof-beyond-a-reasonable-doubt standards for sentences more severe than presumptive guidelines permit. All jurisdictions need a restrictive standard of review. The Minnesota standard that requires judges to provide "substantial and compelling" reasons for departing from the guidelines has worked and made Minnesota the first state to develop an effective system of appellate sentence review (Reitz 1997).

Proposal 11. Appellate Sentence Review: Statutes should be enacted providing (a) in jurisdictions with sentencing guidelines not covered by Blakely *that defendants may appeal any sentence not authorized by applicable guidelines under a presumption that departures will be overturned unless the sentencing judge has provided substantial and compelling reasons for the aggravated sentence and (b) in any other jurisdiction that defendants may appeal any sentence on the basis that it is unreasonable in light of the offense of conviction and the circumstances of the offender.*

6. *Parole Release.* Proposals for abolition of parole release in the 1970s and 1980s were predicated on an assumption that sentences would be imposed under statutory criteria or guidelines that would assure consistency and prevent unwarranted disparities. That did not happen except in a few states that adopted presumptive sentencing guidelines. Sentencing disparities are rife as a result of judicial idiosyncrasy and as a by-product of judges' and prosecutors' efforts to circumvent mandatory minimum sentence laws. Unwarranted disparities remain common.

Lengths of prison sentences in the United States are also extraordinarily long, compared with those in other Western countries. Sentences longer than 1 year are uncommon in most. Longer than 3 years is rare, and longer than 5 years is very rare.

In 2009, the most recent year for which national estimates are available, the mean maximum term for all offenders sentenced to prison in the 75 largest urban counties was 52 months, and the median was 30 months. The means for murder, rape, robbery, and burglary were 373, 142, 90, and 52 months, respectively. Ninety percent of murderers received sentences of 10 years or longer, as did 42 percent of rapists and 20 percent of robbers. Sentences of 6 years or longer were received by 92 percent of murderers, 66 percent of rapists, 40 percent of robbers, and 17 percent of burglars (Reaves 2013, table 25).

Some device is needed to undo the effects of unwarranted sentencing disparities and reexamine the appropriateness of and continuing need for lengthy prison sentences. Reestablishing and reinvigorating parole release is the simplest. Appellate sentence review is the alternative, but in almost all states it is an unsatisfactory one—close to nonexistent in most and cumbersome, expensive, and slow in the rest. Parole boards can do the job faster, more efficiently, and at much less cost.

The parole board's functions and the purposes of its guidelines would vary depending on the nature of the state's sentencing system. For states operating well-designed systems of presumptive sentencing guidelines, the role of parole guidelines might be small in relation to future prisoners (though large in relation to current ones). If ranges of authorized guidelines sentences were broad, however, for example, 36–72 months, rather than narrow, say, 36–42 months, prisoners might be authorized to petition for release when they have served the minimum authorized guidelines sentence. The principal function of parole release under presumptive guidelines would be to review the need for continued confinement of people serving especially long sentences imposed under the guidelines, resulting from imposition of consecutive sentences for multiple offenses, or resulting from sentences imposed for different crimes on different occasions.

For states operating other sentencing guidelines systems or no guidelines at all, the principal function of the parole board would be to create and operate an effective system of standards for release decisions. Well-developed, well-implemented presumptive sentencing guidelines have been a precondition for creation of robust systems of appellate sentence review in the United States (Reitz 1997). States lacking such systems need some other way to prevent unwarranted disparities and unduly long sentences. The evaluations of parole guidelines systems in the 1970s and 1980s showed that well-run parole guidelines systems can implement consistent policies, reduce disparities, and provide meaningful administrative appeals for contested cases (Arthur D. Little, Inc. and Goldfarb and Singer, Esqs., 1981; Blumstein et al. 1983). Where presumptive or voluntary sentencing guidelines systems exist, one especially promising approach would be for the parole board to promulgate identical guidelines, thereby providing a powerful protection against unwarranted disparities.

Proposal 12. Parole Release: Every jurisdiction that does not already have one should establish a parole board, and every state should establish a parole guidelines system.

IV. Unwinding Mass Incarceration

The proposals made thus far concern prospective changes to American sentencing laws, policies, and institutions. If adopted they would greatly reduce the number of people in prison in future years, but their adoption would not significantly reduce the scale of American imprisonment in 2020 or in 2030. Substantially reducing the number of people already in prison will require enactment of new laws authorizing reconsideration of most prison sentences now being served.

Something drastic needs to be done if imprisonment rates in the United States are to reach even the 255 to 315 per 100,000 rates that characterize the Baltic countries of Latvia and Lithuania. These countries, former Soviet Socialist Republics, are admirable in many ways, but would not ordinarily be chosen as targets for American emulation. The imprisonment rates in Western Europe, which average 100 per 100,000, or in the former Warsaw Pact nations of Eastern and Central Europe, which range between 160 and 205 per 100,000, however, are unattainable by 2020.

The mechanisms chosen to review the need for continued confinement of particular prisoners or categories of prisoners are less important than recognition of the need to create some system for shortening sentences of most people now serving long prison terms. That will require decisions that are ultimately based on normative beliefs that too many people have been sent to prison for too long and that something must be done about it. The mechanics will not simply take care of themselves, but the normative change of heart will lay the necessary foundations.

Something similar happened with drug courts beginning in the early 1990s. They proliferated because many judges came to believe them to be a better approach than lengthy prison sentences for dealing with drug-dependent offenders. A credible body of methodologically strong evidence showing that well-targeted and well-managed drug courts can reduce drug dependence and crime has accumulated only in recent years, yet several thousand drug courts were established before the evidence was in (Mitchell 2011; Mitchell et al. 2012).

Likewise reentry programs. The term came into use only in the late 1990s (Travis 2000). Like most community corrections programs, many reentry programs are underdeveloped and underfunded (Jonson and Cullen 2015). They offer the same kinds of services to people released from prison as are offered in traditional probation and parole programs generally. Since a credible case can be made that many or most corrections programs are not adequately funded, especially well-managed, or conspicuously successful, there are "same old same old" grounds for skepticism about the likely effectiveness of reentry programs. Yet thousands have since been established. Corrections officials and other policy makers believe them to be the right thing to do.

The enormous reduction in the prison population that is needed could be accomplished in any of several ways. Prison populations could be substantially reduced, and quickly, by use of large-scale amnesties or commutations. They could be reduced by judges on a case-by-case basis. They could be reduced by a parole board or a special purpose administrative agency. Only the last of these is viable in the United States.

A. Amnesties and Mass Pardons

One or more large-scale amnesties or mass pardons could be used in each jurisdiction, as happens regularly in France and Italy and irregularly elsewhere (Whitman 2003; Lévy 2007). An Italian amnesty in 2006, an effort to deal with prison overcrowding, reduced that country's imprisonment rate by 40 percent. French collective pardons and amnesties often reduce the prison population by 20 percent. Typically they provide for release of all prisoners having unexpired terms of specified lengths, for example, 18 or 24 months, or all prisoners convicted of designated offenses. Amnesties and mass pardons need not, however, be blanket: they can exclude certain categories of prisoners, for example, people convicted of especially violent or organized crime offenses. Or they can shorten all current sentences by a fixed period, say, 18 months: anyone with fewer than 18 months to serve would be released, and all other prisoners' release eligibility dates would be advanced by that much.

Large-scale amnesties and pardons are not a viable option in the United States. However simple, effective, and efficient they might be, the ways of thinking associated with the tough on crime period are too deeply entrenched. Policy makers typically want to create systems in which individual offenders who might benefit are reviewed on a case-by-case basis to prevent releases of people who might be deemed to present unacceptable public safety risks. The US Sentencing Commission delayed the effective date of its retrospective 2014 changes to drug offenders' sentences for 18 months to give federal judges plenty of time for case-by-case consideration of individual cases. Another approach, proposed by former US Attorney General Eric Holder, would be for reviews to be made of the need for continued confinement of designated categories of prisoners with a view to formulating individualized recommendations to the president for commutation of sentence (Apuzzo 2014*a*, *b*). Neither federal approach is likely to result in thousands of releases.

B. Judicial Resentencing

California voters in referenda in 2012 and 2014 authorized resentencing of three-strikes prisoners. Resentencing is also happening pursuant to retrospective changes to federal drug sentences adopted by the US Sentencing Commission. Section 305.6 of the Model Penal Code—Sentencing has proposed enactment of "second look" laws that would authorize "a judicial panel or other judicial decision maker" to consider the need for continuing confinement of prisoners serving long sentences (American Law Institute 2011). However, the proposal envisions that only "a small share of all prison sentences" would be affected, probably only those serving "pronounced terms of more than 20 years" (p. 78). Unsuccessful applicants would be allowed to reapply at intervals no greater than 10 years.

The Model Penal Code provision contemplates a new and expensive sentencing procedure with the full panoply of procedural provisions, victim notifications, and appeals that characterize initial sentencing hearings. It is fundamentally inadequate for two reasons. First, it accepts the legitimacy of sentences measured in decades and lifetimes, something that is rare to nonexistent in most Western countries. I provided illustrative data on sentencing in other countries in chapter 1. Second, it is not premised on the need to reduce mass incarceration and could play no useful role in substantial reduction of the number of people held in American prisons. Even if the minimum eligibility period were substantially reduced, say, to 5 years, the provision's requirement of case-by-case judicial processes would make it impossibly slow, cumbersome, and costly.

C. Parole Boards and Other Administrative Agencies

Other possibilities exist in the executive branch. Parole boards with well-designed release guidelines created for prospective use, for example, could be given statutory authority to apply them retrospectively to all or designated current prisoners. There is a tidiness to this proposal, since it would result in the evenhanded application of the same standards to current and future prisoners, thereby enhancing the prospects for consistency over time.

Alternatively, legislation could be enacted to empower a specially constituted specialized agency to review the need for continued confinement of every inmate held in prison on a specified date. Decisions could be made according to rules but on a case-by-case basis, thereby allowing consideration of whether some individuals pose unacceptably high risks to public safety. The overriding criterion, however, for every case subject to review should be whether a strong case can be made for continued confinement. For reasons given in the second section of this chapter, convincing empirical evidence of likely deterrent or incapacitative effects of continued confinement of individuals would seldom be available.

Administrative agencies, whether parole boards or new special-purpose emergency release agencies, are much more likely than courts to be effective. Well-run administrative agencies can establish general policies, rules, and guidelines and enforce compliance with them much more effectively and less expensively than courts can. Except under the special situation of the mandatory federal sentencing guidelines, American appellate courts have traditionally been loath to subject sentencing decisions by lower courts to close review. That is why meaningful appellate sentence review occurs only in a handful of states with presumptive guidelines systems. Judicial processes are expensive, and, as commentary to the Model Penal Code—Sentencing's second-look provision points out, judges are exceedingly reluctant to take on new responsibilities when they believe courts are underfunded, dockets overcrowded, and themselves overworked.

Proposal 13. Routine Review of Long Sentences: Parole boards or specially created administrative agencies should be given authority to consider the need for continuing confinement of all prisoners meeting statutory eligibility criteria.

Legislation should be enacted that sets criteria to govern the retrospective release authority of parole boards or special purpose release agencies. It should authorize the agency to disregard mandatory minimum, truth-in-sentencing, LWOP, and all similar laws. Inmates over a designated age, say, 35, who have served more than a specified period, say, 3 years, and every inmate who has served more than 5 years should be eligible to apply for release.

Those ages and minimum terms may seem modest in early twenty-first-century America. They were not modest during the indeterminate sentencing era in the United States when few prisoners spent more than a few years behind bars. They are not modest today in other English-speaking countries and Western Europe in which terms longer than a year or two are rare.

Americans in recent decades have for some reason been willing to deprive offenders of large proportions of their lives. Ten years is a quarter of an adult's productive life; 20 years is half. Alabama trial and later federal district court judge Inge Johnson reflected on the disconnect between most peoples' senses of time in their own lives and the lengths of time taken away from offenders. In an article entitled, "'Time' for Prisoners and for Judges," she observed:

> One colleague of mine was asked if he could think of a really LONG period of his life when he could not do everything he would normally do or move about as he wished. He answered—the year he served in the American Armed Forces in Vietnam. That one year, he said, felt like an eternity.
>
> We value time in our own lives differently from how we measure the length of prison terms. Think of the length of a college education. Think of nine months of a pregnancy. . . . Think about waiting for a meal when you are hungry. In all these examples, not one exceeded five years, the longest being an average college education of four years. Yet judges throughout the United States commonly mete out 5-, 10-, and 20-year sentences. (Johnson 1990, p. 8)

Little good is realized from lengthy prison sentences and much harm is done. Eligibility to apply for release, of course, does not mean release would be granted. The evidence from criminal careers research on natural desistance and residual criminal careers indicates that lengthy confinement is not a plausible crime prevention strategy. The evidence that two-thirds of first-time prisoners do not return to prison confirms it (Tonry 2004). In any case, mass incarceration in America will not end unless and until means are developed to release many thousands of people serving unnecessarily and unjustly long prison sentences.

> *Proposal 14. Eligibility for Release: Every state should enact legislation making all prisoners serving fixed terms longer than 5 years, or indeterminate terms, eligible for consideration for release at the expiration of 5 years, and all prisoners aged 35 or over eligible for consideration for release after serving 3 years.*

A weak form of such legislation would merely make long-term prisoners eligible to apply for consideration for release. A stronger form would direct the appropriate authority to release any prisoner serving such a sentence on or after the release eligibility date unless an individualized finding was made of the existence of strong reasons for continued confinement. That was the parsimonious approach of the original Model

Penal Code, which created a presumption that all prisoners be released on parole when they became eligible to apply. If mass incarceration is to be unwound, the stronger form is necessary.

V. Moving Forward

It took less than 30 years, a surprisingly short time, for America's imprisonment rate to increase fivefold, from 150–60 per 100,000 population in 1973, not then the highest among Western developed countries, to 753 in 2007, a level four times that of any other country with which the United States might ordinarily be compared and more than seven times the average European level. That happened because legislatures enacted sentencing laws of historically unprecedented severity that were intended to send more people to prison for much longer periods than had previously been common.

The challenge now is to reverse America's extraordinary use of imprisonment. During the period when crime rates rose, Americans generally supported calls for harsher punishments. Politicians were happy to oblige. Although in the 1970s many liberal politicians favored policies that addressed the underlying causes of crime and aimed to develop better and stronger treatment and diversion programs, it became clear that few politicians could risk, or were willing to risk, the accusation of being soft on crime. By the late 1980s, a political stalemate had set in (Edsall and Edsall 1991). The 1988 presidential election was the last in which crime was a major issue. Major tough-on-crime legislation was enacted federally and in all 50 states in 1984–96, and almost none after that. However, despite declining crime rates since 1991 and negligible voter interest in the subject, prison populations and rates peaked only in 2007.

I rehearse this depressing story to point out that there was little powerful political or sizable public opposition to the tough-on-crime legislation of 1984–96. Small wonder it passed and became increasingly more severe over time. In the intervening years, there has been precious little powerful political support for repealing the laws that led to mass incarceration. It is not clear there is now. It is likely that there will be major political opposition to measures meant to shorten sentences and substantially reduce the numbers in prison.

Unwinding mass incarceration will be much harder than creating it was. Little will happen unless powerful political groups want to unwind it and are willing to spend political capital to make that happen. There are some signs that support for toughness at all costs is waning. The actions of voters in referendums and judges striking down some sentencing laws offer one set of examples. The hundreds of legislative nibbles around the edges of tough-on-crime sentencing laws offer another set. Initiatives like the Model Penal Code's second-chance proposals and the federal commutation and drug sentencing initiatives illustrate yet another set. All are small steps in the right direction. By themselves they cannot roll back mass incarceration. Bigger steps could.

American mass incarceration, absolutely and especially in its effects on black people, will be seen by our descendants as an extraordinary moral failure, a classic instance of man's inhumanity to man. Americans did it, and only Americans can undo it. It is time to start.

REFERENCES

Advisory Council of Judges, National Council on Crime and Delinquency. 1963. *Model Sentencing Act*. Hackensack, NJ: National Council on Crime and Delinquency.

———. 1972. *Model Sentencing Act*, 2nd ed. Hackensack, NJ: National Council on Crime and Delinquency.

Advisory Council on the Penal System. 1978. *Sentences of Imprisonment: A Review of Maximum Penalties*. London: Home Office.

Aebi, Marcelo, and Natalia Delgrande. 2014. *Council of Europe Annual Penal Statistics—SPACE I, Prison Populations, 2013 Survey*. Council of Europe and University of Lausanne: Strasburg and Lausanne.

Aebi, Marcelo F., Bruno Aubusson de Cavarlay, Gordon Barclay, Beata Gruszczyńska, Stefan Harrendorf, Markku Heiskanen, Vasilika Hysi, Véronique Jaquier, Jörg-Martin Jehle, Martin Killias, Olena Shostko, Paul Smit, and Rannveig Þórisdóttir. 2010. *European Sourcebook of Crime and Criminal Justice Statistics: 2010*, 4th ed. The Hague: Research and Documentation Centre, Netherlands Ministry of Justice.

Aebi, Marcelo F., Galma Akdeniz, Gordon Barclay, Claudia Campistol, Stefano Caneppele, Beata Gruszczyńska, Stefan Harrendorf, Markku Heiskanen, Vasilika Hysi, Jörg-Martin Jehle, Anniina Jokinen, Annie Kensey, Martin Killias, Chris J. Lewis, Ernesto Savona, Paul Smit, and Rannveig Þórisdótter. 2014. *European Sourcebook of Crime and Criminal Justice Statistics: 2014*, 5th ed. Hensinki: HEUNI.

Albrecht, Hans-Jörg. 2001. "Post-adjudication Dispositions in Comparative Perspective." In *Sentencing and Sanctions in Western Countries*, edited by Michael Tonry and Richard S. Frase. New York: Oxford University Press.

Alexander, Michelle. 2012. *The New Jim Crow: Mass Incarceration in the Age of Colorblindness*. New York: New Press.

Allen, Francis A. 1959. "Legal Values and the Rehabilitative Ideal." *Journal of Criminal Law, Criminology, and Police Science* 50:226–32.

———. 1964. "Legal Values and the Rehabilitative Ideal." In *The Borderland of Criminal Justice: Essays in Law and Criminology*. Chicago: University of Chicago Press.

Allen, Francis A. 1981. *The Decline of the Rehabilitative Ideal*. New Haven, CT: Yale University Press.

Alschuler, Albert. 1993. "Monarch, Lackey, or Judge." *Colorado Law Review* 64:723–35.

American Bar Association. 1994. *Criminal Justice Standards for Sentencing Alternatives and Procedures*. Chicago: American Bar Association.

American Civil Liberties Union. 2012. *Promising Beginnings: Bipartisan Criminal Justice Reform in Key States*. New York: American Civil Liberties Union.

American Friends Service Committee. 1971. *Struggle for Justice: A Report on Crime and Punishment in Americ*a. New York: Hill & Wang.

American Law Institute. 1962. *Model Penal Code—Proposed Official Draft*. Philadelphia: American Law Institute.

———. 2007. *Model Penal Code—Sentencing*, Tentative Draft No.1. Philadelphia: American Law Institute.

———. 2011. *Model Penal Code—Sentencing*, Tentative Draft No. 2. Philadelphia: American Law Institute.

Anderson, David C. 1995. *Crime and the Politics of Hysteria: How the Willie Horton Story Changed American Justice*. New York: Crown.

Anglin, M. Douglas, and Yih-Ing Hser. 1990. "Treatment of Drug Abuse." In *Drugs and Crime*, edited by Michael Tonry and James Q. Wilson. Vol. 13 of *Crime and Justice: A Review of Research*, edited by Michael Tonry. Chicago: University of Chicago Press.

Apel, Robert, and Daniel Nagin. 2011. "General Deterrence: A Review of Recent Evidence." In *The Oxford Handbook of Crime and Criminal Justice*, edited by Michael Tonry. New York: Oxford University Press.

Apuzzo, Matt. 2014*a*. "Holder Endorses Proposal to Reduce Drug Sentences in Latest Sign of Shift." *New York Times* (March 14), p. A18.

———. 2014*b*. "Justice Dept. Expands Eligibility for Clemency." *New York Times* (April 24), p. A16.

Arthur D. Little, Inc. and Goldfarb and Singer, Esqs. 1981. *An Evaluation of Parole Guidelines in Four Jurisdictions*. Washington, DC: National Institute of Corrections.

Ashworth, Andrew. 2001. "The Decline of English Sentencing and Other Stories." In *Sentencing and Sanctions in Western Countries*, edited by Michael Tonry and Richard S. Frase. New York: Oxford University Press.

———. 2010. *Sentencing and Criminal Justice*, 5th ed. Cambridge, UK: Cambridge University Press.

———. 2011. "Re-evaluating the Standards for Aggravation and Mitigation at Sentencing." In *Mitigation and Aggravation at Sentencing*, edited by Julian V. Roberts. Cambridge, UK: Cambridge University Press.

Asp, Petter. 2010. "Previous Convictions and Proportionate Punishment under Swedish Law." In *Previous Convictions at Sentencing: Theoretical and Applied Perspectives*, edited by Julian V. Roberts and Andrew von Hirsch. Oxford: Hart.

———. 2012. "The Prosecutor in Swedish Law." In *Prosecutors and Politics: A Comparative Perspective,* edited by Michael Tonry. Vol. 41 of *Crime and Justice: A Review of Research*, edited by Michael Tonry. Chicago: University of Chicago Press.

Association of Chief Police Officers. 2012. *Restorative Justice (RJ) Guidelines and Minimum Standards*. London: Association of Chief Police Officers.

Austin, James, Eric Cadora, Todd R. Clear, Kara Dansky, Judith Greene, Vanita Gupta, Marc Mauer, Nicole Porter, Susan Tucker, and Malcolm C. Young. 2013. *Ending Mass Incarceration: Charting a New Justice Reinvestment.* Washington, DC: The Sentencing Project.

Austin, James, John Clark, Patricia Hardyman, and D. Alan Henry. 2000. *Three Strikes and You're Out: The Implementation and Impact of Strike Laws.* Final Report submitted to the US National Institute of Justice. Washington, DC: US Department of Justice, National Institute of Justice.

Austin, James, Charles Jones, John Kramer, and Phil Renninger. 1994. *National Assessment of Structured Sentencing.* Washington, DC: US Department of Justice, Bureau of Justice Assistance.

Austin, James, and Barry Krisberg. 1982. "The Unmet Promise of Alternatives to Incarceration." *Crime & Delinquency* 28:374–409.

Australia, Legal and Constitutional Affairs References Committee. 2013. *Value of a Justice Reinvestment Approach to Criminal Justice in Australia.* Canberra: Senate Printing Unit, Department of the Senate, Parliament House.

Australian Law Reform Commission. 1980. *Sentencing of Federal Offenders*. Canberra: Australian Government Publishing Service.

Baker, Estella, and Andrew Ashworth. 2010. "The Role of Previous Convictions in England and Wales." In *Previous Convictions at Sentencing: Theoretical and Applied Perspectives,* edited by Julian V. Roberts and Andrew von Hirsch. Oxford: Hart.

Bales, William D., and Alex Piquero. 2011. "Assessing the Impact of Imprisonment on Recidivism." *Journal of Experimental Criminology* 8(1):71–101.

Baron-Evans, Amy, and Kate Stith. 2012. "Booker Rules." *University of Pennsylvania Law Review* 160:1631–743.

Barr, William. 1992. *The Case for More Incarceration*. Washington, DC: US Department of Justice, Office of Policy Development.

Beale, Sara Sun. 1989. *Sentencing Guidelines*. Staff memorandum prepared for the Federal Court Study Committee. Federal Courts Study Committee—Working Papers. Washington, DC: Federal Judicial Center.

Beccaria, Cesare. 2007 [1764]. *On Crimes and Punishments, and Other Writings,* translated by Aaron Thomas and Jeremy Parzen. Toronto: University of Toronto Press.

Beha, James A., II. 1977. "'And Nobody Can Get You Out': The Impact of a Mandatory Prison Sentence for the Illegal Carrying of a Firearm on the Use of Firearms and on the Administration of Criminal Justice in Boston." *Boston University Law Review* 57:96–146 (part 1), 289–333 (part 2).

Bendavid, Naftali. 1993. "Sentencing Panel's Political Firestorm: As New Era Dawns, US Commission Rocked by Jostling over Leadership, Goals." *Legal Times*, September 13, 16:10–18.

———. 1994*a*. "Who's Minding the Sentencing Store?" *Legal Times*, April 4, 16:1, 12–14.

———. 1994*b*. "Sentencing Commission at the Brink: Plagued by Vacancies, Panel's Expiration Looms." *Legal Times*, August 17, 17:10–18.

Bennett, Christopher. 2010. "'More to Apologise For': Can We Find a Basis for the Recidivist Premium in a Communicative Theory of Punishment?" In *Previous Convictions at Sentencing: Theoretical and Applied Perspectives*, edited by Julian V. Roberts and Andrew von Hirsch. Oxford: Hart.

Bennett, William J., John J. DiIulio, and John P. Walters. 1996. *Body Count: Moral Poverty . . . and How to Win America's War against Crime and Drugs*. New York: Simon & Schuster.

Bentham, Jeremy. 1970 [1789]. "The Utilitarian Theory of Punishment." In *An Introduction to Principles of Morals and Legislation*, edited by Jeremy Bentham, J. H. Burns, and H. L. A. Hart. London: Athlone.

———. 2008 [1830]. *The Rationale of Punishment*. Amherst, NY: Kessinger.

Bibas, Stephanos. 2004. "The Feeney Amendment and the Continuing Rise of Prosecutorial Power to Plea Bargain." *Journal of Criminal Law and Criminology* 94(2):295–308.

Block, Michael K. 1989. "Emerging Problems in the Sentencing Commission's Approach to Guidelines Amendments." *Federal Sentencing Reporter* 1:451–55.

Blumstein, Alfred, and Allen Beck. 1999. "Population Growth in US Prisons, 1980–1996." In *Prisons*, edited by Michael Tonry and Joan Petersilia. Vol. 26 of *Crime and Justice: A Review of Research*, edited by Michael Tonry. Chicago: University of Chicago Press.

Blumstein, Alfred, Jacqueline Cohen, and P. Hsieh. 1982. *The Duration of Adult Criminal Careers*. Final report submitted to the National Institute of Justice, US Department of Justice. Pittsburgh, PA: Heinz School of Urban and Public Affairs, Carnegie-Mellon University.

Blumstein, Alfred, Jacqueline Cohen, Susan E. Martin, and Michael Tonry, eds. 1983. *Research on Sentencing: The Search for Reform*. 2 vols. Washington, DC: National Academy Press.

Blumstein, Alfred, Jacqueline Cohen, and Daniel Nagin, eds. 1978. *Deterrence and Incapacitation: Estimating the Effects of Criminal Sanctions on Crime Rates*. Washington, DC: National Academy of Sciences.

Blumstein, Alfred, Jacqueline Cohen, Jeffrey A. Roth, and Christy A. Visher, eds. 1986. *Criminal Careers and "Career Criminals."* Washington, DC: National Academies Press.

Bobo, Lawrence D., and Victor Thompson. 2006. "Unfair by Design: The War on Drugs, Race, and the Legitimacy of the Criminal Justice System." *Social Research* 73(2):445–70.

———. 2010. "Racialized Mass Incarceration: Poverty, Prejudice, and Punishment." In *Doing Race: 21 Essays for the 21st Century*, edited by Hazel Rose Markus and Paula M. L. Moya. New York: Norton.

Boerner, David. 1992. "Confronting Violence: In the Act and in the World." *University of Puget Sound Law Review* 15:525–77.

———. 1995. "Sentencing Guidelines and Prosecutorial Discretion." *Judicature* 78:196–200.

———. 2012. "Prosecution in Washington State." In *Prosecutors and Politics: A Comparative Perspective*, edited by Michael Tonry. Vol. 41 of *Crime and Justice: A Review of Research*, edited by Michael Tonry. Chicago: University of Chicago Press.

Boerner, David, and Roxanne Lieb. 2001. "Sentencing Reform in the Other Washington." In *Crime and Justice: A Review of Research*, vol. 28, edited by Michael Tonry. Chicago: University of Chicago Press.

Bogan, Kathleen, and David Factor. 1997. "Oregon Guidelines, 1989–1994." In *Sentencing Reform in Overcrowded Times*, edited by Michael Tonry and Kathleen Hatlestad. New York: Oxford University Press.

Bonczar, Thomas. 2011. *National Corrections Reporting Program: Time Served in State Prison, by Offense, Release Type, Sex, and Race*. Washington, DC: US Department of Justice, Bureau of Justice Statistics.

Bonnie, Richard J., Robert L. Johnson, Betty M. Chemers, and Julie Schuck, eds. 2012. *Reforming Juvenile Justice: A Developmental Approach*. Washington, DC: National Academies Press.

Bottoms, Anthony E. 1977. "Reflections on the Renaissance of Dangerousness." *Howard Journal of Criminal Justice* 16(2):70–96.

Braithwaite, John. 1989. *Crime, Shame, and Reintegration*. Cambridge, UK: Cambridge University Press.

———. 2001*a*. "Republicanism and Restorative Justice: An Explanatory and Normative Connection." In *Restorative Justice: Philosophy to Practice*, edited by John Braithwaite and Heather Strang. Burlington, VT: Ashgate.

———. 2001*b*. *Restorative Justice and Responsive Regulation*. Oxford: Oxford University Press.

Braithwaite, John, and Philip Pettit. 1990. *Not Just Deserts: A Republican Theory of Criminal Justice*. Oxford: Clarendon.

———. 2001. "Republicanism and Restorative Justice: An Explanatory and Normative Connection." In *Restorative Justice: Philosophy to Practice*, edited by John Braithwaite and Heather Strang. Burlington, VT: Ashgate.

Breyer, Stephen. 1988. "The Federal Sentencing Guidelines and the Key Compromises upon Which They Rest." *Hofstra Law Review* 17:1–50.

———. 1999. "Federal Sentencing Guidelines Revisited." *Federal Sentencing Reporter* 11:180–86.

Brockway, Zebulon Reed. 1912. *Fifty Years of Prison Service: An Autobiography.* New York: Charities Publications.

Brown Commission. 1971. See National Commission on Reform of Federal Criminal Laws (1971).

Bureau of Justice Statistics. 1990. *Compendium of Federal Justice Statistics—1985.* Washington, DC: US Department of Justice, Bureau of Justice Statistics.

Burgess, Anthony. 1962. *A Clockwork Orange.* London: Heinemann.

Cahalan, Margaret Werner. 1986. *Historical Corrections Statistics in the United States, 1850–1984.* Washington, DC: US Department of Justice, Bureau of Justice Statistics.

Canada, Standing Committee on Justice and the Solicitor General. 1993. *Crime Prevention in Canada: Toward a National Strategy.* Thirty-Fourth Canadian Parliament, 1991–92–93, 3rd session.

Canadian Sentencing Commission. 1987. *Sentencing Reform: A Canadian Approach.* Ottawa: Canadian Government Publishing Centre.

Carlson, Kenneth. 1982. *Mandatory Sentencing: The Experience of Two States.* Washington, DC: US Government Printing Office.

Carrow, Deborah M., Judith Feins, Beverly N. W. Lee, and Lois Olinger. 1985. *Guidelines without Force: An Evaluation of the Multi-jurisdictional Sentencing Guidelines Field Test.* Report to the National Institute of Justice. Cambridge, MA: Abt Associates.

Carson, E. Ann. 2014. *Prisoners in 2013.* Washington, DC: US Department of Justice, Bureau of Justice Statistics.

Carson, E. Ann, and Daniela Golinelli. 2013. *Prisoners in 2012—Trends in Admissions and Releases, 1991–2012.* Washington, D.C.: U.S. Department of Justice, Bureau of Justice Statistics.

Carson, E. Ann, and William J. Sabol. 2012. *Prisoners in 2011.* Washington, DC: US Department of Justice, Bureau of Justice Statistics.

Caulkins, Jonathan P., and Robert MacCoun. 2003. "Limited Rationality and the Limits of Supply Reduction." *Journal of Drug Issues* 33(2):433–64.

Chaiken, Jan M., and Marcia Chaiken. 1982. *Varieties of Criminal Behavior.* Santa Monica, CA: Rand Corporation.

Chandler, R. K., B. W. Fletcher, and N. D. Volkow. 2009. "Treating Drug Abuse and Addiction in the Criminal Justice System: Improving Public Health and Safety." *Journal of the American Medical Association* 301(2):183–90.

Chen, Elsa Y. 2008. "Impacts of 'Three Strikes and You're Out' on Crime Trends in California and Throughout the United States." *Journal of Contemporary Criminal Justice* 24:345–70.

Cohen, Jacqueline. 1983. "Incapacitation as a Strategy for Crime Control: Possibilities and Pitfalls." In *Crime and Justice: A Review of Research*, vol. 5, edited by Michael Tonry and Norval Morris. Chicago: University of Chicago Press.

Cohen, Jacqueline, and Michael Tonry. 1983. "Sentencing Reforms and Their Impacts." In *Research on Sentencing: The Search for Reform*, vol. 2, edited by Alfred

Blumstein, Jacqueline Cohen, Susan E. Martin, and Michael Tonry. Washington, DC: National Academy Press.

Cohen, Mark A. 1988. "Pain, Suffering, and Jury Awards: A Study of the Cost of Crime to Victims." *Law and Society Review* 22(3):537–56.

———. 2005. *The Costs of Crime and Justice*. Abingdon, Oxon, UK: Routledge.

Cohen, Mark A., Roland T. Rust, Sara Steen, and Simon T. Tidd. 2004. "Willingness-to-Pay for Crime Control Programs." *Criminology* 42(1):89–109.

Cohen, Thomas H., and Tracey Kyckelhahn. 2010. *Felony Defendants in Large Urban Counties, 2006*. Washington, D.C.: U.S. Department of Justice, Bureau of Justice Statistics.

Cook, Philip J. 1980. "Research in Criminal Deterrence: Laying the Groundwork for the Second Decade." In *Crime and Justice: A Review of Research*, vol. 2, edited by Norval Morris and Michael Tonry. Chicago: University of Chicago Press.

Cook, Philip J., Jens Ludwig, Sudhir Alladi Venkatesh, and Anthony A. Braga. 2007. "Underground Drug Markets." *Economic Journal* 117(Nov):F1–F29.

Council of Europe. 2014. *Annual Penal Statistics—Prison Stock on 01 Jan. 2013 and 2014*. Strasburg: Council of Europe.

Cullen, Francis. 2013. "Rehabilitation: Beyond Nothing Works." In *Crime and Justice in America: 1975–2025*, edited by Michael Tonry. Vol. 42 of *Crime and Justice: A Review of Research,* edited by Michael Tonry. Chicago: University of Chicago Press.

Cullen, Francis, and Cheryl Lero Jonson. 2015. "Prisoner Reentry Programs." In *Crime and Justice: A Review of Research*, vol. 44, edited by Michael Tonry. Chicago: University of Chicago Press.

Cullen, Francis, Cheryl Jonson, and Daniel S. Nagin. 2011. "Prisons Do Not Reduce Recidivism." *Prison Journal* 91(3):48–65.

Darley, John M. 2010. "Citizens' Assignments of Punishments for Moral Transgressions: A Case Study in the Psychology of Punishment." *Ohio State Journal of Criminal Law* 8:101–17.

Davis, Kenneth Culp. 1969. *Discretionary Justice: A Preliminary Inquiry*. Baton Rouge: Louisiana State University Press.

Dawson, Robert O. 1969. *Sentencing*. Boston: Little, Brown.

de Keijser, Jan. 2011. "Never Mind the Pain; It's a Measure! Justifying Measures as Part of the Dutch Bifurcated System of Sanctions." In *Retributivism Has a Past: Has It a Future?*, edited by Michael Tonry. New York: Oxford University Press.

Dershowitz, Alan. 1976. *Fair and Certain Punishment*. New York: Twentieth Century Fund.

Dills, Angela K., Jeffrey A. Miron, and Garrett Summers. 2008. "What Do Economists Know about Crime?" Working Paper no. 13759. Cambridge, MA: National Bureau of Economic Research.

Ditton, Paula M., and Doris James Wilson.1999. *Truth in Sentencing in State Prisons*. Washington, DC: US Department of Justice, Bureau of Justice Statistics.

Doob, Anthony N. 1989. "Sentencing Aids Final Report." Unpublished manuscript. Toronto: University of Toronto, Institute of Criminology.

———. 1990. "Computerized Sentencing Information for Judges. An Overview of Progress Reports on the Sentencing Aids Project." Unpublished report. Toronto: University of Toronto, Institute of Criminology.

———. 1995. "The United States Sentencing Commission Guidelines: If You Don't Know Where You Are, You Might Not Get There." In *The Politics of Sentencing Reform*, edited by Chris Clarkson and Rod Morgan. Oxford: Clarendon.

Doob, Anthony N., and Norman W. Park. 1987. "Computerized Sentencing Information for Judges: An Aid to the Sentencing Process." *Criminal Law Quarterly* 30(1):54–72.

Duff, R. Antony. 1986. *Trials and Punishments*. Cambridge, UK: Cambridge University Press.

———. 2001. *Punishment, Communication, and Community*. New York: Oxford University Press.

———. 2002. "Restorative Punishment and Punitive Restoration." In *Restorative Justice and the Law*, edited by Lode Walgrave. Cullompton, UK: Willan.

———. 2011. "Responsibility, Restoration, and Retribution." In *Retributivism Has a Past: Has It a Future?*, edited by Michael Tonry. New York: Oxford University Press.

Durlauf, Steven N., and Daniel S. Nagin. 2011. "Imprisonment and Crime: Can Both Be Reduced?" *Criminology and Public Policy* 10(1):13–54.

Dworkin, Ronald. 1986. *Law's Empire*. Cambridge, MA: Harvard University Press.

Edsall, Thomas, and Mary Edsall. 1991. *Chain Reaction: The Impact of Race, Rights, and Taxes on American Politics*. New York: Norton.

Eisner, Manuel. 2008. "Modernity Strikes Back. A Historical Perspective on the Latest Increase in Interpersonal Violence (1960–1990)." *International Journal on Conflict and Interpersonal Violence* 2:288–316.

Evans, William N., and Emily G. Owens. 2007. "COPS and Crime." *Journal of Public Economics* 91:181–201.

Farrington, David P. 1986. "Age and Crime." In *Crime and Justice: A Review of Research*, vol. 7, edited by Michael Tonry and Norval Morris. Chicago: University of Chicago Press.

———. 2003. "Developmental and Life-Course Criminology: Key Theoretical and Empirical Issues." *Criminology* 41:221–55.

Federal Courts Study Committee. 1990. *Report*. Washington, DC: Administrative Office of the US Courts.

Federal Judicial Center. 1989. *Annual Report 1989*. Washington, DC: Federal Judicial Center.

Feinberg, Joel, ed. 1970. "The Expressive Function of Punishment." *Doing and Deserving: Essays in the Theory of Responsibility*. Princeton, NJ: Princeton University Press.

Ferri, Enrico. 1917. *Criminal Sociology*. Boston: Little, Brown.

———. 1921. *Relazione sul Progetto Preliminare di Codice Penale Italiano*. Milan: L'Universelle.

Fleming, MacKlin. 1974. *The Price of Perfect Justice: The Adverse Consequences of Current Legal Doctrine on the American Courtroom*. New York: Basic Books.

Fletcher, George. 1978. *Rethinking Criminal Law*. Boston: Little, Brown.

Flood, Gerald F. 1963. "The Model Sentencing Act: A Higher Level of Penal Law." *Crime and Delinquency* 9(4):370–80.

Fogel, David. 1979. *We Are the Living Proof: The Justice Model for Corrections*. Cincinnati: Anderson.

Frankel, Marvin. 1972. "Lawlessness in Sentencing." *Cincinnati Law Review* 41(1):1–54.

———. 1973. *Criminal Sentences: Law without Order*. New York: Hill & Wang.

Frase, Richard. 2005. "Sentencing Guidelines in Minnesota, 1978–2003." In *Crime and Justice: A Review of Research*, vol. 32, edited by Michael Tonry. Chicago: University of Chicago Press.

———. 2009*a*. "Limiting Excessive Prison Sentencing." *University of Pennsylvania Journal of Constitutional Law* 11(1):43–46.

———. 2009*b*. "What Explains Persistent Racial Disproportionality in Minnesota's Prison and Jail Populations?" In *Crime and Justice: A Review of Research*, edited by Michael Tonry. Chicago: University Press.

———. 2011. "Can Above-Desert Penalties Be Justified by Competing Deontological Theories?" In *Retributivism Has a Past: Has It a Future?*, edited by Michael Tonry. New York: Oxford University Press.

———. 2013. *Just Sentencing: Principles and Procedures for a Workable System*. New York: Oxford University Press.

Freeborn, Beth A., and Monica E. Hartmann. 2010. "Judicial Discretion and Sentencing Behavior: Did the Feeney Amendment Rein in District Judges?" *Journal of Empirical Legal Studies* 7(2):355–78.

Freiberg, Arie. 2001. "Three Strikes and You're Out—It's Not Cricket: Colonization and Resistance in Australian Sentencing." In *Sentencing and Sanctions in Western Countries*, edited by Michael Tonry and Richard S. Frase. New York: Oxford University Press.

———. 2007. "Jurisprudential Miscegenation: Strict Liability and the Ambiguity of Crime." In *Governance and Regulation in Social Life: Essays in Honour of W. G. Carson*, edited by A. Brannigan and G. Pavlich. Oxford: Routledge-Cavendish.

———. 2014. *Fox and Freiberg's Sentencing: State and Federal Law in Victoria*, 3rd ed. Melbourne: Thomson Reuters.

Garland, David. 2001. *The Culture of Control*. Chicago: University of Chicago Press.

Germany. 2006. *Second Report on the State of Interior/Domestic Security in Germany*. Periodischer Sicherheitsbericht. Berlin: Ministries of Justice and Interior.

Gest, Ted. 2001. *Crime and Politics: Big Government's Erratic Campaign for Law and Order*. New York: Oxford University Press.

Gilliard, Darrell K., and Allen J. Beck. 1997. *Prison and Jail Inmates at Midyear 1996*. Washington, DC: US Department of Justice, Bureau of Justice Statistics.

Gingrich, Newt, and Van Jones. 2014. "Prison System Is Failing America." http://CNN.com (May 22). http://www.cnn.com/2014/05/21/opinion/gingrich-jones-prison-system-fails-america/index.html.

Gingrich, Newt, and Pat Nolan. 2011. "Prison Reform: A Smart Way for States to Save Money and Lives." *Washington Post* (January 7). http://www.washingtonpost.com/wp-dyn/content/article/2011/01/06/AR2011010604386.html.

Glueck, Sheldon. 1928. "Principles of a Rational Penal Code." *Harvard Law Review* 41(4):453–82.

Gottfredson, Don M., Leslie T. Wilkins, and Peter B. Hoffman. 1978. *Guidelines for Parole and Sentencing*. Lanham, MD: Lexington.

Gottschalk, Marie. 2015. *Caught: The Prison State and the Lockdown of American Politics*. Princeton, NJ: Princeton University Press.

Greenfeld, Lawrence. 1988. *Prisoners in 1987*. Washington, DC: US Department of Justice, Bureau of Justice Statistics.

Griset, Pamela. 1991. *Determinate Sentencing: The Promise and the Reality of Retributive Justice*. Albany: State University of New York Press.

Guerino, Paul, Paige M. Harrison, and William J. Sabol. 2011. *Prisoners in 2010*. Washington, DC: US Department of Justice, Bureau of Justice Statistics.

Gwin, James S. 2010. "Juror Sentiment on Just Punishment: Do the Federal Sentencing Guidelines Reflect Community Values." *Harvard Law and Policy Review* 4:173–200.

Hampton, Jean. 1984. "The Moral Education Theory of Punishment." *Philosophy and Public Affairs* 13(3):208–38.

Harrison, Ross. 1995. "Jeremy Bentham." In *The Oxford Companion to Philosophy*, edited by Ted Honderich. Oxford: Oxford University Press.

Hart, H. L. A. 1959. "Prolegomenon to the Principles of Punishment." *Proceedings of the Aristotelian Society*, n.s., 60:1–26.

———. 1968. *Punishment and Responsibility: Essays in the Philosophy of Law*. Oxford: Oxford University Press.

Hay, Douglas. 1975. "Property, Authority, and the Criminal Law." In *Albion's Fatal Tree: Crime and Society in Eighteenth Century England*, edited by Douglas Hay, Peter Linebaugh, E. P. Thompson, and Cal Winslow. New York: Pantheon.

Heaney, Gerald W. 1991. "The Reality of Guidelines Sentencing: No End to Disparity." *American Criminal Law Review* 28:161–233.

Hegel, G. W. F. 1991 [1821]. "Wrong [Das Unrecht]." In *Elements of the Philosophy of Right*, edited by Allen W. Wood, translated by H. B. Nisbet. Cambridge, UK: Cambridge University Press.

Heumann, Milton, and Colin Loftin. 1979. "Mandatory Sentencing and the Abolition of Plea Bargaining: The Michigan Felony Firearms Statute." *Law and Society Review* 13:393–430.

Hinkkanen, Ville, and Tapio Lappi-Seppälä. 2011. "Sentencing Theory, Policy, and Research in the Nordic Countries." In *Crime and Justice in Scandinavia*, edited by Michael Tonry and Tapio Lappi-Seppälä. Vol. 40 of *Crime and*

Justice: A Review of Research, edited by Michael Tonry. Chicago: University of Chicago Press.

Hofer, Paul J. 1990. "Sentencing Procedures and the Federal Guidelines." Draft research report approved for Federal Judicial Center publication but later withdrawn. Washington, DC: Federal Judicial Center.

———. 2011. "Beyond the 'Heartland': Sentencing under the Advisory Federal Guidelines." *Duquesne Law Review* 49:675–705.

———. 2012. "Review of the US Sentencing Commission's Report to Congress: Mandatory Minimum Penalties in the Federal Criminal Justice System." *Federal Sentencing Reporter* 24(3):193–213.

Hoffman, Peter B. 1976. "Salient Factor Score Validation: A 1972 Release Cohort." *Journal of Criminal Justice* 6:69–76.

———. 1983. "Screening for Risk: A Revised Salient Factor Score (SFS 81)." *Journal of Criminal Justice* 11(6):539–47.

———. 1995. "Twenty Years of Operational Use of a Risk Prediction Instrument: The United States Parole Commission's Salient Factor Score." *Journal of Criminal Justice* 22(6):477–94.

Home Office. 1990. *Crime, Justice, and Protecting the Public*. London: Home Office.

Hough, Mike, Jessica Jacobson, and Andrew Millie. 2003. *The Decision to Imprison: Sentencing and the Prison Population*. London: Prison Reform Trust.

Hubbard, Amy. 2012. "624-Year Sentence for Rapist; Plus Other Eye-Popping Jail Terms." *Los Angeles Times* (August 15).

Husak, Douglas. 2008. *Overcriminalization: The Limits of the Criminal Law*. New York: Oxford University.

———. 2011. "Retributivism, Proportionality, and the Challenge of the Drug Court Movement." In *Retributivism Has a Past: Has It a Future?*, edited by Michael Tonry. New York: Oxford University Press.

Jacobs, James B. 1981. "The Prisoner's Rights Movement and Its Impacts, 1960–80." In *Crime and Justice: A Review of Research*, vol. 2, edited by Norval Morris and Michael Tonry. Chicago: University of Chicago Press.

———. 2015. *The Eternal Criminal Record*. Cambridge, MA: Harvard University Press.

Jacobsen, J., and M. Hough. 2010. *Unjust Deserts: Imprisonment for Public Protection*. London: Prison Reform Trust.

Jehle, Jörg-Martin, Paul Smit, and Josef Zila. 2008. "The Public Prosecutor as Key-Player: Prosecutorial Case-Ending Decisions." *European Journal of Criminal Policy and Research* 14:161–79.

Jenkins, Philip. 1998. *Moral Panic: Changing Concepts of the Child Molester in Modern America*. New Haven: Yale University Press.

Johnson, Brian D. 2012. "Sentencing." In *The Oxford Handbook of Crime and Criminal Justice, edited by* Michael Tonry. New York: Oxford University Press.

———. 2014. *The Missing Link: Examining Prosecutorial Decision-Making across Federal District Courts*. Final Report to the National Institute of Justice (grant no. 2010-IJ-CX-0012). Washington, DC: US Department of Justice, National Institute of Justice.

Johnson, Inge. 1990. "'Time' for Prisoners and for Judges." *Overcrowded Times* 1(4):7–8.

Joint Committee on New York Drug Law Evaluation. 1978. *The Nation's Toughest Drug Law: Evaluating the New York Experience*. Washington, DC: US Government Printing Office.

Jonson, Cheryl Lero, and Francis Cullen. 2015. "Prisoner Reentry Programs." In *Crime and Justice: A Review of Research*, vol. 44, edited by Michael Tonry. Chicago: University of Chicago Press.

Kaiser, Kimberly A., and Cassia Spohn. 2014. "Fundamentally Flawed?: Exploring the Use of Policy Disagreements in Judicial Downward Departures for Child Pornography Sentences." *Criminology and Public Policy* 13(2):241–70.

Kant, Immanuel. 1965 [1798]. "The Penal Law and the Law of Pardon." In *The Metaphysical Elements of Justice*, translated by John Ladd. Indianapolis: Liberal Arts Press/Bobbs-Merrill.

Kassebaum, Gene, David Ward, and Daniel Wilner. 1971. *Prison Treatment and Parole Survival: An Empirical Assessment*. New York: John Wiley.

Kirk, David S., and Robert J. Sampson. 2012. "Juvenile Arrest and Collateral Educational Damage in the Transition to Adulthood." *Sociology of Education* 86:36–62.

Kleiman, Mark A. R. 1997. "The Problem of Replacement and the Logic of Drug Law Enforcement." *Drug Policy Analysis Bulletin* 3:8–10.

———. 2009. *When Brute Force Fails: How to Have Less Crime and Less Punishment*, Princeton: Princeton University Press.

Kleinig, John. 1973. *Punishment and Desert*. New York: Springer.

Knapp, Kay A. 1984. *The Impact of the Minnesota Sentencing Guidelines: Three-Year Evaluation*. St. Paul: Minnesota Sentencing Guidelines Commission.

———. 1991. "Arizona: Unprincipled Sentencing, Mandatory Minimums, and Prison Crowding." *Overcrowded Times* 2(5):10–12.

———. 1993. "Allocation of Discretion and Accountability within Sentencing Structures." *University of Colorado Law Review* 64:679–706.

Knapp, Kay A., and Denis J. Hauptly. 1992. "State and Federal Sentencing Guidelines: Apples and Oranges." *University of California at Davis Law Review* 25:679–94.

Kommers, Donald P. 1997. *The Constitutional Jurisprudence of the Federal Republic of Germany*, 2nd ed. Durham, NC: Duke University Press.

Kramer, John H., and Jeffrey T. Ulmer. 2008. *Sentencing Guidelines: Lessons from Pennsylvania*. Boulder, CO: Lynne Rienner.

Kress, Jack M. 1980. *Prescription for Justice: The Theory and Practice of Sentencing Guidelines*. Cambridge, MA: Ballinger.

Lappi-Seppälä, Tapio. 2001. "Sentencing and Punishment in Finland: The Decline of the Repressive Ideal." In *Sentencing and Sanctions in Western Countries*, edited by Michael Tonry and Richard S. Frase. New York: Oxford University Press.

———. 2007. "Penal Policy in Scandinavia." In *Crime, Punishment, and Politics, in Comparative Perspective*, edited by Michael Tonry. Vol. 36 of *Crime and*

Justice: A Review of Research, edited by Michael Tonry. Chicago: University of Chicago Press.

———. 2008. "Trust, Welfare, and Political Culture: Explaining Differences in National Penal Policies." In *Crime and Justice: A Review of Research*, vol. 37, edited by Michael Tonry. Chicago: University of Chicago Press.

———. 2011. "Sentencing and Punishment in Finland: The Decline of the Repressive Ideal." In *Why Punish? How Much?*, edited by Michael Tonry. New York: Oxford University Press.

———. 2016. "Sentencing Policy in Scandinavia." In *Sentencing and Punishment in Western Countries since 2000*. Vol. 45 of *Crime and Justice: A Review of Research*, edited by Michael Tonry. Chicago: University of Chicago Press. Forthcoming.

Lappi-Seppälä, Tapio, and Michael Tonry. 2011. "Crime, Criminal Justice, and Criminology in the Nordic Countries." In *Crime and Justice in Scandinavia*, edited by Michael Tonry and Tapio Lappi-Seppälä. Vol. 40 of *Crime and Justice: A Review of Research*, edited by Michael Tonry. Chicago: University of Chicago Press.

LaVigne, Nancy, Samuel Bieler, Lindsey Cramer, Helen Ho, Cybele Kotonias, Deborah Mayer, David McClure, Laura Pacifici, Erika Parks, Bryce Peterson, and Julie Samuels. 2014. *Justice Reinvestment Initiative State Assessment Report*. Washington, D.C.: Urban Institute.

Lawrence, Pamela B., and Paul J. Hofer. 1992. *An Empirical Study of the Application of Relevant Conduct Guidelines*. Washington, DC: Federal Judicial Center.

Lee, Youngjae. 2010. "Repeat Offenders and the Question of Desert." In *Previous Convictions at Sentencing: Theoretical and Applied Perspectives*, edited by Julian V. Roberts and Andrew von Hirsch. Oxford: Hart.

Lerman, Amy, and Vesla Weaver. 2014. *Arresting Citizenship: The Democratic Consequences of American Crime Control*. Chicago: University of Chicago Press.

Levitt, Steven D., and Sudhir Alladi Venkatesh. 2000. "An Economic Analysis of a Drug Selling Gang's Finances." *Quarterly Journal of Economics* 115(3):755–89.

Lévy, René. 2007. "Pardons and Amnesties as Policy Instruments in Contemporary France." In *Crime, Punishment, and Politics in Comparative Perspective*, edited by Michael Tonry. Vol. 36 of *Crime and Justice: A Review of Research*, edited by Michael Tonry. Chicago: University of Chicago Press.

Lewis, C. S. 2011 [1949]. "The Humanitarian Theory of Punishment." In *Why Punish? How Much?*, edited by Michael Tonry. New York: Oxford University Press.

Lipton, Douglas, Robert Martinson, and Judith Wilks. 1975. *Effectiveness of Correctional Treatment: A Survey of Treatment and Evaluation Studies*. New York: Praeger.

Loftin, Colin, Milton Heumann, and David McDowall. 1983. "Mandatory Sentencing and Firearms Violence: Evaluating an Alternative to Gun Control." *Law and Society Review* 17:287–318.

Loftin, Colin, and David McDowall. 1981. "'One with a Gun Gets You Two': Mandatory Sentencing and Firearms Violence in Detroit." *Annals of the American Academy of Political and Social Science* 455:150–67.

Lovegrove, Austin. 1988. *Judicial Decision-Making.* New York: Springer-Verlag.

———. 1997. *The Framework of Judicial Sentencing: A Study in Legal Decision Making.* Cambridge, UK: Cambridge University Press.

Luna, Erik, and Marianne Wade, eds. 2012. *The Prosecutor in Transnational Perspective.* New York: Oxford University Press.

Lynch, Gerard E. 2003. "Screening versus Plea Bargaining: Exactly What Are We Trading Off?" *Stanford Law Review* 55:1399–1408.

MacCoun, Robert, and Karin D. Martin. 2009. "Drugs." In *The Oxford Handbook on Crime and Public Policy,* edited by Michael Tonry. New York: Oxford University Press.

MacKenzie, Doris Layton. 2006. *What Works in Corrections: Reducing the Criminal Activities of Offenders and Delinquents.* Cambridge, UK: Cambridge University Press.

Mackie, John L. 1982. "Morality and the Retributive Emotions." *Criminal Justice Ethics* 1(1):3–10.

Markel, Dan. 2010. "Bentham on Stilts: The Bare Relevance of Subjectivity to Retributive Justice." *California Law Review* 98:907–87.

Martin, Susan. 1984. "Interests and Politics in Sentencing Reform: The Development of Sentencing Guidelines in Pennsylvania and Minnesota." *Villanova Law Review* 29:21–113.

Martin, Susan, Lee Sechrest, and Robin Redner, eds. 1981. *New Directions in the Rehabilitation of Criminal Offenders.* Washington, DC: National Academies Press.

Martinson, Robert. 1974. "What Works? Questions and Answers about Prison Reform." *Public Interest* 35(2):22–54.

Marvell, Thomas B. 1995. "Sentencing Guidelines and Prison Population Growth." *Journal of Criminal Law and Criminology* 85:696–706.

Marvell, Thomas B., and Carlisle E. Moody. 1996. "Determinate Sentencing and Abolishing Parole: The Long-Term Impacts on Prisons and Crime." *Criminology* 34:107–38.

Mason, David P. 2004. "Barking Up the Wrong Tree: The Misplaced Furor over the Feeney Amendment as a Threat to Judicial Independence." *William and Mary Law Review* 46:731–85.

Mauer, Marc, and Nazgol Ghandnoosh. 2013. "Can We Wait 88 Years to End Mass Incarceration?" *Huffington Post* (December 20). http://www.huffingtonpost.com/marc-mauer/88-years-mass-incarceration_b_4474132.html.

McCoy, Candace, and Patrick McManimon. 2004. "New Jersey's 'No Early Release Act': Its Impact on Prosecution, Sentencing, Corrections, and Victim Satisfaction." Final Report to the National Institute of Justice, US Department of Justice. Rutgers University, School of Criminal Justice. Obtainable from the National Criminal Justice Reference Service.

McDonald, Douglas C., and Kenneth E. Carlson. 1992. *Federal Sentencing in Transition, 1986–90*. Washington, DC: US Department of Justice, Bureau of Justice Statistics.

Mennel, Robert M. 1983. *Thorns and Thistles: Juvenile Delinquents in the United States, 1825–1940*. Hanover: University of New Hampshire Press.

Merritt, Nancy, Terry Fain, and Susan Turner. 2006. "Oregon's Get Tough Sentencing Reform: A Lesson in Justice System Adaptation." *Criminology and Public Policy* 5(1):5–36.

Messinger, Sheldon L., John E. Berecochea, David Rauma, and Richard A. Berk. 1985. "Foundations of Parole in California." *Law and Society Review* 19:69–106.

Messinger, Sheldon L., and Phillip E. Johnson. 1978. "California's Determinate Sentencing Statute: History and Issues." In *Determinate Sentencing: Reform or Regression*, edited by the National Institute of Justice. Washington, DC: US Government Printing Office. http://scholarship.law.berkeley.edu/cgi/viewcontent.cgi?article=2883&context=facpubs.

Michael, Jerome, and Mortimer Adler. 1933. *Crime, Law, and Social Science*. New York: Harcourt Brace.

Michael, Jerome, and Herbert Wechsler. 1937. "A Rationale of the Law of Homicide II." *Columbia Law Review* 37:1261–1325.

———. 1940. *Criminal Law and Its Administration*. Chicago: Foundation.

Miller, Marc L., and Samantha Caplinger. 2012. "Prosecution in Arizona: Practical Problems, Prosecutorial Accountability, and Local Solutions." In *Prosecutors and Politics: A Comparative Perspective*, edited by Michael Tonry. Vol. 41 of *Crime and Justice: A Review of Research*, edited by Michael Tonry. Chicago: University of Chicago Press.

Minton, Todd D. 2012. *Jail Inmates at Mid-year 2011*. Washington, DC: US Department of Justice, Bureau of Justice Statistics.

Minton, Todd D., and Daniela Golinelli. 2014. *Jail Inmates at Midyear 2013—Statistical Tables*. Washington, DC: US Department of Justice, Bureau of Justice Statistics.

Mitchell, Ojmarrh. 2011. "Drug and Other Problem-Solving Courts." In *The Oxford Handbook of Crime and Criminal Justice*, edited by Michael Tonry. New York: Oxford University Press.

Mitchell, Ojmarrh, David B. Wilson, Amy Eggers, and Doris L. MacKenzie. 2012. "Assessing the Effectiveness of Drug Courts on Recidivism: A Meta-analytic Review of Traditional and Non-traditional Drug Courts." *Journal of Criminal Justice* 40:60–71.

Moore, Michael S. 1993. "Justifying Retributivism." *Israeli Law Review* 27:15–36.

Moore, Nina M. 2015. *The Political Roots of Political Tracking in American Government*. New York: Cambridge University Press.

Morris, Herbert. 1966. "Persons and Punishment." *Monist* 52:475–501.

———. 1981. "A Paternalist Theory of Punishment." *American Philosophical Quarterly* 18:263–71.

Morris, Norval. 1951. *The Habitual Criminal*. London: Longmans.

———. 1953. "Sentencing Convicted Criminals." *Australian Law Review* 27:186–208.

———. 1974. *The Future of Imprisonment*. Chicago: University of Chicago Press.

Morris, Norval, and Michael Tonry. 1990. *Between Prison and Probation: Intermediate Punishments in a Rational Sentencing System*. New York: Oxford University.

Murakawa, Naomi. 2014. *The First Civil Right: How Liberals Built Prison America*. New York: Oxford University Press.

Murphy, Jeffrey. 1973. "Marxism and Retribution." *Philosophy and Public Affairs* 2:217–43.

Murray, Joseph, David P. Farrington, Catrien C. J. H. Bijleveld, and Rolf Loeber. 2014. *Effects of Parental Incarceration on Children: Cross-National Comparative Studies*. Washington, DC: American Psychological Association.

Nagel, Ilene H. 1990. "Foreword: Structuring Sentencing Discretion: The New Federal Sentencing Guidelines." *Journal of Criminal Law and Criminology* 80(4):883–943.

Nagel, Ilene H., and Stephen J. Schulhofer. 1992. "A Tale of Three Cities: An Empirical Study of Charging and Bargaining Practices under the Federal Sentencing Guidelines." *Southern California Law Review* 66:501–79.

Nagel, Thomas. 1986. *The View from Nowhere*. New York: Oxford University Press.

Nagin, Daniel S. 1978. "General Deterrence: A Review of the Empirical Evidence." In *Deterrence and Incapacitation*, edited by Alfred Blumstein, Jacqueline Cohen, and Daniel Nagin. Washington, DC: National Academy Press.

———. 2013. "Deterrence in the Twenty-First Century." In *Crime and Justice in America: 1975–2025*, edited by Michael Tonry. Vol. 42 of *Crime and Justice: A Review of Research*, edited by Michael Tonry. Chicago: University of Chicago Press.

Nagin, Daniel S., Francis Cullen, and Cheryl Lero Jonson. 2009. "Imprisonment and Re-offending." In *Crime and Justice: A Review of Research*, vol. 38, edited by Michael Tonry. Chicago: University of Chicago Press.

Nagin, Daniel S., and John V. Pepper, eds. 2012. *Deterrence and the Death Penalty*. Washington, DC: National Academies Press.

National Advisory Commission on Criminal Justice Standards and Goals. 1973. *A National Strategy to Reduce Crime*. Washington, DC: US Government Printing Office.

National Commission on Law Observance and Enforcement. 1931. *Report on Penal Institutions, Probation, and Parole*. Washington, DC: US Government Printing Office.

National Commission on Reform of Federal Criminal Laws. 1971. *Report*. Washington, DC: US Government Printing Office. Also known as "Brown Commission."

National Conference of State Legislatures. 2015. *State Sentencing and Corrections Legislation Database.* http://www.ncsl.org/issues-research/justice/state-sentencing-and-corrections-legislation.aspx.

National Institute on Drug Abuse. 2014. *Principles of Drug Abuse Treatment for Criminal Justice Populations: A Research-Based Guide.* Bethesda, MD: National Institute on Drug Abuse.

Nelken, David. 2013. "Can Prosecutors Be Too Independent? An Italian Case Study." In *European Penology?*, edited by Tom Daems, Sonja Snacken, and Dirk Van Zyl Smit. Oxford: Hart.

Nellis, Ashley. 2013. *Life Goes On: The Historic Rise in Life Sentences in the United States.* Washington, DC: The Sentencing Project.

Newman, Donald. 1966. *Conviction.* Boston: Little, Brown.

Nicholson-Crotty, Sean. 2004. "The Impact of Sentencing Guidelines on State-Level Sanctions: An Analysis over Time." *Crime and Delinquency* 50(3):395–411.

Nimmer, Raymond T. 1971. *Two Million Unnecessary Arrests: Removing a Social Service Concern from the Criminal Justice System.* Chicago: American Bar Foundation.

O'Donnell, Pierce, Dennis Curtis, and Michael Churgin. 1977. *Toward a Just and Effective Sentencing System.* New York: Praeger.

Ogletree, Charles J., Jr., and Austin Sarat, eds. 2012. *Life without Parole: America's New Death Penalty?* New York: New York University Press.

O'Hear, Michael. 2011. "Drug Treatment Courts as Communicative Punishment." In *Retributivism Has a Past: Has It a Future?*, edited by Michael Tonry. New York: Oxford University Press.

Orland, Leonard, and Kevin R. Reitz. 1993. "Epilogue: A Gathering of State Sentencing Commissions." *Colorado Law Review* 64:837–45.

Parent, Dale G. 1988. *Structuring Criminal Sentences: The Evolution of Minnesota's Sentencing Guidelines.* New York: LEXIS Law Publications.

Parnas, Raymond I., and Michael B. Salerno. 1978. "The Influence behind, Substance, and Impact of the New Determinate Sentencing Law in California." *University of California at Davis Law Review* 11:29–41.

Perlman, Harvey S., and Josephine R. Potuto. 1979. "The Uniform Law Commissioners' Model Sentencing and Corrections Act: An Overview." *Nebraska Law Review* 58:925–64.

Petersilia, Joan, and Richard Rosenfeld, eds. 2007. *Parole, Desistance from Crime, and Community Integration.* Washington, DC: National Academy Press.

Pew Charitable Trusts. 2014. *States Project 3% Increase in Prisoners by 2018.* Philadelphia: Pew Charitable Trusts.

Pifferi, Michele. 2012. "Individualization of Punishment and the Rule of Law: Reshaping Legality in the United States and Europe between the 19th and the 20th Century." *American Journal of Legal History* 52(3):325–76.

Piquero, Alex R., David P. Farrington, and Alfred Blumstein. 2003. "The Criminal Career Paradigm." In *Crime and Justice: A Review of Research*, vol. 30, edited by Michael Tonry. Chicago: University of Chicago Press.

Piquero, Alex R., David P. Farrington, and Alfred Blumstein. 2007. *Key Issues in Criminal Career Research: New Analyses of the Cambridge Study in Delinquent Development*. New York: Cambridge University Press.

Platt, Anthony M. 1969. *The Child Savers: The Invention of Delinquency*. Chicago: University of Chicago Press.

Platt, Tony, and Paul Takagi. 1977. "Intellectuals for Law and Order: A Critique of the New 'Realists.'" *Crime and Social Justice* 8:1–24.

Porter, Nicole D. 2014. *The State of Sentencing 2013: Developments in Policy and Practice*. Washington, DC: The Sentencing Project.

———. 2015. *The State of Sentencing 2014: Developments in Policy and Practice*. Washington, DC: The Sentencing Project.

Pratt, Travis C., Francis T. Cullen, Kristie R. Blevins, Leah H. Daigle, and Tamara D. Madensen. 2006. "The Empirical Status of Deterrence Theory: A Meta-Analysis." In *Taking Stock: The Status of Criminological Theory*, edited by Francis T. Cullen, John Paul Wright, and Kristie R. Blevins. New Brunswick, NJ: Transaction.

President's Commission on Law Enforcement and Administration of Justice. 1967. *The Challenge of Crime in a Free Society*. Washington, DC: US Government Printing Office.

President's Commission on Model State Drug Laws. 1993. *Final Report*. Washington, DC: US Government Printing Office.

Probation Officers Advisory Group. 1996. "Survey." *Federal Sentencing Reporter* 8:303–306.

Raphael, Steven, and Michael A. Stoll. 2013. *Why Are So Many Americans in Prison?* New York: Russell Sage Foundation.

Rawls, John. 1955. "Two Concepts of Rules." *Philosophical Review* 44:3–13.

———. 1958. "Justice as Fairness: Political not Metaphysical." *Philosophy and Public Affairs* 14:223–51.

———. 1971. *A Theory of Justice*. Cambridge, MA: Harvard University.

Reaves, Brian A. 2013. *Felony Defendants in Large Urban Counties, 2009—Statistical Tables*. Washington, DC: US Department of Justice, Bureau of Justice Statistics.

Reiss, Albert J., Jr., and Jeffrey Roth, eds. 1993. *Understanding and Controlling Violence*. Washington, DC: National Academy Press.

Reitz, Kevin. 1993. "Sentencing Facts: Travesties of Real-Offense Sentencing." *Stanford Law Review* 45:523–73.

———. 1997. "Sentencing Guideline Systems and Sentence Appeals: A Comparison of Federal and State Experiences." *Northwestern University Law Review* 91:1441–1505.

———. 2006. "Don't Blame Determinacy: US Incarceration Growth Has Been Driven by Other Forces." *Texas Law Review* 84:1787–1802.

———. 2010. "The Illusion of Proportionality: Desert and Repeat Offenders." In *Previous Convictions at Sentencing: Theoretical and Applied Perspectives*, edited by Julian V. Roberts and Andrew von Hirsch. Oxford: Hart.

———. 2011. "Proof of Aggravating and Mitigating Facts at Sentencing." In *Mitigation and Aggravation at Sentencing*, edited by Julian V. Roberts. Cambridge, UK: Cambridge University Press.

———. 2012. "The 'Traditional' Indeterminate Sentencing Model." In *The Oxford Handbook of Sentencing and Corrections*, edited by Joan Petersilia and Kevin R. Reitz. New York: Oxford University Press.

Reitz, Kevin, and Curtis R. Reitz. 1993. "The American Bar Association's New Sentencing Standards." *Federal Sentencing Reporter* 11(3):169–73.

Remington, Frank. 1969. "Introduction." In *Sentencing*, edited by Robert Dawson. Boston: Little, Brown.

Reuter, Peter, Robert J. MacCoun, and Patrick Murphy. 1990. *Money from Crime: The Economics of Drug Dealing in Washington, DC.* Santa Monica, CA: RAND, Drug Policy Research Center.

Rhodes, William. 1992. "Sentence Disparity, Use of Incarceration, and Plea Bargaining: The Post-Guideline View from the Commission." *Federal Sentencing Reporter* 5:153–55.

Rich, William D., L. Paul Sutton, Todd D. Clear, and Michael J. Saks. 1982. *Sentencing by Mathematics: An Evaluation of the Early Attempts to Develop Sentencing Guidelines.* Williamsburg, VA: National Center for State Courts.

Roberts, Julian V. 1997. "The Role of Criminal Record in the Sentencing Process." In *Crime and Justice: A Review of Research*, vol. 22, edited by Michael Tonry. Chicago: University of Chicago Press.

———. 2008. *Punishing Persistent Offenders: Exploring Community and Offender Perspectives.* Oxford: Oxford University Press.

———. 2010. "First-Offender Sentencing Discounts: Exploring the Justifications." In *Previous Convictions at Sentencing: Theoretical and Applied Perspectives*, edited by Julian V. Roberts and Andrew von Hirsch. Oxford: Hart.

———. 2012. "Structured Sentencing in Canada and England and Wales: A Tale of Two Jurisdictions." *Criminal Law Forum* 23(4):319–45.

Roberts, Julian V., Loretta J. Stalans, David Indermaur, and Mike Hough. 2003. *Penal Populism and Public Opinion: Lessons from Five Countries.* Oxford: Oxford University Press.

Roberts, Julian V., and Andrew von Hirsch. 2010. *Previous Convictions at Sentencing: Theoretical and Applied Perspectives.* Oxford: Hart.

Robinson, Paul. 1987*a*. *Dissenting View of Commissioner Paul H. Robinson on the Promulgation of Sentencing Guidelines by the United States Sentencing Commission.* Washington, DC: US Government Printing Office.

———. 1987*b*. "Hybrid Principles for the Distribution of Criminal Sanctions." *Northwestern Law Review* 82:19–42.

———. 2003. "The Virtues of Restorative Processes, the Vices of 'Restorative Justice.'" *Utah Law Review* 2003(1):375–88.

Robinson, Paul. 2008. *Distributive Principles of Criminal Law: Who Should Be Punished? How Much*? New York: Oxford University Press.

Robinson, Paul. 2013. *Intuitions of Justice and the Utility of Desert*. New York: Oxford University Press.

Robinson, Paul H., Robert Kurzban, and Owen D. Jones. 2007. "The Origins of Shared Intuitions of Justice." *Vanderbilt Law Review* 60:1633–88.

Roeder, Oliver, Lauren-Brooke Eisen, and Julia Bowling. 2015. *What Caused the Crime Decline?* New York: Brennan Center, New York University.

Rosenmerkel, Sean, Matthew Durose, and Donald Farole. 2009. *Felony Sentences in State Courts, 2006—Statistics Tables*. Washington, DC: US Department of Justice, Bureau of Justice Statistics. http://bjs.ojp.usdoj.gov/content/pub/pdf/fssc06st.pdf.

Rossman, David, Paul Froyd, Glen Pierce, John McDevitt, and William Bowers. 1979. *The Impact of the Mandatory Gun Law in Massachusetts*. Report to the National Institute of Law Enforcement and Criminal Justice. Washington, DC: US Government Printing Office.

Rothman, David. 1971. *The Discovery of the Asylum: Social Order and Disorder in the New Republic*. Boston: Little, Brown.

———. 1980. *Conscience and Convenience: The Asylum and Its Alternatives in Progressive America*. Boston: Little, Brown.

Sabol, William J., Katherine Rosich, Kamala Mallik Kane, David Kirk, and Glenn Dubin. 2002. *Influences of Truth-in-Sentencing Reforms on Changes in States' Sentencing Practices and Prison Populations*. Washington, DC: Urban Institute.

Saris, Patti B. 2011. *Prepared Testimony of Judge Patti B. Saris, Chair, United States Sentencing Commission, before the Subcommittee on Crime, Terrorism, and Homeland Security, Committee on the Judiciary, United States House of Representatives, October 12, 2011*. Washington, DC: US Sentencing Commission.

———. 2013. *Prepared Statement by Judge Patti B. Saris, Chair, United States Sentencing Commission, for the Hearing on "Reevaluating the Effectiveness of Federal Mandatory Minimum Sentences" before the Committee on the Judiciary, United States Senate, September 18, 2013*. Washington, DC: US Sentencing Commission.

Schulhofer, Stephen J., and Ilene Nagel. 1989. "Negotiated Pleas under the Federal Sentencing Guidelines: The First Fifteen Months." *American Criminal Law Review* 27:231–88.

Schulhofer, Stephen J., and Irene Nagel. 1997. "Plea Negotiations under the Federal Sentencing Guidelines: Guideline Circumvention and Its Dynamics in the Post-*Mistretta* Period." *Northwestern University Law Review* 91:1284–316.

Schwartz, Louis B. 1983. "Options in Constructing a Sentencing System: Sentencing Guidelines under Legislative or Judicial Hegemony." In *Reform and Punishment: Essays on Criminal Sentencing*, edited by Michael Tonry and Franklin E. Zimring. Chicago: University of Chicago Press.

Schwartzer, William W. 1991. "Judicial Discretion in Sentencing." *Federal Sentencing Reporter* 4:339–41.

Scott, Ryan W. 2010. "Inter-Judge Sentencing Disparity after Booker: A First Look." *Stanford Law Review* 63:1–66.

Sechrest, Lee, Susan O. White, and Elizabeth D. Brown, eds. 1979. *The Rehabilitation of Criminal Offenders: Problems and Prospects*. Washington, DC: National Academy Press.

Sessions, William K., III. 2011. "At the Crossroads of the Three Branches: The US Sentencing Commission's Attempts to Achieve Sentencing Reform in the Midst of Inter-Branch Power Struggles." *Journal of Law and Policy* 26:305–57.

Shane-DuBow, Sandra, Alice P. Brown, and Erik Olsen. 1985. *Sentencing Reform in the United States: History, Content, and Effect*. Washington, DC: US Government Printing Office.

Shermer, Lauren O'Neill, and Brian D. Johnson. 2009. "Criminal Prosecutions: Examining Prosecutorial Discretion and Charge Reductions in U.S. Federal District Courts." *Justice Quarterly* 27(3):394–430.

Simester, Andrew P., and Andreas von Hirsch. 2011. *Crimes, Harms, and Wrongs: On the Principles of Criminalisation*. Oxford: Hart.

Simon, Jonathan. 2007. *Governing through Crime: How the War on Crime Transformed American Democracy and Created a Culture of Fear*. New York: Oxford University Press.

Singer, Richard G. 1979. *Just Deserts: Sentencing Based on Equality and Desert*. Lexington, MA: Ballinger.

Slobogin, Christopher, and Lauren Brinkley-Rubenstein. 2014. "Putting Desert in Its Place." *Stanford Law Review* 65(1):77–136.

Smith, Michael E., and Walter J. Dickey. 1999. *Reforming Sentencing and Corrections for Just Punishment and Public Safety*. Washington, DC: US Department of Justice, National Institute of Justice.

Spelman, William. 2009. "Crime, Cash, and Limited Options: Explaining the Prison Boom." *Criminology and Public Policy* 8(1):29–77.

Spohn, Cassia C. 2008. *How Do Judges Decide? The Search for Fairness and Justice in Punishment*, 2nd ed. Thousand Oaks, CA: Sage.

Starr, Sonja. 2014. "Evidence-based Sentencing and the Scientific Rationalization of Discrimination." *Stanford Law Review* 66:803–72.

Stemen, Don, Andres Rengifo, and James Wilson. 2006. *Of Fragmentation and Ferment: The Impact of State Sentencing Policies on Incarceration Rates, 1975–2002*. Final Report to the National Institute of Justice. Washington, DC: National Institute of Justice.

Stith, Kate, and José Cabranes. 1998. *Fear of Judging: Sentencing Guidelines in the Federal Courts*. Chicago: University of Chicago Press.

Stith, Kate, and Steve Yoh. 1993. "The Politics of Sentencing Reform: The Legislative History of the Federal Sentencing Guidelines." *Wake Forest Law Review* 28:233–90.

Stuntz, William J. 2011. *The Collapse of American Criminal Justice*. Cambridge: Harvard University Press.

Subramanian, Ram, and Ruth Delaney. 2014. "Playbook for Change? States Reconsider Mandatory Sentences." *Federal Sentencing Reporter* 26(3):198–211.

Subramanian, Ram, Rebecka Moreno, and Sharon Broomhead. 2014. *Recalibrating Justice: A Review of 2013 State Sentencing and Corrections Trends*. New York: Vera Institute of Justice.

Sutherland, Edward H. 1950a. "The Diffusion of Sexual Psychopath Laws." *American Sociological Review* 56(2):142–48.

Sutherland, Edward H. 1950b. "The Sexual Psychopath Laws." *Journal of Criminal Law and Criminology* 40(5):543–54.

Sweeten, Gary, Alex R. Piquero, and Laurence Steinberg. 2013. "Age and the Explanation of Crime, Revisited." *Journal of Youth and Adolescence* 42(6):921–38.

Tak, Peter J. 2001. "Sentencing and Punishment in the Netherlands." In *Sentencing and Sanctions in Western Countries*, edited by Michael Tonry and Richard S. Frase. New York: Oxford University Press.

Tappan, Paul W. 1949. "Habitual Offender Laws in the United States." *Federal Probation* 13:28–31.

Tonry, Michael. 1981. "Real Offense Sentencing: The Model Sentencing and Corrections Act." *Journal of Criminal Law and Criminology* 72:1550–96.

———. 1982. "Criminal Law: The Missing Element in Sentencing Reform." *Vanderbilt Law Review* 35:607–41.

———. 1987. *Sentencing Reform Impacts*. Washington, DC: US Government Printing Office.

———. 1988. "Sentencing Guidelines and the Model Penal Code." *Rutgers Law Review* 19:823–48.

———. 1992*a*. "GAO Report Confirms Failure of U.S. Sentencing Commission's Guidelines." *Federal Sentencing Reporter* 5:144–52.

———. 1992*b*. "Salvaging the Sentencing Guidelines in Seven Easy Steps." *Federal Sentencing Reporter* 4:355–59.

———. 1996. *Sentencing Matters*. New York: Oxford University Press.

———, ed. 2001*a*. *Penal Reform in Overcrowded Times*. New York Oxford University Press.

———. 2001*b*. "Punishment Policies and Patterns in Western Countries." In *Sentencing and Sanctions in Western Countries*, edited by Michael Tonry and Richard S. Frase. New York: Oxford University Press.

———. 2004. *Thinking about Crime: Sense and Sensibility in American Penal Culture*. New York: Oxford University Press.

———. 2007. "Determinants of Penal Policies." In *Crime, Punishment, and Politics in Comparative Perspective*, edited by Michael Tonry. Vol. 35 of *Crime and Justice: A Review of Research*, edited by Michael Tonry. Chicago: University of Chicago Press.

———. 2009*a*. "The Mostly Unintended Effects of Mandatory Penalties: Two Centuries of Consistent Findings." In *Crime and Justice: A Review of Research*, vol. 38, edited by Michael Tonry. Chicago: University of Chicago Press.

———. 2009*b*. "Emerging Explanations of American Punishment Policies: A Natural History." *Punishment and Society* 11:377–94.

———. 2009*c*. "The Untold Story of America's First Sentencing Commission," *Federal Sentencing Reporter* 21(4):265–70.

———. 2010. "The Questionable Relevance of Previous Convictions to Punishments for Later Crimes." In *Previous Convictions at Sentencing: Theoretical and Applied Perspectives*, edited by Julian Roberts and Andrew von Hirsch. Oxford: Hart.

———. 2011*a*. *Punishing Race: An American Dilemma Continues*. New York: Oxford University Press.

———. 2011*b*. "Can Twenty-First Century Punishment Policies Be Justified in Principle?" In *Retributivism Has a Past: Has It a Future?*, edited by Michael Tonry. New York: Oxford University Press.

———, ed. 2012*a*. *Prosecutors and Politics: A Comparative Perspective*, edited by Michael Tonry. Vol. 41 of *Crime and Justice: A Review of Research*, edited by Michael Tonry. Chicago: University of Chicago Press.

———. 2012*b*. "Prosecutors and Politics in Comparative Perspective." In *Prosecutors and Politics: A Comparative Perspective*, edited by Michael Tonry. Vol. 41 of *Crime and Justice: A Review of Research*, edited by Michael Tonry. Chicago: University of Chicago Press.

———. 2013. "Sentencing in America, 1975–2025." In *Crime and Justice in America, 1975–2025*, edited by Michael Tonry. Vol. 42 of *Crime and Justice: A Review of Research*, edited by Michael Tonry. Chicago: University of Chicago Press.

———. 2014. "Why Crime Rates Are Falling Throughout the Western World." In *Why Crime Rates Fall and Why They Don't*, edited by Michael Tonry. Vol. 43 of *Crime and Justice: A Review of Research*, edited by Michael Tonry. Chicago: University of Chicago Press.

———, ed. 2016. *Sentencing and Punishment in Western Countries since 2000*. Volume 45 of *Crime and Justice: A Review of Research*, edited by Michael Tonry. Chicago: University of Chicago Press. Forthcoming.

Tonry, Michael, and Richard S. Frase, eds. 2001. *Sentencing and Sanctions in Western Countries*. New York: Oxford University Press.

Törnudd, Patrik. 1993. *Fifteen Years of Declining Prisoner Rates*. Research Communication no. 8. Helsinki: National Research Institute of Legal Policy.

Travis, Jeremy. 2000. "But They All Come Back: Rethinking Prisoner Reentry." Papers from the Executive Sessions on Sentencing and Corrections. Washington, D.C.: U.S. Department of Justice, National Institute of Justice.

Travis, Jeremy, Bruce Western, and Steve Redburn, eds. 2014. *The Growth of Incarceration in the United States: Exploring Causes and Consequences*. Washington, DC: National Academies Press.

Turner, Susan, Terry Fain, Peter W. Greenwood, Elsa Y. Chen, and James R. Chiesa. 2001. *National Evaluation of the Violent Offender Incarceration/Truth-in-Sentencing Incentive Grant Program*. Final Report to the US National Institute of Justice. Santa Monica, CA: RAND.

Turner, William Bennett. 1971. "Establishing the Rule of Law in Prisons: A Manual for Prisoners' Rights Litigation." *Stanford Law Review* 23:473–518.

Uniform Law Commissioners. 1979. *Model Sentencing and Corrections Act*. Washington, DC: National Institute of Law Enforcement and Criminal Justice, U.S. Department of Justice.

US Courts. 2014. *Judicial Facts and Figures—2012*. http://www.uscourts.gov/uscourts/Statistics/JudicialFactsAndFigures/2012/Table101.pdf.

US General Accounting Office. 1990. *US Sentencing Commission: Changes Needed to Improve Effectiveness*. Washington, DC: US General Accounting Office.

———. 1992. *Sentencing Guidelines: Central Questions Remain Unanswered*. Washington, DC: US General Accounting Office.

US Sentencing Commission. 1986. *Preliminary Draft: Sentencing Guidelines, United States Sentencing Commission*. Washington, DC: US Sentencing Commission.

———. 1987*a*. *Sentencing Commission Guidelines Manual*. Washington, DC: US Sentencing Commission.

———. 1987*b*. *Sentencing Guidelines and Policy Statements, April 13, 1987*. Washington, DC: US Government Printing Office.

———. 1987*c*. *Supplemental Report on the Initial Sentencing Guidelines and Policy Statements, June 18, 1987*. Washington, DC: US Government Printing Office.

———. 1990*a*. *Annual Report—1989*. Washington, DC: US Sentencing Commission.

———. 1990*b*. *The Federal Offender: A Program of Intermediate Punishments*. Report from the Alternatives to Imprisonment Project. Washington, DC: US Sentencing Commission.

———. 1991*a*. *The Federal Sentencing Guidelines: A Report on the Operation of the Guidelines System and Short-Term Impacts on Disparity in Sentencing, Use of Incarceration, and Prosecutorial Discretion and Plea Bargaining*. Washington, DC: US Sentencing Commission.

———. 1991*b*. *Special Report to the Congress: Mandatory Minimum Penalties in the Federal Criminal Justice System*. Washington, DC: US Sentencing Commission.

———. 1994. *Annual Report—1993*. Washington, DC: US Sentencing Commission.

———. 1995*a*. *Special Report to Congress: Cocaine and Federal Sentencing Policy*. Washington, DC: US Sentencing Commission.

———. 1995*b*. *Report to Congress: Analysis of Penalties for Federal Rape Cases*. Washington, DC: US Sentencing Commission.

———. 1995*c*. *Report to Congress: Adequacy of Penalties for the Intentional Exposure of Others, through Sexual Activity, to Human Immunodeficiency Virus*. Washington, DC: US Sentencing Commission.

———. 1995*d*. *Report to Congress: Adequacy of Penalties for Fraud Offenses Involving Elderly Victims*. Washington, DC: US Sentencing Commission.

———. 1996*a*. *Report to the Congress: Adequacy of Federal Sentencing Guideline Penalties for Computer Fraud and Vandalism Offenses*. Washington, DC: US Sentencing Commission.

———. 1996*b*. *Report to the Congress: Sex Crimes against Children*. Washington, DC: US Sentencing Commission.

——— 1996*c*. *Annual Report—Fiscal Year 1995*. Washington, DC: US Sentencing Commission.

——— 1996*d*. *Simplification Draft Paper*. Working Group on Guideline Simplification. Washington, DC: US Sentencing Commission.

——— 1996*e*. *Staff Discussion Paper: Sentencing Options under the Guidelines*. Washington, DC: US Sentencing Commission.

——— 1997*a*. *Special Report to Congress: Cocaine and Federal Sentencing Policy*. Washington, DC: US Sentencing Commission.

——— 1997*b*. *Sentencing Policy for Money Laundering Offenses, including Comments on Department of Justice Report*. Washington, DC: US Sentencing Commission.

——— 1998. *Report to the Congress: Telemarketing Fraud Offenses—Explanation of Recent Guideline Amendments*. Washington, DC: US Sentencing Commission.

——— 2002. *Special Report to Congress: Cocaine and Federal Sentencing Policy*. Washington, DC: US Sentencing Commission.

——— 2003*a*. *Report to the Congress: Increased Penalties for Campaign Finance Offenses and Legislative Recommendations*. Washington, DC: US Sentencing Commission.

——— 2003*b*. *Report to the Congress: Increased Penalties for Cyber Security Offenses*. Washington, DC: US Sentencing Commission.

——— 2003*c*. *Report to the Congress: Increased Penalties under the Sarbanes Oxley Act of 2002*. Washington, DC: US Sentencing Commission.

——— 2004. *15 Years of Guidelines Sentencing: An Assessment of How Well the Federal Criminal Justice System Is Achieving the Goals of Sentencing Reform*. Washington, DC: US Sentencing Commission.

——— 2005. Annual Report—Fiscal Year 2004. Washington, DC: US Sentencing Commission.

——— 2007. *Special Report to Congress: Federal Cocaine Sentencing Policy*. Washington, DC: US Sentencing Commission.

——— 2008. *Report to the Congress: Amendments to the Federal Sentencing Guidelines in Response to the Emergency Disaster Assistance Fraud Penalty Enhancement Act of 2007*. Washington, DC: US Sentencing Commission.

——— 2009. *The Federal Offender: A Program of Intermediate Punishments*. Washington, DC: US Sentencing Commission.

——— 2010. *Results of Survey of United States District Judges—January 2010 through March 2010*. Washington, DC: US Sentencing Commission.

———. 2011. *Report to the Congress: Mandatory Minimum Penalties in the Federal Criminal Justice System*. Washington, DC: US Sentencing Commission.

——— 2012*a*. *Report to the Congress: Federal Child Pornography Offenses*. Washington, DC: US Sentencing Commission.

——— 2012*b*. *Report to the Congress: Report on the Continuing Impact of United States v. Booker on Federal Sentencing*. Washington, DC: US Sentencing Commission.

——— 2013. *2013 Sourcebook of Federal Sentencing Statistics*. Washington, DC: US Sentencing Commission.

——— 2014*a*. "Comment of Honorable Patti B. Saris, Chair, US Sentencing Commission, on Amendment Reducing Drug Guidelines becoming Effective

Tomorrow." News Release, October 31. Washington, DC: US Sentencing Commission.

US Sentencing Commission 2014*b*. *Sentencing Commission Guidelines Manual.* Washington, DC: US Sentencing Commission.

——— 2014*c*. "Summary of Key Data Regarding Retroactive Application of the 2014 Drug Guidelines Amendment." Office of Research and Data Memorandum, July 25. Washington, DC: US Sentencing Commission.

——— 2014*d*. "US Sentencing Commission Selects Policy Priorities for 2014–2015 Guidelines Amendment Cycle—Continued Work on Mandatory Minimum Penalties, Review of Fraud Guidelines on List of Priorities." News Release, August 14. Washington, DC: US Sentencing Commission.

——— 2015. *2014 Drug Guidelines Amendments. Retroactivity Data Report.* U.S. Sentencing Commission: Washington, D.C.

US Surgeon General. 2001. *Youth Violence: A Report of the Surgeon General.* National Center for Injury Prevention and Control. Rockville, MD: Office of the Surgeon General.

van de Bunt, Henk, and Jean-Louis van Gelder. 2012. "The Dutch Prosecution Service." In *Prosecutors and Politics: A Comparative Perspective*, edited by Michael Tonry. Vol. 41 of *Crime and Justice: A Review of Research*, edited by Michael Tonry. Chicago: University of Chicago Press.

van den Haag, Ernst. 1975. *Punishing Criminals.* New York: Basic Books.

van Dijk, Jan, John van Kesteren, and Paul Smit. 2007. *Criminal Victimisation in International Perspective: Key Findings from the 2004–2005 ICVS and EU ICS.* The Hague: Netherlands Ministry of Justice.

van Zyl Smit, Dirk, and Sonja Snacken. 2009. *Principles of European Prison Law and Policy: Penology and Human Rights.* Oxford: Oxford University Press.

Villettaz, Patrice, Gwladys Gilliérion, and Martin Killias. 2014. *The Effects on Re-offending of Custodial versus Non-custodial Sanctions.* Stockholm: National Council for Crime Prevention.

Virginia Criminal Sentencing Commission. 2010. *Manual*, 13th ed. Richmond: Virginia Criminal Sentencing Commission.

von Hirsch, Andrew. 1976. *Doing Justice.* New York: Hill & Wang.

——— 1981. "Desert and Previous Convictions in Sentencing." *Minnesota Law Review* 65:591–634.

——— 1985. *Past and Future Crimes: Deservedness and Dangerousness in Sentencing Criminals.* New Brunswick, NJ: Rutgers University Press.

——— 1988. "Federal Sentencing Guidelines: The United States and Canadian Schemes Compared." Occasional Papers from the Center for Research in Crime and Justice, no. 4. New York: New York University Law School.

——— 2010. "Proportionality and the Progressive Loss of Mitigation: Some Future Reflections." In *Previous Convictions at Sentencing: Theoretical and Applied Perspectives*, edited by Julian V. Roberts and Andrew von Hirsch. Oxford: Hart.

——— 2011. "Reflections on Punishment Futures: The Desert-Model Debate and the Importance of the Criminal Law Context." In *Retributivism Has a Past: Has It a Future?*, edited by Michael Tonry. New York: Oxford University Press.

von Hirsch, Andrew, and Andrew Ashworth. 2005. *Proportionate Sentencing: Exploring the Principles*. Oxford: Oxford University Press.

von Hirsch, Andrew, Anthony E. Bottoms, Elizabeth Burney, and Per-Olof Wikström. 1999. *Criminal Deterrence and Sentence Severity: An Analysis of Recent Research*. Cambridge, UK: University of Cambridge.

von Hirsch, Andrew, and Kathleen J. Hanrahan. 1979. *The Question of Parole: Retention, Reform, or Abolition?* Cambridge, MA: Ballinger.

von Hirsch, Andrew, Kay A. Knapp, and Michael Tonry. 1987. *The Sentencing Commission and Its Guidelines*. Boston: Northeastern University Press.

von Hirsch, Andrew, Julian V. Roberts, Anthony E. Bottoms, Kent Roach, and Mara Schiff, eds. 2003. *Restorative Justice and Criminal Justice: Competing or Reconcilable Paradigms?* Oxford: Hart.

Walgrave, Lode. 2008. *Restorative Justice, Self-interest, and Responsible Citizenship*. Cullompton, UK: Willan.

Walker, Nigel. 1991. *Why Punish?* Oxford: Oxford University Press.

———. 1996. *Dangerous People*. London: Blackstone.

Walmsley, Roy. 2014. *World Prison Brief*, 10th ed. Colchester, UK: International Centre for Prison Studies, University of Essex.

Wechsler, Herbert, and Jerome Michael. 1937. "A Rationale of the Law of Homicide I." *Columbia Law Review* 37:701–61.

Weigend, Thomas. 2001. "Sentencing and Punishment in Germany." In *Sentencing and Sanctions in Western Countries*, edited by Michael Tonry and Richard S. Frase. New York: Oxford University Press.

——— 2016. "Sentencing in Germany." In *Sentencing and Punishment in Western Countries since 2000*. Vol. 45 of *Crime and Justice: A Review of Research*, edited by Michael Tonry. Chicago: University of Chicago Press. Forthcoming.

Weisburd, David. 1992. "Sentencing Disparity and the Guidelines: Taking a Closer Look." *Federal Sentencing Reporter* 5:149–52.

Welsh, Brandon C., and David P. Farrington, eds. 2006. *Preventing Crime: What Works for Children, Offenders, Victims, and Places*. New York: Springer.

Wexler, David. 1995. "Reflections on the Scope of Therapeutic Jurisprudence." *Psychology, Public Policy, and Law* 1(1):230–36.

——— 2008*a*. *Rehabilitation Lawyers: Principles of Therapeutic Jurisprudence for Criminal Law Practice*. Durham, NC: Carolina Academic Press.

——— 2008*b*. "Two Decades of Therapeutic Jurisprudence." *Toronto Law Review* 24:7–29.

Wexler, David B., and Bruce Winick, eds. 2003. *Judging in a Therapeutic Key: Therapeutic Jurisprudence and the Courts*. Durham, NC: Carolina Academic Press.

Whitman, James. 2003. *Harsh Justice*. New York, NY: Oxford University Press.

Wilcox, A., Richard Young, and Carolyn Hoyle. 2004. *An Evaluation of the Impact of Restorative Cautioning: Findings from a Reconviction Study*. London: Home Office.

Wilson, David B., Doris L. MacKenzie, and Fawn Ngo Mitchell. 2008. *Effects of Correctional Boot Camps on Offending*. Campbell Systematic review no. 1 (First published January 8, 2003; updated February 12, 2008). http://www.campbell-collaboration.org/lib/project/1/.

Wilson, James Q. 1975. *Thinking about Crime*. New York: Basic Books.

Windlesham, Lord David. 1998. *Politics, Punishment, and Populism*. New York: Oxford University Press.

Wines, Enoch. 1880. *The State of Prisons and of Child-Saving Institutions in the Civilized World*. Cambridge, UK: University Press, John Wilson.

Winick, Bruce J. 1997. "The Jurisprudence of Therapeutic Jurisprudence." *Psychology, Public Policy, and Law* 3(1):184–206.

——— 2005. *Civil Commitment: A Therapeutic Jurisprudence Model*. Durham, NC: Carolina Academic Press.

Wright, Ronald. 2002. "Counting the Cost of Sentencing in North Carolina, 1980–2000." *Crime and Justice: A Review of Research*, vol. 29, edited by Michael Tonry. Chicago: University of Chicago Press.

——— 2012. "Persistent Localism in the Prosecutor Services of North Carolina." In *Prosecutors and Politics: A Comparative Perspective*, edited by Michael Tonry. Vol. 41 of *Crime and Justice: A Review of Research*, edited by Michael Tonry. Chicago: University of Chicago Press.

——— 2013. "The Wickersham Commission and Local Control of Criminal Prosecution." *Marquette Law Review* 96:1199–1219.

Yankelovich, Daniel. 1991. *Coming to Public Judgment: Making Democracy Work in a Complex World*. Syracuse, NY: Syracuse University Press.

Zeisel, Hans, and Shari Seidman Diamond. 1977. "Search for Sentencing Equity: Sentence Review in Massachusetts and Connecticut." *American Bar Foundation Research Journal* 2(4):881, 883–940.

Zimring, Franklin E., Gordon Hawkins, and Sam Kamin. 2001. *Punishment and Democracy: Three Strikes and You're Out in California*. New York: Oxford University Press.

INDEX

Figures and tables are indicated by "f" and "t" following the page numbers.